DATA ANALYSIS

FOR

CONTINUOUS SCHOOL
IMPROVEMENT

SECOND EDITION

VICTORIA L. BERNHARDT, Ph.D.
Executive Director
Education for the Future Initiative

Professor
Department of Professional Studies in Education
College of Communication and Education
California State University, Chico, CA

EYE ON EDUCATION
6 Depot Way West
Larchmont, NY 10538
(914) 833-0551
(914) 833-0761 Fax
http://www.eyeoneducation.com/

Library of Congress Cataloging—in—Publication Data

Bernhardt, Victoria L., 1952-
    Data analysis for continuous school improvement / by Victoria L. Bernhardt. — 2nd ed.
        p.   cm.
    Rev. ed. of Data analysis for comprehensive schoolwide improvement. ©1998.
    Includes bibliographical references (p.) and index.
    ISBN 1-930556-74-8
    1. Computer managed instruction—United States. 2. School improvement programs
United States—Data processing. 3. Educational planning—United States—Statistical
methods. I. Title: Data analysis. II. Bernhardt, Victoria L., 1952—Data analysis for
comprehensive schoolwide improvement. III. Title.

    LB1028.46.B47 2004
    371.2'00973--dc22
                                                                    2003064330

10 9 8 7

ACKNOWLEDGEMENTS

As was the case with the first edition of this book, this second edition is dedicated with appreciation to the hard-working staff of the *Education for the Future Initiative.* This acknowledgement only begins to convey my appreciation for the individual dedication, hard work, and willingness of the *Education for the Future* staff to go beyond the call of duty for the benefit of schools and for the improvement of student learning. I am indebted to Lynn Varicelli, Brad Geise, Marcy Lauck, Alicia Hamilton, Sally Withuhn, Mary Foard, and Thiago Jorge for their contributions to this book and for all they do for the *Initiative* every day. Lynn, Brad, Alicia, Sally, Mary, and Thiago do amazing work every day, keeping me on the road with the cutting edge work that we do. Marcy, serving as our depth charge in San Jose Unified School District, helps us know that it is possible to do this work on a large scale and that it can be sustainable over time.

Lynn Varicelli once again did a fabulous job on the layout of this book and with all the numerous drafts and updates. There is no one more dedicated, committed, loyal, and supportive than Lynn. There is no one who does a better job than she does on book layouts. I am lucky to know and be able to work with her for close to a decade now. These books could never be done without her.

Because this was a second edition and not an entirely new book, I left my usual tradition of asking about 50 practicing educators to review its contents. I asked a very small group of special people from across the country, and Japan, to review the updated content which included feedback from thousands of participants from a decade of data analysis workshops. Those people deserving of much more than mere thanks are:

- ▼ Dr. William Johnston, Greenville, South Carolina
- ▼ Joy Rose, Columbus, Ohio
- ▼ Andy Mark, Forest Ranch, California
- ▼ Laurel Eisinger, DODDS–Japan
- ▼ Sue Clayton, Montpelier, Vermont
- ▼ Dr. Paul Preuss, Queensbury, New York
- ▼ Judy English, Columbia, Missouri
- ▼ Marcy Lauck, San Jose, California

Joy Rose, my editor "extraordinaire," was available no matter what was going on in her life to read another chapter another time. I am so humbled by Joy's dedication to these books and to the *Education for the Future* staff and mission. I wish I could truly show her how much I appreciate her support and quality work. Joy is another one who makes it possible for me to travel and write books. Without her support, I would not have the confidence or editorial support to keep writing.

A special thanks to the schools that gave me data to use in the examples. In concert with our agreements, I will not reveal who you are or your real locations. We all appreciate the opportunity to learn from you.

Vanessa Wolfe from *MC² Design Group* did a fabulous job on the design of the cover—one of my all-time favorites. The others at *MC²*, Brian Curtis and Judy Sherwood, have been a treat to work with in this publication and to get to know over the years. Not only do they do a fabulous job on this project, their overall support for our work is phenomenal. (See *http://www.MC2design.com*.)

Tom Devol, our fabulous professional photographer (that's loved spelled backwards), provided many of the pictures in this book and continues to be there for us whenever we need him. The quality of his photos is unmatched.

The analyses in this book do not look that extensive until you try to do them yourself. Luckily, I have the support of *TetraData Corporation* and their fabulous data warehouse and data analyzer product called *EASE-E* so I could do all the analyses in this book in a day (had all the data been in the warehouse). *TetraData* has the best tool out there for data analysis work in schools and school districts. They have been nothing but supportive of the work I do with school districts. I send my most gracious thanks to each and every person in that company. Thank you for all you do for me, for *Education for the Future,* and for all of our futures.

I thank my husband, Jim Richmond, for again providing his brand of support for my work. He does a lot of what I should be doing around the house so I can pursue these publications and the work I cannot not do.

A huge thanks to my publisher, affectionately known as *Cousin Bob,* Mr. Robert Sickles. I continue to be grateful for all you do for us. Thank you.

This acknowledgement section could not be complete without thanking you, the reader, and you, the school personnel working with continuous school improvement, who have believed in and tried *Education for the Future* products and processes.

I do hope this second edition exceeds your expectations; and if it does, it is because of the continuous improvement that has resulted from your insights, direction, assistance, and support all along the way. Thank you.

Vickie Bernhardt
December 2004

TABLE OF CONTENTS

ABOUT THE AUTHOR

Victoria L. Bernhardt, Ph.D., is Executive Director of the *Education for the Future Initiative*, a not-for-profit organization whose mission is to build the capacity of all schools at all levels to gather, analyze, and use data to continuously improve learning for all students. She is also a Professor, on leave, in the Department of Professional Studies in Education, College of Communication and Education, at California State University, Chico. Dr. Bernhardt is the author of 14 books *(including this one)* eleven of which are still in print, all published by Eye on Education, Larchmont, New York:

▼ *From Questions to Actions: Using Questionnaire Data for Continuous School Improvement* (2009).

▼ *Data, Data Everywhere: Bringing All the Data Together for Continuous School Improvement* (2009).

▼ *Translating Data into Information to Improve Teaching and Learning* (2007).

▼ A four-book collection of using data to improve student learning—*Using Data to Improve Student Learning in Elementary Schools* (2003); *Using Data to Improve Student Learning in Middle Schools (2004); Using Data to Improve Student Learning in High Schools (2005);* and *Using Data to Improve Student Learning in School Districts* (2006).

▼ *Data Analysis for Continuous School Improvement* (First Edition, 1998; Second Edition, 2004).

▼ *The School Portfolio Toolkit: A Planning, Implementation, and Evaluation Guide for Continuous School Improvement,* and CD-Rom (2002).

▼ *The Example School Portfolio* (2000).

▼ *The School Portfolio: A Comprehensive Framework for School Improvement* (First Edition, 1994; Second Edition, 1999).

Dr. Bernhardt is passionate about her mission of helping all educators continuously improve student learning in their classrooms, their schools, their districts, and states by gathering, analyzing, and using actual data—as opposed to using hunches and "gut-level" feelings. She has made numerous presentations at professional meetings and has conducted thousands of workshops on the school portfolio, data analysis, and school improvement at local, state, regional, national, and international levels.

Dr. Bernhardt can be reached at:

Victoria L. Bernhardt
Executive Director, *Education for the Future Initiative*
400 West First Street, Chico, CA 95929-0230
Tel: 530-898-4482 — Fax: 530-898-4484
e-mail: vbernhardt@csuchico.edu — web: *http://eff.csuchico.edu*

FOREWORD

TetraData Corporation is a software and services company that focuses on tools that support continuous improvement in education. *TetraData* continues to be proudly associated with Victoria L. Bernhardt, one of the most dedicated, capable, and energetic leaders in school improvement today. Our firm shares a common passion, i.e., that data-driven decision-making can provide each state, each regional service center, each district, each school, each class, and each student with a reliable way to facilitate continuous improvement in education processes and outcomes. We also share a common vision of a world where education is moving toward increased knowledge, increased caring, and where we focus societal resources on some of the most important people that we know—the children of our world.

The first edition of the book *Data Analysis for Comprehensive Schoolwide Improvement* is *the* book of data-driven decision-making books that explains what data should be analyzed, how it can be turned into meaningful diagnostic information, and what should be communicated. The whole intent of the first edition was to bring us the wake-up call that we will not improve education unless we analyze the data, turn it into meaningful information, and then change the processes that are impacting school improvement.

This second edition by Dr. Bernhardt, *Data Analysis for Continuous School Improvement* is truly a representation of "Good to Great," to borrow a modern phrase. The first edition is *Good* because it helped all of us initiate our data-driven decision-making efforts in education. It also helped raise our eyes above the individual test scores to longitudinal analyses and to analyze other data sources, i.e., the *demographics, perceptions,* and *processes* that can impact and influence education outcomes.

This newest edition of Victoria's takes us an important step forward—it moves us to *Great*. Based upon Dr. Bernhardt's excellent research and thoughtful application, this newest edition takes into account fresh and relevant field-level information. This work is full of practical examples of how educators have used data analysis and continuous improvement processes to not only recognize and isolate symptoms, but how educators discovered the core causes and actually modified their processes, thus overcoming problems for today and tomorrow. In addition, the second edition helps us all integrate *No Child Left Behind* (NCLB) into our processes and thinking. Accountability is here to stay, and that can be good news since standards-based testing provides another important data source on our quest for data-driven decision making.

What has not changed is Dr. Bernhardt's most powerful characteristic—*passion*—her passion for children, her passion for making lasting quality change in education, and her passion for helping this generation of children, as well as generations ahead, to learn, grow, and participate productively in society. Enjoy, grow, and embrace the mission as you read *Data Analysis for Continuous School Improvement*, Second Edition.

Martin S. Brutosky
Chairman and CEO
TetraData Corporation
300 Executive Center Drive, Suite 300
Greenville, SC 29615
Tel: (864) 458-8243
http://www.tetradata.com

Schools are powerful organizations. Every day, across the United States, schools are impacting the lives of millions of children and the future of our very existence. Schools become even more powerfully efficient and effective when data play an active role in their operations.

I am passionate about the impact data analyses make on building strong schools, teachers, administrators, and district, county, regional, state, and national education systems. Data not only tell us where we have been, where we are right now, and where we are going; data inform us of the ways to get there, sensibly.

I have worked closely with teachers and schools on systemic change for many years. The one area in which schools continue to have the most difficulty is data analysis.

Data provide power to... make good decisions, work intelligently, work effectively and efficiently, change things in better ways, know the impact of our hard work and how it benefits children, and help us prepare for the future.

The purposes of this book are to update the original *Data Analysis for Comprehensive Schoolwide Improvement* book with new and improved strategies and knowledge, and to clarify:

- ▼ why data are important and what data to gather
- ▼ how data—gathered, analyzed, and properly used—can make a difference in meeting the needs of every student in the school
- ▼ how to communicate and report data results
- ▼ the data analyses required to meet *No Child Left Behind* (NCLB) legislation

This book is not a statistics text. It shows how to use data to gain answers to logical questions and to understand current and future impact. Examples from real schools illustrate the points.

This book works with the four-book *series—Using Data to Improve Student Learning in Elementary Schools; Using Data to Improve Student Learning in Middle Schools; Using Data to Improve Student Learning in High Schools;* and *Using Data to Improve Student Learning in School Districts.* Each of the books in the series shows how to analyze the data at that level and provides tools and templates on accompanying CD-ROMs.

With the enactment of NCLB, data analysis is no longer optional! The requirements take us deep into the data to help us identify and uncover powerful solutions to schools' greatest challenges. I believe we have to look more systematically and deeper than we are used to looking to get to analyses that will make the difference. We must also look at other data sources besides our required state assessments.

This second edition includes updated and new information gathered since the publication of the first edition. It also includes some of the same information included in other books I've written—at the request of the book reviewers and participants in workshops using the *Data Analysis* book. It appears people want a data analysis book with everything in it.

I want this book to contribute to the success of schools and districts throughout the United States and abroad, *because* . . . I want schools to prove that they can help *all* children learn and be all they want to be in the future.

I look forward to hearing from you with questions or feedback for my continuous improvement. Good luck with your data analysis efforts, and please enjoy.

Victoria L. Bernhardt
Executive Director, *Education for the Future Initiative*
400 West First Street, Chico, CA 95929-0230
Tel: 530-898-4482 — Fax: 530-898-4484
e-mail: vbernhardt@csuchico.edu — web: *http://eff.csuchico.edu*

INTRODUCTION

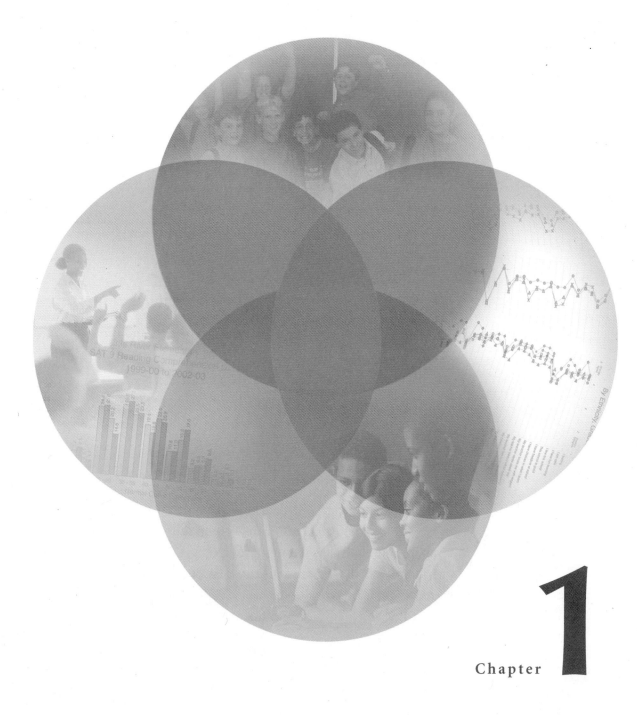

Chapter 1

People without information cannot act. People with information cannot help but act.

Ken Blanchard

Schools that gather, analyze, and use information about their school communities make better decisions, not only about what to change but also how to institutionalize systemic change. Schools that understand the needs of their primary customers—the students—are more successful in planning changes and remain more focused during implementation than those schools that simply gather, but make no sustained effort to analyze and use, data. Schools that use data understand the effectiveness of their reform efforts; those that do not can only assume that effectiveness.

Schools committed to improving student learning analyze data in order to plan for the future through understanding—

▼ the ways in which the school and the community have changed and are continuing to change

▼ the current and future needs of the students, parents, teachers, school, and community

▼ how well current processes meet these customers' needs

▼ the gaps between the results the school is getting and the results it wants

▼ the root causes for the gaps

▼ the types of education programs, expertise, and process adjustments that will be needed to alleviate the gaps and to meet the needs of all customers

▼ how well the new processes being implemented meet the needs of the students, parents, teachers, school, and community

The Importance of Data

Businesses typically use data to determine customers' wants and needs. No matter what occupation we, or our students, aspire to, everyone can appreciate that fact. We can also appreciate the fact that businesses not properly analyzing and using data, more often than not, are not successful. Those of us who work in the business of education, however, may not be as familiar with the ways that *businesses* use *educational* data.

In many states, the prison systems look at the number of students not reading on grade level in grades two, three, or four to determine the number of prison cells to build ten years hence (*Lawmakers Move to Improve Literacy, 2001*). The fact that the prison system can use this prediction formula with great accuracy should make us all cringe, but the critical point is that if businesses can use educational data for predictions, so can educators. Not only can we predict, we can use the same data to *prevent* undesirable results from happening. Nothing would make educators happier than to hear that prison systems do not need as many cells because more students are being successful in school and, therefore, in life.

Schools in the United States have a long history of adopting innovations one after another as they are introduced. Very few schools take the time to use data to understand the needs of the children being served. Few take the time to understand the impact current processes have on these children. Few take the time to determine the root causes of recurring problems, or to measure and analyze the impact of implementing new approaches. Fewer still use sound information to build and stick with a solid long-term plan that will improve learning for all students. Across our country, we have found that schools spend an average of about two years engaged in their school improvement efforts. The sad fact is that most schools really only implement their plans for the first six to twelve months after the plan is completed. Is it any wonder that nothing seems to generate results for these schools?

We find a different story among the schools that measure and analyze the impact of implementing new approaches. These schools know if what they are doing is working, and if not, why not. These schools also stick with their efforts to create change long after most schools have switched to new efforts. These schools get results.

The use of data can make an enormous difference in school reform efforts by helping schools see how to improve school processes and student learning. Data can help to—

- ▼ replace hunches and hypotheses with facts concerning what changes are needed
- ▼ facilitate a clear understanding of the gaps between where the school is and where the school wants to be
- ▼ identify the root causes of these gaps, so the school can solve the problem and not just treat the symptom
- ▼ understand the impact of processes on the student population
- ▼ assess needs to target services on important issues
- ▼ provide information to eliminate ineffective practices
- ▼ ensure the effective and efficient uses of dollars
- ▼ show if school goals and objectives are being accomplished
- ▼ ascertain if the school staffs are *implementing their visions*
- ▼ promote understanding of the impact of efforts, processes, and progress

The use of data can make an enormous difference in school reform efforts by helping schools see how to improve school processes and student learning.

3

▼ generate answers for the community related to: *What are we getting for our children by investing in the school's methods, programs, and processes?*

▼ continuously improve all aspects of the learning organization

▼ predict and prevent failures

▼ predict and ensure successes

One small rural Northern California community learned a valuable lesson regarding the difference between hypotheses and fact while investigating why the majority of their high school graduates dropped out of college before the end of their first year. They learned that a great deal of money and time could have been spent in "solving a symptom" without ever getting to the real issue—the quality of their academic programs.

Each year, for several years, the community watched 80 percent of their graduates go off to college in the fall, 40 percent return to the community by Christmas, and almost 95 percent of those who went off to college return by the end of spring—for good. This recurring problem was discussed widely among teachers and the community. Their hypothesis was that their students lacked experience and social skills. Their students simply did not have the social skills to function in other environments. Everyone "knew" that these students did not interact positively with people they knew, so they could not possibly know how to interact positively with strangers.

Based on this "knowledge," the school district began an extensive restructuring effort centered on working with all K-12 students to develop their social and communication skills. At the request of a consultant brought in to ". . . make this vision a shared community vision," the teachers reluctantly conducted a telephone survey of their graduates, asking them why they had dropped out of college. Almost without exception, graduates said the following: "They made me write. I can't write!" Based on this fact-finding survey, the focus of the restructuring effort changed immediately, and the school district began using data on an ongoing basis to provide a challenging curriculum that kept students engaged in learning, enjoying school—and writing!

One large Southern California elementary school learned the value of disaggregating its data to understand its students and to aid its reform efforts.

School personnel stated that because their population included so many English Learners, the school's scores remained at a low level. They also reported that, because of these children, they could not become a mathematics, science, and technology magnet school.

The standardized achievement tests that had been given during the previous five years were analyzed. It was clear that while the reading and writing scores of the English Learners' abilities were lower than the other students, these same English Learners outscored English-proficient students in science and mathematics. With this and other information, the teachers researched strategies that could be used to everyone's advantage.

The research resulted in the school becoming a mathematics, science, and technology magnet school. It utilized hands-on math, science, and technology activities to build language competence in its targeted population, while increasing all students' science, mathematics, and technology knowledge. The test scores of all students improved tremendously, in just one year.

Another elementary school in California's Central Valley learned through the use of empirical data that it was not "walking the talk." The data provided guidance in establishing a new purpose for the school and in understanding how to reach its goals.

The teachers stated that the purpose of their school was "to prepare students for middle school." As a means of gathering data to understand how well they were accomplishing this goal, a small group of teachers went to the middle and high schools and asked questions of teachers and then former elementary school students. The elementary teachers were mortified to find that the majority of students who left their school with limited English-speaking skills were forever tracked in special programs that did not allow them to take college or career preparation classes. Some students had even dropped out of school.

The teachers came to the consensus that the purpose of their school, which served a mostly (about 85%) English-learning population, was to do much more than prepare them for the middle school. The school needed to be preparing students for any career they might want to pursue in the United States.

These same teachers went back to their school understanding that their highest priority had to be to get their students speaking, reading, and writing English successfully before they left elementary school. They examined the processes used to teach students English. They were teaching English to non-English-speaking children for 20 minutes each day, and moving 35 children into English-speaking classrooms in one year's time— a process they had been using for the past four years. And, because the product of the process was the same every year, a process change was required in order to get different results.

Typically, schools say, "We have lots of data; we just do not know what data to use, or how or when to use them."

By doubling the time spent teaching English to forty minutes each day, the number of students who became fluent in English by the end of that next semester more than doubled. Aside from learning how to measure their processes, the teachers learned the importance of tracking student performance on an ongoing basis, ensuring every student's success.

Barriers to Using Data

Schools do not deliberately ignore data. Typically, schools say, "We have lots of data; we just do not know what data to use, or how or when to use them." When school personnel first get interested in data and want to do more with the data they have, they often hit the proverbial brick wall.

While many schools gather data, barriers begin with attempts to analyze the data to help improve teaching and learning. Barriers can pop-up anywhere, for a variety of reasons:

▼ In contrast to the work culture in business, the work culture in education usually does not focus on data.

▼ Few people in schools and districts are adequately trained to gather and analyze data or to establish and maintain databases.

▼ Administrators and teachers do not see gathering and analyzing data as part of their jobs.

▼ District personnel have job definitions that often do not include, as a priority, helping individual schools with data.

▼ Gathering data is perceived to be a waste of time (after all, we are here every day—we know what the problems are!)

▼ Schools do not have databases that allow for easy access and analysis of data.

▼ Computer systems are outdated and inadequate; appropriate, user-friendly software is not available.

▼ Teachers have been trained to be subject-oriented, not data-oriented; process-oriented, rather than product-oriented.

▼ There is a lack of professional development for teachers to understand why data are important and how data can make a difference in their teaching.

▼ Some teachers see data as another thing that takes away from teaching.

▼ Busy school personnel may view data collecting as just more work to do.

▼ Data are not used systematically from the state to the regional and local levels, nor are they used particularly well.

▼ School personnel have had only negative experiences with data.

▼ There is a perception that data are collected for someone else's purposes.

▼ Data have been used in negative ways in the past.

▼ There is confusion upon which data to focus.

▼ There are not enough good examples of schools gathering, maintaining, and benefiting from the use of data.

▼ The legislature keeps changing the rules.

Whatever it is that keeps us from assessing our progress and products adequately, we must learn to listen, to observe, and to gather data from all sources that will help us know how we are doing, where we are going, and how we can get there.

The Purpose of this Book

The purpose of this book is fourfold:

▼ The first purpose is to update the original *Data Analysis for Comprehensive Schoolwide Improvement* with new and improved strategies and knowledge.

▼ The second purpose is to clarify why data are important and what data to gather.

▼ The third purpose is to share how to use and analyze data for comprehensive and continuous schoolwide improvement.

▼ The fourth purpose is to show how to communicate and report data results.

This edition also clarifies the data analyses required to meet *No Child Left Behind* (NCLB) legislation.

The Structure of this Book

This book begins with an overview of where we are in education and the barriers schools face with respect to data analysis. Chapter 2 describes how to get started, why we gather data, and to what end we use data. Chapter 3 describes what data are important for continuous school improvement. Chapters 4, 5, 6, and 7 deal with the major categories of data described in Chapter 3 (*demographics, perceptions, student learning,* and *school processes*); define each; describe their importance; explain how to gather, analyze, and use these data separately; and show an example. Chapter 8 explores the intersections of these measures—two-way, three-way, and the all-important four-way intersections—that allow schools to predict what they need to do to *prevent* failures. Chapter 9 discusses communicating the results of comprehensive data analyses to staff and the community, with special emphasis on effective displays of data. Chapter 10 reveals the need for data warehousing and offers conclusions and recommendations.

Most of the chapters contain examples of two fictional schools—one high school and one elementary school—using data from real schools. These data are used to illustrate the analyses that could be completed in your school.

Questions at the end of each chapter will assist your school staff in thinking through their own data analyses. The intent is for staff to work through these chapters as they design a comprehensive data analysis process that can be built upon each year to gain those powerful analyses that will help predict and prevent program failure—and to ensure that all students achieve success.

Three appendices, a *Glossary of Data Analysis Terms,* and a *References and Resources* section appear at the end of the book. Appendix A consists of sample questionnaires. Appendix B offers the complete *Education for the Future Initiative Continuous Improvement Continuums,* a self-assessment tool for schools to use to measure their school processes and support their continuous school improvement efforts. Appendix C contains the *Education for the Future Initiative Continuous Improvement Continuums* for measuring district processes.

Summary

Data Analysis for Continuous School Improvement, Second Edition, is about analyzing data at the school level for comprehensive and continuous improvement. This first chapter sets the stage for the deeper work of this book by discussing the importance of data and the barriers to using data. By the end of this book, readers will understand what data to gather, how to analyze the data, how to go deeper into the data, what the analyses look like, how to communicate the analyses that can lead to a school's continuous improvement, and how a data warehousing system can make data analysis doable.

Study questions are provided at the end of each chapter to assist the reader in understanding the content and to encourage study group discussions.

GETTING STARTED WITH DATA ANALYSIS

Chapter 2

It is hard to begin to move when you don't know where you are moving, how to move, or if you are going to get there.

Peter Nivio Zarlenga

How does a school get started with comprehensive data analysis work? How do you know if what you are currently doing is making a difference with respect to what you expect students to know and be able to do? How do you know which strategies ought to be the focus of your school improvement efforts?

If your school is like 95% of the schools in this country, my hunch is that your school improvement committee comes up with achievable school improvement goals each year, often focused on increasing student attendance, involving more parents, or improving one subject area at a time. The school improvement plan is sent to the district, which will allow staff to spend money on things they want to buy. Staff look at the state student assessment results, make statements about how these scores do not reflect what teachers are doing in their classrooms, attempt to explain the results to the school board and to the public, and then hope that the test will go away before students have to take it again next year. Your school might have special externally funded grants or programs that require the collection and analysis of other data. Those who are providing the funds want progress described. Questionnaires are then sent out each year and are analyzed for the funders, not for those who implement the programs. Or, like many schools since the passage of *No Child Left Behind* (NCLB), your school personnel have learned how to analyze your most recent state assessment results. The analysis may lead to the development of strategies by some people to make the changes they feel the data are showing them to make.

At the classroom level, some teachers have adopted rubrics and performance assessment measures. They know their students are learning, but performance assessment measures are not easy to talk about in terms of an entire class, let alone schoolwide progress. It can be done, but it is difficult. And to frustrate the issue even more, some times high performance assessment results do not match high stakes assessment results.

Unfortunately, the scenarios described above are all too familiar in schools across the United States. However, with the increasing scrutiny called for by federal and state legislations and the sincere desire of educators to increase learning for all students, changes are occurring. The major change is that districts, schools, and teachers are seeing the connection between the analysis of data and the school improvement plan to ensure that every student is learning. Most schools are getting better at planning for improvement after looking at data. We still need to get better at planning for whole school change, and not just improving parts.

We want data about all parts of the school gathered and analyzed on a regular basis to understand the entire system, not just student achievement data, and not just when an external force requires it. We want members of the school community to understand not only how to gather and analyze the data, but also how to use data to accurately understand which strategies are not working and what to do differently to get different results. We want data analysis to lead to continuous school improvement.

The real voyage of discovery consists not in seeking new landscapes, but in seeing with new eyes.

Marcel Proust

A Better Way to Start Data Analysis

A system is not the sum of its parts, but rather, the product of the interaction of the parts.

Russell Ackoff

There are many ways to approach data analysis in schools. The approach taken in this book is a systematic, systemic, continuous improvement approach—we want to systematically gather and analyze data that will help us understand the system that produces the results we are getting. Then we want to use the data to continuously improve the system and, ultimately, to improve our results.

When we talk about the "system," we mean *all* the processes and procedures that contribute to student learning. Systems thinking is about viewing the whole and the interrelationships of the parts of the whole to each other. Systems thinking researchers would assign most differences in student performance to the system—not to the student. In other words, we must look carefully at how we deliver instruction and not just the material that is presented. We must look at what we are offering students, and who enrolls in our schools.

By continuous improvement, we mean measuring and evaluating processes on an ongoing basis to identify and implement improvement. *Teams and Tools* (1991) describes continuous improvement as causing us to " . . . think about upstream process improvement, not downstream damage control." This is exactly where we want schools to go with continuous school improvement—to become proactive, not reactive—to

Without continual growth and progress, such words as improvement, achievement, and success have no meaning.

Benjamin Franklin

create a system that will lead to the student learning results we want, and then to continually review and reflect on the results to improve all aspects of the system.

To focus on systemic continuous improvement, one must have *guiding principles* for the system, or school. Guiding principles are the ultimate purpose for the school, the vision of how that purpose will be carried out, based upon core values and beliefs and what we expect students to know and be able to do. By focusing on the guiding principles, we will be focusing our school improvement efforts on our ultimate purpose—why our school exists—to improve student learning. If we are not focusing on guiding principles, the results will lead to random acts of improvement, as shown in Figure 2.1, which I am sure we have all experienced. A focused data analysis process will enhance the continuous improvement process and provide information about how the school is doing in relationship to its guiding principles. Data analysis is focused when schools are clear on their purpose and clear on what they expect students to know and be able to do, and when students and the community are aware of these expectations.

Figure 2.1

Focusing the Data

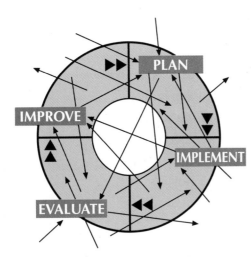

Random Acts of Improvement

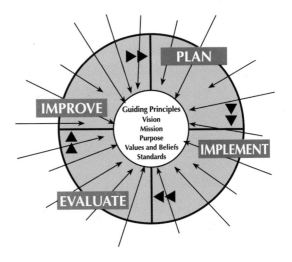

Focused Improvement

Data analyses flow comfortably from questions that staff and administrators naturally ask, to learn if the guiding principles are being met. Contrary to many assumptions about data, data analyses are very logical—we need to think about what we want to know and why, and then think about the data we have, or need, to answer the questions.

If you don't know where you are going, anything you do will get you there.

Anonymous

The most important question is: *What is the purpose of the school?* The answer to this question guides all other questions and answers.

▼ What do you expect students to know and be able to do by the time they leave the school? *(Standards)*

▼ What do you expect students to know and be able to do by the end of each semester? *(Benchmarks)*

▼ How well will students be able to do what they want to do with the knowledge and skills they acquire by the time they leave school? *(Performance)*

▼ Why are you getting the results you are getting? Why are you not getting the results you want? *(School Processes)*

▼ What would your school and educational processes look like if your school were achieving its purpose, goals, and expectations for student learning? *(Vision)*

▼ How will you use the data you gather? *(Implementation)*

To guide the process, to keep it focused, and to ensure that it is used, it is important to understand from the beginning how data analysis information is going to be used and who is going to use it.

Typically, school data are analyzed to—

▼ improve instruction

▼ gain instructional coherence

▼ provide students with feedback on their performance

▼ gain common understanding of what quality performance is and how close we are to achieving it

▼ measure program success and effectiveness

▼ understand if what we are doing is making a difference

▼ make sure students "do not fall through the cracks"

▼ show which programs are getting the results we want

▼ get to the "root causes" of problems

▼ guide curriculum development and revision

▼ promote accountability

▼ meet state and federal requirements

▼ better understand the school

▼ continuously improve the system

Schools that are not gathering, analyzing, and using data in purposeful ways need to transform their thinking about data. If the focus of data analysis efforts is on the continuous improvement of the entire learning organization, it is likely that other data analysis needs—such as external reporting requirements—will be met.

Getting Started Questions

As you begin your data analysis journey, take some time with your school team to think through the following questions. Identify one person as the recorder—the other members contribute ideas.

♦ What is the purpose of your school?

♦ What is the purpose for collecting data at your school?

♦ How do you want to use the data that will be collected?

♦ What are the roadblocks (i.e., people, products, reasons) to *collecting* data at your school?

♦ What are the roadblocks to *analyzing* data at your school?

♦ What are the roadblocks to *using* data at your school?

♦ How can you "get rid of" those roadblocks so data can be used on a systemic and continuous basis?

Summary

Comprehensive data analysis is tied to systematic and systemic continuous improvement. Some very important questions must be answered in order to make the work the school is doing worthwhile—not only the analysis work, but the work that is done for and with students every day. Clarifying the guiding principles of the school sets the stage for all systems and data analysis work.

The chapters that follow will help you think through all of these questions and their importance in your comprehensive data analysis journey. As you go through each of the chapters, think about what data you have now and what other data you need to gather.

WHAT DATA ARE IMPORTANT

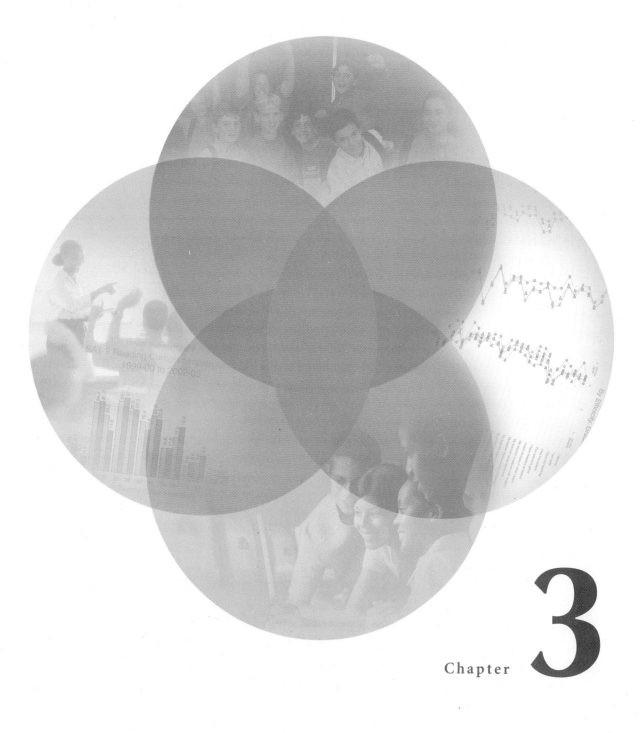

Chapter **3**

Learning does not take place in isolation. Students bring to the learning setting what they have experienced and the values they have been taught at home and in their neighborhoods. This effects how they respond.

National Center
for Education Statistics

If the purpose of school is to ensure that all students learn, what data will help schools understand if they are effectively carrying out their purpose? What data analyses will help schools know if all students are learning?

Learning takes place neither in isolation, nor only at school. Learning is also cumulative. Multiple measures must be considered and used to understand the multifaceted world of learning from the perspective of everyone involved. Using more than one method of assessment allows students to demonstrate their full range of abilities, and collecting data on *multiple occasions* provides students several opportunities to demonstrate their various abilities. If staffs want to know if the school is achieving its purpose and how to continually improve all aspects of the school, multiple measures—gathered from varying points of view—must be used.

Staff must think through the factors that impact student learning to determine data requirements. We need to ask students what they like about the way they learn at school and how they learn best. School processes, such as programs and instructional strategies, need to be described in order for all staff to meet the learning styles that will optimize the learning of all students.

Because students neither learn only at school nor only through teachers, we need to know about the learning environment from the parent and community perspective. Schools may also need to know how employers are perceiving the abilities and skills of former students.

But will these data provide enough information to determine how well the school is meeting the needs of all students? Other factors over which we have little or no control, such as background or demographics, also impact student learning. These data are crucial to our understanding of whom we serve, and whether or not our educational services are meeting the needs of every student.

Analyses of demographics, perceptions, student learning, and school processes provide a powerful picture that will help us understand the school's impact on student achievement. When used together, these measures give schools the information they need to improve teaching and learning and to get positive results.

In Figure 3.1, these four major categories of data are shown as overlapping circles. This figure illustrates the different types of information one can gain from individual measures and the enhanced levels of analyses that can be gained from the intersections of the measures.

Figure 3.1

Multiple Measures of Data

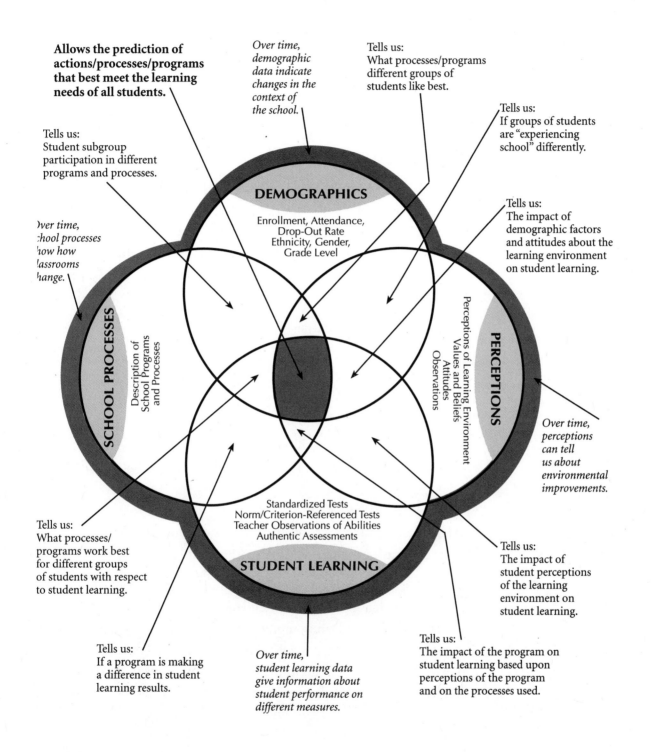

Allows the prediction of actions/processes/programs that best meet the learning needs of all students.

Over time, demographic data indicate changes in the context of the school.

Tells us: What processes/programs different groups of students like best.

Tells us: If groups of students are "experiencing school" differently.

Tells us: Student subgroup participation in different programs and processes.

Tells us: The impact of demographic factors and attitudes about the learning environment on student learning.

Over time, school processes show how classrooms change.

DEMOGRAPHICS

Enrollment, Attendance, Drop-Out Rate Ethnicity, Gender, Grade Level

SCHOOL PROCESSES

Description of School Programs and Processes

Perceptions of Learning Environment Values and Beliefs Attitudes Observations

PERCEPTIONS

Over time, perceptions can tell us about environmental improvements.

Standardized Tests Norm/Criterion-Referenced Tests Teacher Observations of Abilities Authentic Assessments

STUDENT LEARNING

Tells us: What processes/ programs work best for different groups of students with respect to student learning.

Tells us: The impact of student perceptions of the learning environment on student learning.

Tells us: If a program is making a difference in student learning results.

Over time, student learning data give information about student performance on different measures.

Tells us: The impact of the program on student learning based upon perceptions of the program and on the processes used.

Analysis discourages inappropriate actions by filtering out the noise before potential signals are identified. Before you can detect signals within the data, you must first filter out the probable noise. And, to filter out noise, you must start with past data.

Donald J. Wheeler

One measure, by itself, gives useful information. Comprehensive measures, used together and over time, provide much richer information. Ultimately, schools need to be able to predict what they must do to meet the needs of *all* the students they have, or will have in the future. The information gleaned from the intersections of these four measures (*demographics, perceptions, student learning,* and *school processes*), helps us to define the questions we want to ask, and focuses us on what data are necessary in order to find the answers.

Levels of Analysis

Different levels of analysis reveal answers to questions at varying depths of understanding. Each of the four measures, on its own, gives valuable descriptive information. However, more and better quality information can be found by digging deeper into the data through different levels of analysis in which one type of measure is analyzed and compared with other measures, over time.

Below are ten levels of analysis. Each level builds on the previous one to show how past data and intersections of measures provide more comprehensive information than a single measure of data taken for one year. If you feel you are only at level one, hang in there; this book and your own work will help you get to level ten.

Note: Unless otherwise specified, *over time* refers to no less than three years. Definitions of terms appear in the *Glossary* at the back of the book.

Level 1: Snapshots of Measures

Level one refers to the four major measures of data, shown in Figure 3.1, in their current state and independent of each other.

Demographic data provide descriptive information about the school community, such as enrollment, attendance, grade level, ethnicity, gender, and native language. Demographic data are very important for us to understand. They are the part of our educational system from which we can observe trends and glean information for purposes of prediction and planning. Demographic data assist us in understanding the results of all parts of our educational system through the disaggregation of other measures by demographic variables. Demographic data can also give us a glimpse of the system and how the school/district organizes the system.

Perceptions data help us understand what students, parents, staff, and others think about the learning environment. Perceptions can be gathered in a variety of ways—through questionnaires, interviews, focus groups, and observations. Perceptions are important since people act in congruence with what they believe, perceive, or think about different topics. It is important to know student, staff, and parent perceptions of the school so school personnel know what they can do to improve the system. Perceptions data can also tell us what is possible.

Student Learning describes the outcomes of our educational system in terms of standardized test results, grade point averages, standards assessments, and authentic assessments. Schools use a variety of student learning measurements—usually separately—and sometimes without thinking about how these measurements are interrelated. Schools normally think of multiple measures as looking only at different measures of student learning, rather than including demographics, perceptions, and school processes.

School Processes define what the system and teachers are doing to get the results they are getting. For example, how Reading is being taught at grade two, or Math at grade six. School processes include assessments, programs (e.g., English as a second language, special education), instructional strategies, and other classroom practices. This is the measure that seems to be the hardest for teachers to describe. Most often, teachers say they do what they do intuitively, and that they are too busy doing whatever they do to systematically document and reflect on their processes. To change the results schools are getting, teachers and school personnel must begin to document these processes and align them with the results they are getting in order to understand what to change to get different results, and to share their successes with others.

Looking at each of the four measures separately, we get snapshots of data in isolation from any other data at the school level. At this level we can answer questions such as—

▼ How many students are enrolled in the school this year?
  (*Demographics*)

▼ How satisfied are parents, students, and/or staff with the
  learning environment? (*Perceptions*)

▼ How did students at the school score on a test?
  (*Student Learning*)

▼ What programs are operating in the school this year?
  (*School Processes*)

Level 2: Measures, Over Time

At the second level, we start digging deeper into each of the measures by looking over time to answer questions, such as, but not limited to—

- ▼ How has enrollment in the school changed over the past five years? (*Demographics*)

- ▼ How have student perceptions of the learning environment changed over time? (*Perceptions*)

- ▼ Are there differences in student scores on standardized tests over the years? (*Student Learning*)

- ▼ What programs have operated in the school during the past five years? (*School Processes*)

Level 3: Two or More Variables Within Measures

Looking at more than one type of data within each of the circles gives us a better view of the learning organization (e.g., one year's standardized test subscores compared with performance assessment measures). We can answer questions such as—

- ▼ What percentage of the students currently at the school are fluent speakers of languages other than English, and are there equal numbers of males and females? (*Demographics*)

- ▼ Are staff, student, and parent perceptions of the learning environment in agreement? (*Perceptions*)

- ▼ Are students' standardized test scores consistent with teacher-assigned grades and performance assessment rubrics? (*Student Learning*)

- ▼ What are the instructional strategies in the school's mathematics and science programs? (*School Processes*)

Level 4: Two or More Variables Within One Type of Measure, Over Time

Level 4 takes similar measures as Level 3, across time (e.g., standardized test subscores and performance assessment measures compared over the past four years), and allows us to answer deeper questions such as—

- ▼ How has the enrollment of non-English-speaking kindergartners changed in the past three years? (*Demographics*)

- ▼ Are staff, students, and parents more or less satisfied with the learning environment now than they were in previous years? (*Perceptions*)

- ▼ Over the past three years, how do teacher-assigned grades and standardized test scores compare? (*Student Learning*)

- ▼ How have the instructional strategies used in the school's mathematics and science programs changed over time? (*School Processes*)

Level 5: Intersection of Two Types of Measures

Level 5 begins the intersections across two circles (e.g., last year's standardized test results by ethnicity). Level 5 helps us to answer questions such as—

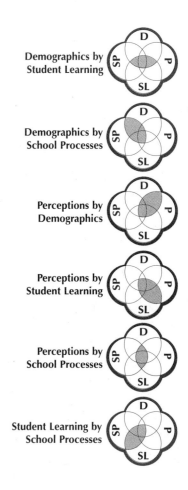

Demographics by Student Learning

Demographics by School Processes

Perceptions by Demographics

Perceptions by Student Learning

Perceptions by School Processes

Student Learning by School Processes

- ▼ Do students who attend school every day perform better on the state assessment than students who miss more than five days per month? (*Demographics by Student Learning*)

- ▼ What instructional strategies do third grade teachers use with students whose native languages are different from that of the teacher? (*Demographics by School Processes*)

- ▼ Is there a gender difference in students' perceptions of the learning environment? (*Perceptions by Demographics*)

- ▼ Do students with positive attitudes about school do better academically, as measured by the state assessment? (*Perceptions by Student Learning*)

- ▼ Are there differences in how students enrolled in different programs perceive the learning environment? (*Perceptions by School Processes*)

- ▼ Do students who were enrolled in active hands-on content courses this year perform better on standardized achievement tests than those who took the content courses in a more traditional manner? (*Student Learning by School Processes*)

Level 6: Intersection of Two Measures, Over Time

Looking at the intersection of two of the measures over time allows us to see trends as they develop (e.g., standardized achievement scores disaggregated by ethnicity over the past three years can help us see if the equality of scores, by ethnicity, is truly a trend or an initial fluctuation). This intersection also begins to show the relationship of the multiple measures and why it is so important to look at all the measures together.

At Level 6 we are looking at the intersection of two of the circles over time. The questions we can answer at this level include, as examples—

- ▼ How have students of different ethnicities scored on standardized tests over the past three years? (*Demographics by Student Learning*)

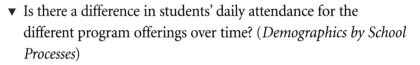

▼ Is there a difference in students' daily attendance for the different program offerings over time? (*Demographics by School Processes*)

▼ Have parent perceptions of the learning environment changed since the implementation of the new mathematics program? (*Perceptions by School Processes*)

Level 7: Intersection of Three Measures

As we intersect three of the measures at the school level (e.g., student learning measures disaggregated by ethnicity compared to student questionnaire responses disaggregated by ethnicity), the types of questions that we are able to answer include the following:

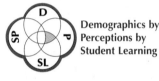

Demographics by Perceptions by Student Learning

Perceptions by Demographics by School Processes

Perceptions by Student Learning by School Processes

School Processes by Student Learning by Demographics

▼ Do students of different ethnicities perceive the learning environment differently, and are their scores on standardized achievement tests consistent with these perceptions? (*Demographics by Perceptions by Student Learning*)

▼ What instructional process(es) did the previously non-English-speaking students enjoy most in their all-English classrooms this year? (*Perceptions by Demographics by School Processes*)

▼ Is there a difference in students' reports of what they like most about the school by whether or not they participate in extracurricular activities? Do these students have higher grade point averages than students who do not participate in extracurricular activities? (*Perceptions by Student Learning by School Processes*)

▼ Which program is making the biggest difference with respect to student achievement for at-risk students this year, and is one group of students responding "better" to the processes? (*School Processes by Student Learning by Demographics*)

Level 8: Intersection of Three Measures, Over Time

Looking at three measures over time allows us to see trends, to begin to understand the learning environment from the students' perspectives, and to know how to deliver instruction to get the desired results from and for all students.

Level 8 takes Level 7 intersections over time (e.g., standardized achievement scores disaggregated by ethnicity compared to student questionnaires disaggregated by ethnicity, for the past four years). Level 8 allows us to answer the following types of questions:

▼ What programs do all types of students like the most every year? (*Demographics by Perceptions by School Processes*)

▼ Have the processes used to teach English to English-learning students been consistent across grade levels so each student is able to build on her/his abilities? (*Demographics by Student Learning by School Processes*)

Level 9: Intersection of All Four Measures

Our ultimate analysis is the intersection of all four measures at the school level (e.g., standardized achievement tests disaggregated by program, by gender, within grade level, compared to questionnaire results for students by program, by gender, within grade level). These intersections allow us to answer questions such as—

▼ Are there differences in achievement scores for 8th grade girls and boys who report that they like school, by the type of program and grade level in which they are enrolled? (*Demographics by Perceptions by School Processes by Student Learning*)

Demographics by
Perceptions by
School Processes by
Student Learning

Level 10: Intersection of All Four Measures, Over Time

It is not until we intersect all four circles, at the school level and over time, that we are able to answer questions that will predict if the actions, processes, and programs that we are establishing will meet the needs of all students. With this intersection, we can answer the ultimate question:

▼ Based on whom we have as students, how they prefer to learn, and what programs they are in, are all students learning at the same rate? (*Student Learning by Demographics by Perceptions by School Processes*)

Level 10 is basically where we want to go to gauge a school's progress over time. It takes into consideration all previous levels. This is also the level that will get us closer to understanding root causes of our undesirable results. The analyses at this level can keep us from repeating processes that are not effective.

If you know why, you figure out how...

W. Edwards Deming

At Level 10, we will not necessarily see one graph disaggregated four ways. What we might see are a number of analyses from Level 1 through 9 used together to understand more about our ultimate Level 10 goal.

The next four chapters (Chapters 4 through 7) will discuss each of these measures of data separately. Intersections of these measures will again be discussed in Chapter 8.

Study Questions for What Data are Important

How will you get started with your school's comprehensive data analysis? What data do you have, or need to gather, to answer the questions discussed in this chapter? Fill in the blank cells in the table below to guide your work. Examples appear in the table for guidance.

Questions	What data do you have or need to answer the questions?	What other data do you have or need to gather?
Demographics	*Student enrollment by grade, by gender, by ethnicity, by free/reduced lunch status, language proficiency, for five years.* *Teachers data by gender, ethnicity, number of years teaching experience, credentials.*	*Information about predicted community changes.* *Administrator information, such as number of years in current position, and number of years teaching.*
Perceptions	*Perceptions: student, staff, parent questionnaires.* *Education for the Future Continuous Improvement Continuums Assessment.*	
Student Learning	*Student achievement results.*	
School Processes	*Extracurricular programs we offer students.*	

Summary

Schools cannot use student achievement measures alone for continuous school improvement. Why? Because the *context* is missing! Relying on only one measure can mislead schools into thinking they are analyzing student learning in a comprehensive fashion. Just looking at student learning measures alone could, in fact, keep teachers from progressing and truly meeting the needs of students, because they are not looking at the other elements that have a great impact on student learning and teaching.

If we want to get different results, we have to change the processes (e.g., instruction, system) that create the results. When we focus only on student learning measures, we see school personnel using their time figuring out how to look better on the student learning measures. We want school personnel to use their time to determine how to do better for *all* students. In order to do that, we must look at intersections of demographic, perceptual, student learning, and school process data, so we can understand the inter-relationships among these elements.

DEMOGRAPHICS

Chapter **4**

Demographics are typically known as the statistical characteristics of human populations (such as age or ethnicity). In education, demographic data translate to items such as—

▼ numbers of students in the school

▼ numbers of students with special needs

▼ ethnicities of the students in the school

▼ number of graduates

▼ number of students who drop out of school each year

▼ number of teachers by years of experience

Demographics clarify who our "clients" are and who the staff are as service providers. Demographics build the *context* of the school and help us begin to predict future conditions, so we can take an active approach to serving the needs of our current and future students. These contextual variables are critical and required for understanding any other information gathered about the school.

Through the study of demographic trends, we can predict with some accuracy such things as the number of students and the ethnic diversity with which the school can expect to work in the future. From an historical perspective, a school can use demographic data to analyze how well it has served its past and current population, and identify changes needed to meet the needs of its future clients.

Demographic data do so much more than just inform us of human characteristics, however; demographics also tell us about the system. The structure of the school, such as class sizes, number of years of teacher experience by grade level, number of students in special education programs, by gender and ethnicity, and the subgroups of students enrolled in different programs, such as advanced placement, or honors, are all part of demographics.

What Demographic Data

Many school districts have much demographic data available. The following list is offered to note the items that are usually available, at school and district offices. It is not a list that says you should seek all of these elements. Use the demographic data that will build the context of your school. To be most useful, much of the data should reflect at least three years of information (over time).

Possible Existing Demographic Data at School and District Levels

Community

- ▼ Location and history
- ▼ Economic base, population trends, and community resources (*www.census.gov* is a great resource for getting information about the community, as is your local chamber of commerce)
- ▼ Community involvement
- ▼ Business partnership

School District

- ▼ Description and history
- ▼ Number of schools, administrators, students and teachers over time, and by grade level

School

- ▼ Description and history, attendance area, location
- ▼ Type of school, e.g., magnet, alternative, charter, private, private management
- ▼ Number of administrators, students and teachers over time, and by grade level
- ▼ Number of students electing to come to the school from out of the attendance area
- ▼ Grants and awards received
- ▼ Title 1/Schoolwide
- ▼ Safety/crime data
- ▼ *State designation as a dangerous school
- ▼ Uniqueness and strengths
- ▼ Class sizes
- ▼ Extracurricular activities
- ▼ After-school programs/summer school
- ▼ Tutoring/peer mentoring
- ▼ Community support-services coordinated
- ▼ Counseling opportunities
- ▼ *Facilities: equipped for networked computers and handicapped
- ▼ Facilities: age, capacity, maintenance
- ▼ Availability of supplies and necessities

Students Over Time, and by Grade Level

- ▼ Living situation/family structure/family size
- ▼ Preschool/Head Start/Even Start
- ▼ Preschool attendance
- ▼ *Number of students

▼ Gender of students

▼ *Race/ethnicity, numbers and percentages

▼ *Free/reduced lunch, numbers and percentages

▼ *Language fluency by language

▼ *Migrant/immigrants, by country, home languages, homeless

▼ *Special Education by disability, gender, ethnicity, language fluency, free/reduced lunch

▼ *Attendance/tardies

▼ Mobility (where students go/come from)

▼ Retention rates by gender, ethnicity, language fluency, free/reduced lunch

▼ *Dropout rates by gender, ethnicity, free/reduced lunch, migrant, and special education (where students go/what they do)

▼ Number of students leaving middle school overall for grade, by gender, ethnicity, language fluency, free/reduced lunch

▼ Extracurricular activity participation/clubs/service learning by gender, ethnicity, language fluency, free/reduced lunch

▼ Number of participants in programs, such as AP, IB, Honors, Upward Bound, Gear-up, college-prep, vocational

▼ Number of home schoolers associated with school

▼ Number of students electing to come to the school from out-of-attendance area

▼ Number of bus riders

▼ Student employment

▼ *Discipline indicators (e.g., suspensions, referrals, types of incidences, number of students carrying weapons on school property)

▼ *Number of drugs on school property (offered, sold, or given illegal drugs)

▼ *Graduation rates by gender, ethnicity, language proficiency, free/reduced lunch, migrant, and special education (where students go/what they do)

▼ Number of students concurrently enrolled in college courses

▼ Number of students meeting college course entrance requirements, by gender, ethnicity, language fluency, free/reduced lunch

▼ Number of scholarships, by gender, ethnicity, language fluency, free/reduced lunch

▼ Number of students completing GEDs

▼ Adult education program

▼ Number and percentage of students going on to college; post-graduate training; and/or employment
▼ Grade-point average in college
▼ Number of graduates ending up in college remedial classes

Staff Over Time

▼ *Number of teachers, administrators, instructional specialists, support staff by roles
▼ *Years of experience, by grade level and/or role, in this school/ in teaching
▼ Ethnicity, gender, languages spoken
▼ Retirement projections
▼ *Types of certifications/licenses/teacher qualifications/ percentage of time teaching in certified area(s)
▼ Grade/subjects teachers are teaching
▼ Degrees
▼ *Educational training of paraprofessionals
▼ Teacher-student ratios by grade level
▼ Teacher turnover rates
▼ Attendance rates
▼ Teacher involvement in extracurricular activities, program participation
▼ *Number of teachers receiving high-quality professional development
▼ *Percent of teachers qualified to use technology for instruction
▼ *National Board for Professional Teaching Standards* (NBPTS) teachers

Parents

▼ Educational levels, home language, employment, socio-economic status
▼ Involvement with their child's learning
▼ Involvement in school activities
▼ Incarceration

What Other Data?

Required for NCLB (includes the numbers required to understand the disaggregated numbers required by NCLB)

Disaggregation is not a problem-solving strategy. It is a problem-finding strategy.

Disaggregation

The separation of results into different subgroups that make up the population is called *disaggregation*. Demographics play an important role in the disaggregation of data. Demographic subgroupings of any achievement or perception measures allow us to isolate variations among different subgroups of students to understand if all students are achieving or experiencing school in the same way.

Disaggregation provides powerful information in the analysis of school variables, test scores, and questionnaire results. Schools need to disaggregate their important student achievement, perceptions, and school process data by demographic variables that impact student learning to understand all aspects of the population of the school, and enable them to look for problems and root causes. For *No Child Left Behind* (NCLB), schools must disaggregate their student achievement results by:

▼ ethnicity/race

▼ indicators of poverty

▼ English language proficiency

▼ special education disabilities

Disaggregation helps us understand if we are truly meeting the purpose and mission of our school. If we are acting on the belief that all students can achieve, any breakdown of subgroups of students should show few differences. Disaggregation also helps us find subgroups that are not responding to our processes in the way that others are—enabling us to understand why and to search for new processes so all students can learn.

It is best to disaggregate for few rather than many subpopulations at a time. When too many subpopulations are used, group sizes may become so small that individuals can easily be identified, and the reliability of the results diminish. In fact, most states have official subgroup sizes that they believe will lead to unreliable results. NCLB uses 40.

Choose general demographic variables that may be associated with student achievement, such as—

▼ gender

▼ ethnicity

▼ socioeconomic status

▼ grade level

▼ attendance

▼ number of years at the school

How to Analyze Demographic Information

A comprehensive demographic study begins with a school profile. A school profile typically displays data from the general to the specific. A good profile systematically describes the context of the school. Most schools have student information systems that house their demographic data, gathered on an ongoing basis. You will need to indicate the point in time you take data for demographic analysis. Most states have an official date in the fall for census information. Make sure the point in time used to describe your demographics is both noted and typical of what your state uses, and NCLB requires. Example profiles for an elementary and a high school are shown as Figures 4.1 and 4.2, respectively. *(Note: Using Data to Improve Student Learning in Elementary Schools; Middle Schools; High Schools;* and *School Districts,* provide graphing templates and examples on accompanying CDs for doing this work [Bernhardt, 2003, 2004].)*

Our Example Schools

Figure 4.1

Archer Elementary School Demographic Profile

Archer Elementary School is a pre-kindergarten through grade five school located in the Midwest. According to the 2001 census, the city in which Archer is located has a population of around 80,000, up approximately 10,000 from the 1991 census *(http://www.census.gov)*. The census data also show that the average family income in 1991 was about $26,000, while in 2001, the average family income was approximately $31,219. The city is home to the main and largest of four university campuses, with 23,300 students. The university, the school district, and the university hospital are the major stable employers in this city.

Archer Elementary is part of the Park School District, which currently serves 16,451 students in 28 schools: eighteen elementary (K-5), three middle (6-7), three junior high (8-9), three senior high (10-12), and a career center. Nine years ago, 14,022 students were served by the district. The percent increase in the student population mirrors the percent increase in the community population. This 2,429 student increase in overall district enrollment during the last ten years is shown in Figure A.

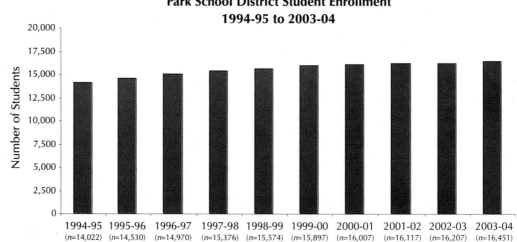

Figure A
Park School District Student Enrollment
1994-95 to 2003-04

Archer Elementary School currently serves 472 students, down 109 students from four years earlier (Figure B).

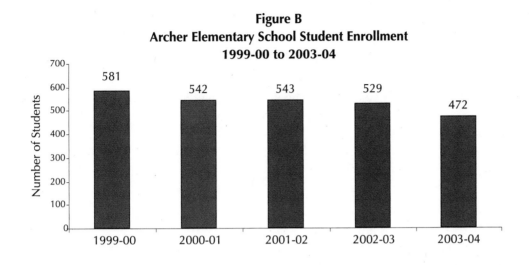

Figure B
Archer Elementary School Student Enrollment
1999-00 to 2003-04

Figure C shows the current population consists of 235 Black (49.8%), 218 White (46.2%), 8 Hispanic/Latino (1.7%), 8 Asian (1.7%), and 3 American Indian (.6%) students.

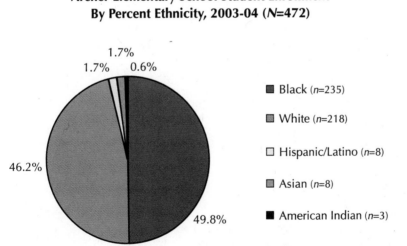

Figure C
Archer Elementary School Student Enrollment
By Percent Ethnicity, 2003-04 (*N*=472)

■ Black (*n*=235)

■ White (*n*=218)

□ Hispanic/Latino (*n*=8)

■ Asian (*n*=8)

■ American Indian (*n*=3)

As shown in Figure D, over the past five years, the proportion of Black students to the total school population dipped from 39.9% (*n*=232) to 38.7% (*n*=210), increased to 45.1% (*n*=245), continued to increase to 47.4% (*n*=251), and then to 49.8% (*n*=235). The proportion of White students decreased from 58.2% (*n*=338) to 46.2% (*n*=218) over the five years. The number of Hispanic/Latino students generally increased over four years and decreased a bit by the fifth year. The numbers of American Indian and Asian students have remained small (less than 1%) over the five years, with the exception of a percentage increase of Asian students in 2003-04.

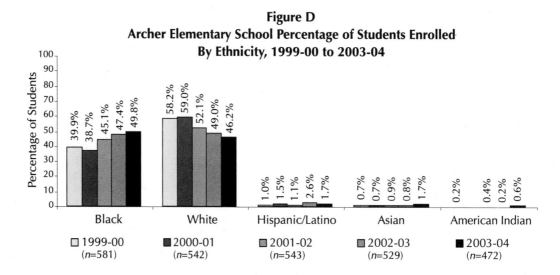

Figure D
Archer Elementary School Percentage of Students Enrolled
By Ethnicity, 1999-00 to 2003-04

One can also see the fluctuating population of this school attendance area (Figure E) reflected in the school enrollment by grade level over the last five years. (The total numbers do not match previous graph because pre-K was taken out of the total numbers.)

Note: Looking at the same grade level over time is called *trend analysis*.

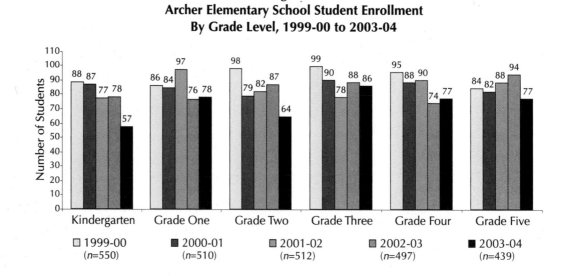

Figure E
Archer Elementary School Student Enrollment
By Grade Level, 1999-00 to 2003-04

Figure F shows the cohorts of students passing through grade levels together. One can see how much fluctuation there is in subgroups progressing through the grades together.

Note: Reorganizing the data to look at the groups of students progressing through the grades together over time is called a *cohort analysis.* If we were looking at the same students, as opposed to the groups of students, it would be called *matched cohorts.*

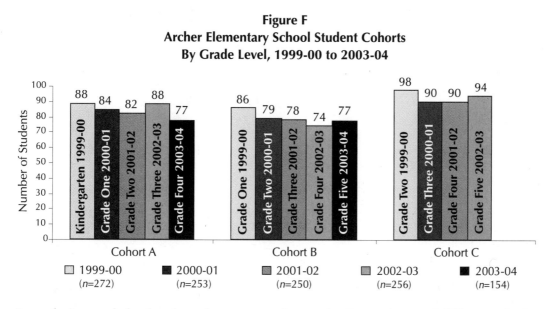

Figure F
Archer Elementary School Student Cohorts
By Grade Level, 1999-00 to 2003-04

By analyzing grade level and gender, one can also see the fluctuations and differences in the numbers and percentages of males and females over time, within any grade level (Figure G).

Figure G
Archer Elementary School
Numbers and Percentages of Students
By Grade Level and Gender, 1999-00 to 2003-04

Grade Level	Gender	1999-00 (n=550)		2000-01 (n=510)		2001-02 (n=512)		2002-03 (n=497)		2003-04 (n=439)	
Kindergarten	Male	45	51%	51	59%	37	48%	40	51%	33	58%
	Female	43	49%	36	41%	40	52%	38	49%	24	42%
Grade One	Male	38	44%	46	55%	58	60%	33	43%	36	46%
	Female	48	56%	38	45%	39	40%	43	57%	42	54%
Grade Two	Male	51	52%	33	42%	42	51%	53	61%	31	48%
	Female	47	48%	46	58%	40	49%	34	39%	33	52%
Grade Three	Male	44	44%	43	48%	33	42%	43	49%	50	58%
	Female	55	56%	47	52%	45	58%	45	51%	36	42%
Grade Four	Male	52	55%	37	42%	43	48%	34	46%	37	48%
	Female	43	45%	51	58%	47	52%	40	54%	40	52%
Grade Five	Male	45	54%	41	50%	37	42%	48	51%	40	52%
	Female	39	46%	41	50%	51	58%	46	49%	37	48%

Over this same five-year period, Figure H shows the percentage of students qualifying for Free/Reduced Lunch has increased from 51% of the school population to 60%, an indicator of an increase in the percentage of families living in poverty. The actual number of students qualifying for Free/Reduced Lunch decreased from 2002-03 to 2003-04.

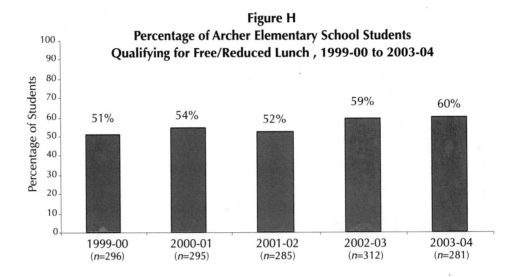

Figure H
Percentage of Archer Elementary School Students
Qualifying for Free/Reduced Lunch , 1999-00 to 2003-04

Archer students have maintained an average of about 91% yearly attendance rate during the last five years. With 94% attending, students in 2003-04 had the highest rate for the past five years (Figure I).

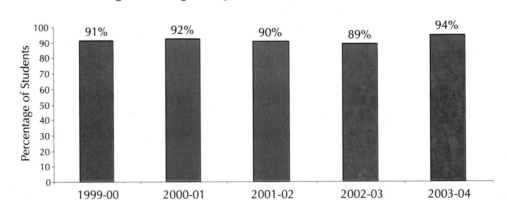

Figure I
Archer Elementary School
Average Percentage Yearly Attendance, 1999-00 to 2003-04

Twenty-seven classroom teachers currently work at Archer, down from 28 in 2002-03, 31 in 2001-02, 30 in 2000-01, and 28 in 1999-00 (Figure J). All classroom teachers in 2002-03 are White, as is the female principal. There is one male teacher who teaches third grade. The average class size is 18 students. The number of classroom teachers is shown in Figure J, by grade level over time.

Figure J
Number of Archer Elementary School Teachers
By Grade Level, 1999-00 to 2003-04

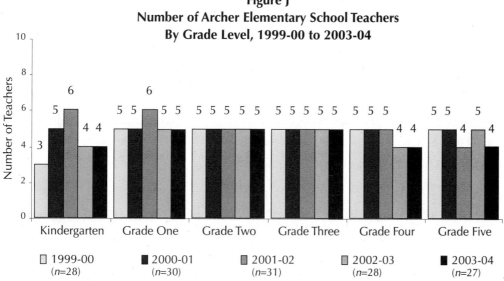

| | 1999-00 (*n*=28) | | 2000-01 (*n*=30) | | 2001-02 (*n*=31) | | 2002-03 (*n*=28) | | 2003-04 (*n*=27) |

Figure K shows the total number of years of teaching experience, by grade taught, for each of the classroom teachers at Archer Elementary for 2002-03. The principal has been the leader of this school for five years. The scatter plot of data reveals that teachers with the least experience have a tendency to teach lower grades, while those with many years of experience teach the higher grades.

Figure K
Archer Elementary School
Teaching Experience by Grade Level and Teacher, 2003-04

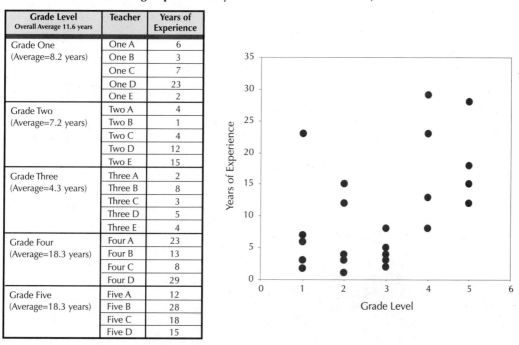

Grade Level Overall Average 11.6 years	Teacher	Years of Experience
Grade One (Average=8.2 years)	One A	6
	One B	3
	One C	7
	One D	23
	One E	2
Grade Two (Average=7.2 years)	Two A	4
	Two B	1
	Two C	4
	Two D	12
	Two E	15
Grade Three (Average=4.3 years)	Three A	2
	Three B	8
	Three C	3
	Three D	5
	Three E	4
Grade Four (Average=18.3 years)	Four A	23
	Four B	13
	Four C	8
	Four D	29
Grade Five (Average=18.3 years)	Five A	12
	Five B	28
	Five C	18
	Five D	15

Note: The Archer School profile would continue to systematically describe the demographic data. Other data to include in a comprehensive school profile are listed earlier in this chapter, *Possible Existing Data at School and District Levels* (pages 33-35).

Figure 4.2

Majestic High School Demographic Profile

Majestic High School currently serves 241 students. Over the past ten years, the population of Majestic High School has fluctuated between 205 and 243. The lump-sum increase is 36 students (15%), in ten years, as shown in Figure A below.

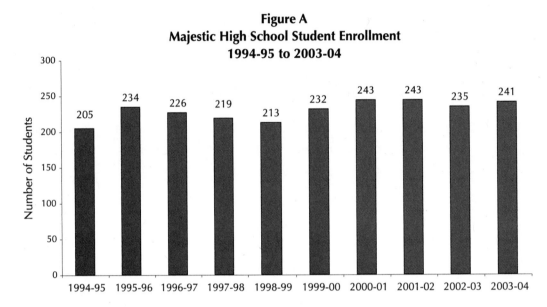

Figure A
Majestic High School Student Enrollment
1994-95 to 2003-04

Majestic's student population has some ethnic diversity. Figure B shows the current student population consists of 157 White (65.1%), 33 Asian (13.7%), 23 Hispanic/Latino (9.5%), 21 Black (8.7%), and 7 American Indian (2.9%) students.

Figure B
Majestic High School Student Enrollment
By Percent Ethnicity, 2003-04 (N=241)

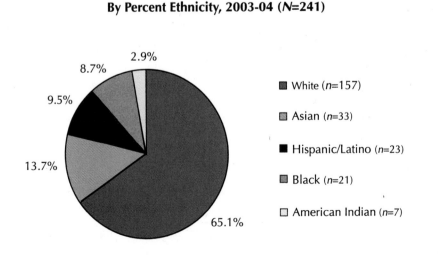

Over the past six years, as shown in Figure C, the number of American Indian students has remained small and has increased from 2 to a high of 9, and then back down to 5 in the six years. The number of Asian students increased from 27 to 34. There was only 1 Pacific Islander student enrolled—in 2000-01. The number of Hispanic/Latino students decreased from 30 to 24, over the six years. The number of Black students increased to 25 in 2000-01 and then dipped back to 22 in 2003-04. The number of White students increased from 132 in 1998-99 to 165 in 2002-03 and then dipped to 156 in 2003-04.

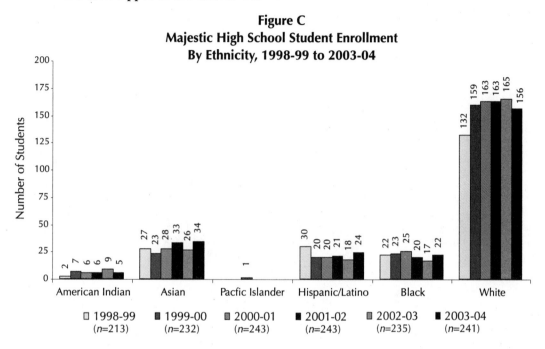

Figure C
Majestic High School Student Enrollment
By Ethnicity, 1998-99 to 2003-04

One can see the fluctuating population of this school attendance area reflected in the school enrollment by grade level over the last six years (Figure D).

Note: Looking at the same grade level over time is called *trend analysis.*

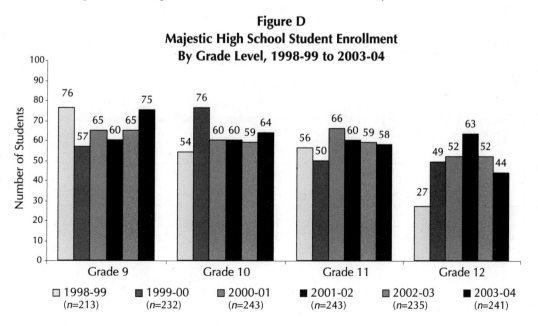

Figure D
Majestic High School Student Enrollment
By Grade Level, 1998-99 to 2003-04

Looking at the cohorts of these students over time (Figure E), one can see that in every cohort, the number of students decreased by grade twelve.

Note: Reorganizing the data to look at the groups of students progressing through the grades together over time is called a *cohort analysis.* If we were looking at the same students, as opposed to the groups of students, the analysis would be called *matched cohort analysis.*

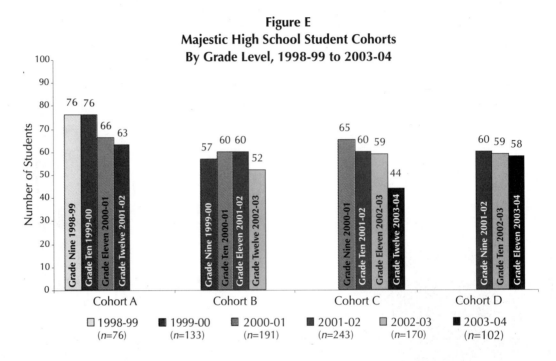

Figure E
Majestic High School Student Cohorts
By Grade Level, 1998-99 to 2003-04

By analyzing grade level and gender, one can also see the fluctuations and the differences in the numbers and percentages of males and females over time, within any grade level (Figure F), and diagonally over time.

Figure F
Majestic High School
Numbers and Percentages of Students
By Grade Level and Gender, 2000-01 to 2003-04

Grade Level	Gender	2000-01 (n=243)		2001-02 (n=243)		2002-03 (n=235)		2003-04 (n=241)	
Grade Nine	Male	36	62%	28	46%	37	56%	32	42%
	Female	29	38%	32	54%	28	44%	43	58%
Grade Ten	Male	26	43%	36	60%	32	54%	33	51%
	Female	34	57%	24	40%	27	46%	31	49%
Grade Eleven	Male	31	46%	24	40%	35	59%	33	56%
	Female	35	54%	36	60%	24	41%	25	44%
Grade Twelve	Male	26	50%	28	44%	21	40%	29	65%
	Female	26	50%	35	56%	31	60%	15	35%

Figure G shows the number of students by grade level, ethnicity, and gender from 2000-01 through 2003-04.

Figure G
Majestic High School
Numbers and Percentages of Students
By Grade Level and Gender, 2000-01 to 2003-04

Grade Level	Ethnicity	2000-01 (n=243)		2001-02 (n=243)		2002-03 (n=235)		2003-04 (n=241)	
		Male	Female	Male	Female	Male	Female	Male	Female
Grade Nine	American Indian	1				1		1	1
	Asian	3	4	5	4	3		5	8
	Hispanic/Latino	1	2	3	1	2	3	3	6
	Black	4	4	3	1	1	3	2	4
	White	27	19	17	26	30	22	21	24
Grade Ten	American Indian	1	2	1		2	1		
	Asian	2	6	3	5	6	5	3	
	Pacific Islander							1	
	Hispanic/Latino	3	2	1	3	3	3	2	4
	Black		3	3	4	3	1	1	4
	White	20	21	28	12	18	17	26	23
Grade Eleven	American Indian	1	1	1	2	2		2	1
	Asian	3	6		6	3	4	6	5
	Hispanic/Latino	1	6	3	4		2	3	2
	Black	5	2	1	2	3	4	3	1
	White	21	20	19	22	27	14	19	16
Grade Twelve	American Indian			1	1	1	2	2	
	Asian	1	3	2	8		5	3	3
	Pacific Islander		1						
	Hispanic/Latino	3	2		6	3	2		3
	Black	3	4	4	2	1	1	3	3
	White	19	16	21	18	16	21	21	6

As shown in Figure H, the percentage of students qualifying for free/reduced lunch in the last ten years has changed from 72% (*n*=205) in 1994-95, to 93% (*n*=232) in 1999-00, to 68% (*n*=241) in 2003-04.

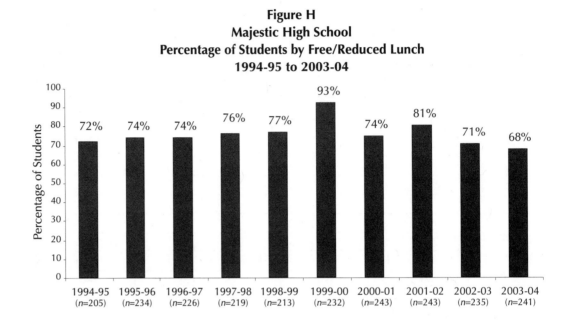

Figure H
Majestic High School
Percentage of Students by Free/Reduced Lunch
1994-95 to 2003-04

Over the past nine years, Majestic High has experienced dropout percentages between 1.5% and 6.4%. 1997-98 had the highest percentage of dropouts (Figure I). The percentages have steadily decreased since that time to 2.6% in 2002-03.

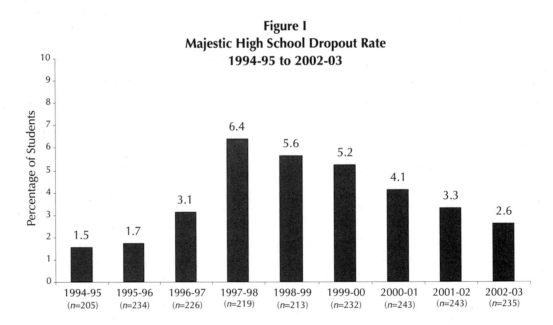

Figure I
Majestic High School Dropout Rate
1994-95 to 2002-03

Majestic High School has 17 regular classroom teachers. The average years of teaching experience increased from 16.5 years in 1998-99 to 19.5 years in 2003-04 (Figure J).

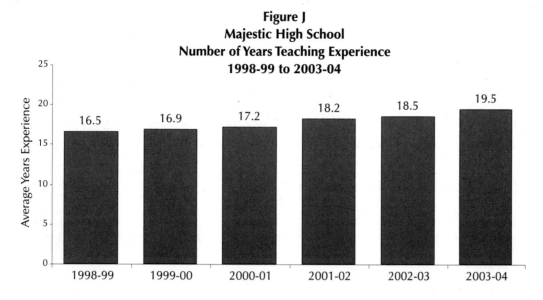

Figure J
Majestic High School
Number of Years Teaching Experience
1998-99 to 2003-04

Comparing teaching experience to the district, county, and state in 2003-04, Majestic High School teachers have taught an average of 19.5 years, while teachers representing the three other larger entities taught fewer years on average—district teachers average 16.9 years, county teachers average 17.5, and state teachers average 12.7 years. Majestic High teachers have been in the district an average of 15.5 years, while district teachers overall have been in the district an average of 13.2 years, teachers have taught in the county an average of 13.8 years, and in the state 10.4 years (Figure K).

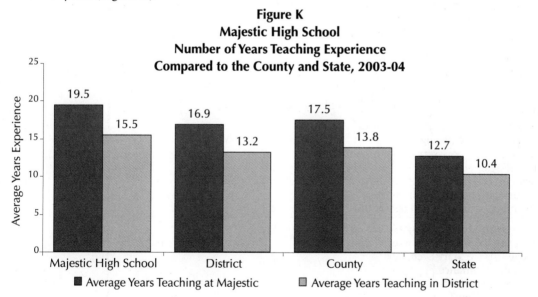

Figure K
Majestic High School
Number of Years Teaching Experience
Compared to the County and State, 2003-04

Majestic had no first or second year teachers in 2002-03, while the district had 5, the county had 24, and the state had 42,788 first and second year teachers. Majestic High School staff is essentially one-half male (9), and one-half female (8). All of the teaching staff have Bachelor's degrees. Two have Master's degrees.

Note: Majestic High School's profile would continue with demographic data that are listed earlier in this chapter, *Possible Existing Data at School and District Levels* (pages 33-35).

Study Questions for Demographics

Below, think about the demographic data you have that will describe your school. How many years of complete and useable data do you have? How many years of data do you want to use in your analysis?

Also, think about other demographic information you want to include in your analyses and how you will want to disaggregate and graph this information.

Demographic Data	Number of Years of Data Existing	Number of Years of Data Desired
Community Location and history Economic base, population trends, and community resources Community involvement Business partnerships		
School District Description and history Number of schools, administrators, students and teachers over time, and by grade level		
School Description and history, attendance area, location Type of school, e.g., magnet, alternative, charter, private, private management Number of administrators, students and teachers over time, and by grade level Number of students electing to come to the school from out of the attendance area Grants and awards received Title 1/Schoolwide Safety/crime data *State designation as a dangerous school Uniqueness and strengths Class sizes After-school programs/summer school Extracurricular activities Advisors for extracurricular activities Tutoring/peer mentoring Community support-services coordinated Counseling opportunities *Facilities: equipped for networked computers and handicapped Facilities: age, capacity, maintenance Availability of supplies and necessities		
Students Over Time, and by Grade Level Living situation/family structure/family size Preschool/Head Start/Even Start Preschool attendance *Number of students Gender of students *Race/ethnicity numbers and percentages *Free/reduced lunch numbers and percentages *Language fluency by language *Migrant/immigrants, by country, home languages *Homeless *Special Education by disability, gender, ethnicity, language fluency, free/reduced lunch *Attendance/tardies Mobility (where students go/come from) Retention rates by gender, ethnicity, language fluency, free/reduced lunch *Dropout rates by gender, ethnicity, free/reduced lunch, migrant, and special education (where students go/what they do)		

*Required for NCLB (includes the numbers required to understand the disaggregated numbers required by NCLB)

Demographic Data	Number of Years of Data Existing	Number of Years of Data Desired
Students Over Time, and by Grade Level *(continued)*		
Number of students leaving school overall by gender, ethnicity, language fluency, free/reduced lunch		
Extracurricular activity participation/clubs/service learning by gender, ethnicity, language fluency, free/reduced lunch		
Number of participants in programs, such as AP, IB, Honors, Upward Bound, GEAR UP, college-prep, vocational		
Number of home schoolers associated with school		
Number of students electing to come to the school from out-of-attendance area		
Number of bus riders and distances they ride		
Student employment		
*Discipline indicators (e.g., suspensions, referrals, types of incidences, number of students carrying weapons on school property)		
*Number of drugs on school property (offered, sold, or given illegal drugs)		
*Graduation rates by gender, ethnicity, language proficiency, free/reduced lunch, migrant, and special education (where students go/what they do)		
Number of high school students concurrently enrolled in college courses		
Number of students meeting college course entrance requirements, by gender, ethnicity, language fluency, free/reduced lunch		
Number of middle students concurrently enrolled in high school courses		
Number of scholarships by gender, ethnicity, language proficiency, free/reduced lunch		
Number of students completing GEDs		
Adult education program		
Number and percentage of students going on to college, post-graduate training, and/or employment		
Grade-point average in college		
Number of graduates ending up in college remedial classes		
Staff Over Time		
*Number of teachers, administrators, instructional specialists, support staff by roles		
*Years of experience, by grade level and/or role, in this school/in teaching		
Ethnicity, gender, languages spoken		
Retirement projections		
*Types of certifications/licenses/teacher qualifications/percentage of time teaching in certified area(s)		
Grades/subjects teachers are teaching		
Degrees		
*Educational training of paraprofessionals		
Teacher-student ratios by grade level		
Teacher turnover rates		
Attendance rates		
Teacher involvement in extracurricular activities, program participation		
*Number of teachers receiving high-quality professional development		
*Percent of teachers qualified to use technology for instruction		
National Board for Professional Teaching Standards (NBPTS) teachers		
Parents		
Educational levels, home language, employment, socioeconomic status		
Involvement with their child's learning		
Involvement in school activities		
Incarceration		
Other Data?		

*Required for NCLB (includes the numbers required to understand the disaggregated numbers required by NCLB)

Summary

Demographic data are very important in comprehensive data analysis for continuous school improvement. Demographics establish the context of the school and describe the trends of the past. Trends help staffs predict and plan for the future, as well as understand all other measures with which they work in their school improvement efforts. Demographics inform about the structure of the school—the system.

From the examples, one can see how the demographics begin the stories of the schools. When demographic variables are crossed, an even more comprehensive story of the condition of schools is told. One does not have to go back 10 years to get a complete look at the population changes; however, sometimes it is required to really understand when and how the population changed.

The analysis of demographic data sets the stage for comprehensive data analysis.

PERCEPTIONS

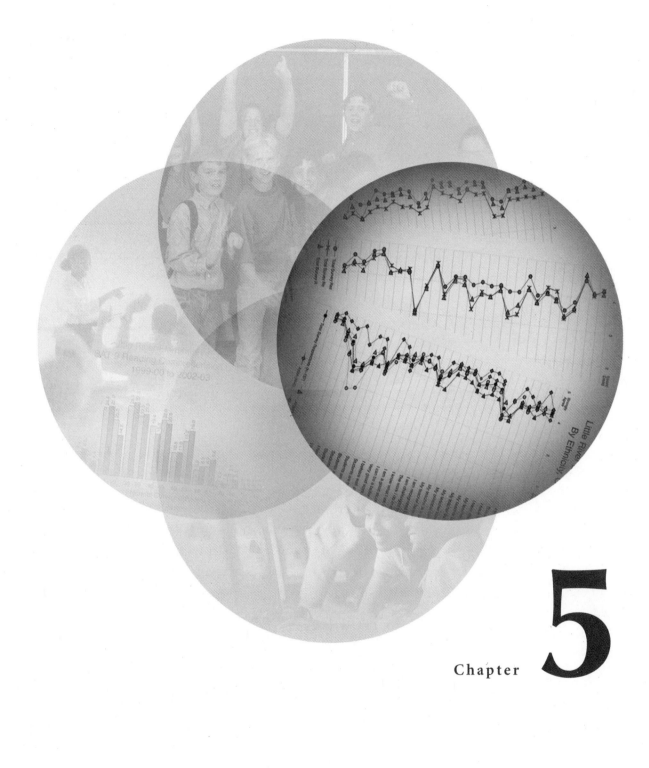

Chapter

5

> *Not to understand another person's way of thinking does not make that person confused.*
>
> Michael Quinn Patten

The definition of *perceptions* and its synonyms provides almost enough information to understand why it is important to know the perceptions of our students, teachers, administrators, and parents.

The word *perception* leads us to such words as "observation" and "opinion," with definitions that include—

▼ a view, judgment, or appraisal formed in the mind about a particular matter

▼ a belief stronger than impression and less strong than positive knowledge

▼ a generally held view

▼ a formal expression of judgment or advice

▼ a judgment one holds as true

Synonyms offered by the *Merriam-Webster Dictionary* include opinion, view, belief, conviction, persuasion, and sentiment. The implications of these synonyms to comprehensive data analysis are discussed in the following text:

▼ *Opinion* implies a conclusion thought out yet open to dispute.

▼ *View* suggests a subjective opinion.

▼ *Belief* implies often deliberate acceptance and intellectual assent.

▼ *Conviction* applies to a firmly and seriously held belief.

▼ *Persuasion* suggests a belief grounded on assurance (as by evidence) of its truth.

▼ *Sentiment* suggests a settled opinion reflective of one's feelings.

All of us have perceptions of the way the world operates. We act upon those perceptions everyday as if they are reality. Basically, we do not act differently from what we value, believe, or perceive. In organizations, if we want to know what is possible (i.e., if we want to know how others are perceiving what is possible), we need to know the perceptions of the people who make up the organization. This might be the only way we can know that a shared vision truly exists.

Changing Perceptions

Is it possible to change perceptions? Absolutely. How do we get perceptions to change? The most effective approach is through behavior changes. That means if a constituency does not believe in an approach we are taking in the classroom, one way to change the constituency's collective minds is to increase their understanding of the approach and give them an opportunity to experience it. Awareness and experience can lead to basic shifts in opinions first, then attitudes and beliefs. That is why many schools have parent nights when there is a change in a math or technology curriculum. Giving parents an opportunity to understand and *experience* the approach helps them understand a different perspective, which could make them more supportive of the program.

Another way to change perceptions is through *cognitive dissonance.* Cognitive dissonance is the discomfort one feels when holding two thoughts, opinions, or ideas that are inconsistent. Cognitive dissonance creates perception changes when people experience a conflict between what they believe and what they, or trusted sources, experience.

In order to change the way business is done, schools establish guiding principles which include the purpose and mission of the school. These principles grow out of the values and beliefs of the individuals who make up the school community. Sometimes school communities adopt guiding principles that they *want* and *hope* to believe in, as opposed to those that they *do* believe in. The idea is that those who try out behaviors that are consistent with these principles will see a positive impact, leading to change in their internal thinking and belief in those principles. This is okay. Changed attitudes represent change at the deepest level of an organization's culture.

Too often, schools think of their guiding principles as being sacred and static. They might be sacred, but they should never be static. Even if a school keeps its guiding principles intact, their meanings evolve as people reflect and talk about them and as the principles are applied to guide decisions and actions.

An example of behavior changes preceding perception changes follows.

> Blossom Middle School teachers were given a questionnaire about their values and beliefs about technology—how they believed technology would increase student learning, and in what ways e-mail, the Internet, and videoconferencing used in instructional units would impact student learning. Additionally, the students were given a questionnaire asking them similar questions and their impressions of the impact of technology on their learning.
>
> For two years, the results were almost the same; nothing was happening with respect to the implementation of technology or perceptions about technology in the classroom. In the meantime, teachers were given professional development with demonstration and coaching components;

It is what teachers think, what teachers believe, and what teachers do at the level of the classroom that ultimately shapes the kind of learning that young people get.

Andy Hargreaves and
Michael Fullan

When we survey teachers about making desired changes in their classrooms, very close to 100% of the teachers who are not implementing the vision or teaching to the standards will say they are not doing so because they do not know what it would look like if they were implementing these concepts in their classrooms.

administration placed typical staff meeting items on e-mail requiring teachers to begin implementing technology for personal use. With the coaching, and demonstration lessons, teachers began implementing technology in their classrooms leading to major behavior changes.

During the following year, it became clear from the questionnaire results that the classrooms were different because teachers were using technology—first for their own benefit, and then with and for students. When their actions changed in the classroom with the use of technology, their ideas and attitudes changed about the impact technology could have with respect to increasing student learning. It was also easy to see in the student questionnaire that student perceptions of the impact technology could have on their learning also changed—after the teachers' behaviors and attitudes changed.

Again, if we want perceptions to change—and we usually do as we implement new concepts and innovations—we need to change behaviors. As the example above also illustrates, to change student perceptions, teacher perceptions must change, which requires teacher behavior to change.

Just a quick note about changing teacher behaviors. When we survey teachers about making desired changes in their classrooms, very close to 100% of the teachers who are not implementing the vision or teaching to the standards will say they are not doing so because they do not know what it would look like if they were implementing these concepts in their classrooms. The implications for how professional development is conducted and supported are huge. (For more information on behavior changes, see *References and Resources*.)

Assessing Perceptions

Common approaches to understanding perceptions in schools include the use of questionnaires, interviews, and focus groups.

Interviews with individuals allow for in-depth understandings of topics and content. Interviews can be done in person or on the telephone.

Focus groups are small groups of representative people who are asked their opinions. Focus groups of students are often used to understand what the larger group of students is thinking or why they responded in a certain way. The majority of this chapter focuses on questionnaires.

Questionnaires

Questionnaires are an excellent way to assess perceptions because they can be completed anonymously and readministered to assess the changes in perceptions over time.

How questionnaires are used and the type of information sought will vary from purpose-to-purpose and from school-to-school. For example, your staff might solicit information from teachers to understand if you truly have a shared vision. You might want to ask students and parents about their perceptions of the school, what they think are the strengths of the school, or what they feel needs to be improved. You might want to understand shifts in parent attitudes about the way you teach "new math" before Family Math Night and after Family Math Night.

A questionnaire is a system for collecting information to describe, compare, and explain knowledge, attitudes, perceptions, or behavior. Good questionnaires have the following features:

▼ A strong purpose for participants to complete the questionnaire which is relayed to them

▼ Short and to the point

▼ Include questions that everyone can understand in the same way

▼ Include everyone because we want all participants to feel their opinions are valued, plus we want the results to be used later

▼ Start with more general items and lead to more specific items

▼ Have response options that make sense for the questions

▼ Use analyses appropriate to the questions and their response options

▼ Result in reports that truly present the results clearly and accurately

Whatever type of questionnaire you decide to use for data gathering, the questionnaire must be based upon an underlying assumption that the respondents will give truthful answers. To this end, you must ask questions that are—

▼ valid—ask the right questions

▼ reliable—will result in the same answers if given more than once

▼ understandable—respondents know what you are asking

▼ quick to complete—brain-compatible, designed well, and short

▼ able to get the first response from the respondent—quality administration and set-up

▼ able to get what you want in the end—validity

Requiring respondents to read questions over and over in order to understand what one is asking, or making it necessary for the respondents to gather information before they can complete the questionnaire, will increase the possibility of inaccurate responses, question responses left blank, or no response at all.

Designing Questionnaires: Begin with the End in Mind

The diagram in Figure 5.1 outlines useful steps for thinking through and selecting the most appropriate criteria when designing questionnaires for your particular purpose. When designing questionnaires, you must know the purpose and what you want the final results to look like before beginning. The steps in questionnaire design follow.

Plan for the Questionnaire

It is next to impossible to put together a valid (the "right" content), understandable questionnaire that is easy to complete and analyze without thinking through the elements of questionnaire construction and analysis before starting. Notice that as you go through the elements profiled in Figure 5.1, one answer could impact previous elements. That is why it is important to go through these questions before writing a questionnaire. There are many issues that need to be taken into consideration, with a great deal of rethinking needed along the way.

Determine the Purpose

What do you really want to know? Why are you administering a questionnaire? To what end are you asking these questions? You might want to know perceptions of parents, students, teachers, and administrators with respect to a shared vision—what each constituency values and believes about school, education, teaching, and learning. These might be questions that you want to continue to ask over time to watch the responses change as new ideas and innovations are being implemented. One might also want to know about standards implemented in classrooms: the degree to which standards are being implemented, why not, and what would help teachers implement the standards.

Questionnaires that have been used with *Education for the Future Initiative* schools are offered as examples in Appendix A. The results of these questionnaires are used to understand the perceptions of students, staffs, and parents with respect to a shared vision, instructional coherence, and to help us get to root causes of problems (discussed in Chapter 8), and to get everyone's input into the vision for the school.

Identify How the Information will be Used

To what end is this data collection activity directed? How will the information be used? How do you want to disseminate the findings? Do you need to present this information to a funding agency, to your school board, or to staff for improving instructional practices? The intended use of the information collected has a major impact on the steps used to construct the questionnaire. Example: *Education for the Future* designed the example questionnaires in the Appendix A to be used over time so school staffs could see progress being made, as well as to understand what has to change to get different results.

Check for Existing Data

Another important question to ask yourself, as you begin the arduous task of putting together a questionnaire, is—can we get this information without doing a questionnaire? Too often, inexperienced staff will want to ask questions that can be answered through other means. Consider a parent example question: *Did you attend Back to School Night?* If the purpose for asking the question is to find out how many parents came to Back to School Night, there are other ways to know that information which might, in fact, produce more accurate data. Usually there is a guest book at Back to School Night functions, or someone is put in charge of counting the number of attendees. Use that source of information, and reserve questionnaires for important questions that cannot be answered in other ways.

Identify Sources of Information

As you think through the purpose, also consider whether the questionnaires will be given anonymously, if you will code them to link them with other databases, or if you will ask for respondents' names. If you want honest, non-threatened responses, you might consider not asking for names or information that could identify the respondents.

With respect to the purpose for administering the questionnaire and how it will be used, who or what are the logical sources of information? Who

Figure 5.1

Begin With the End in Mind

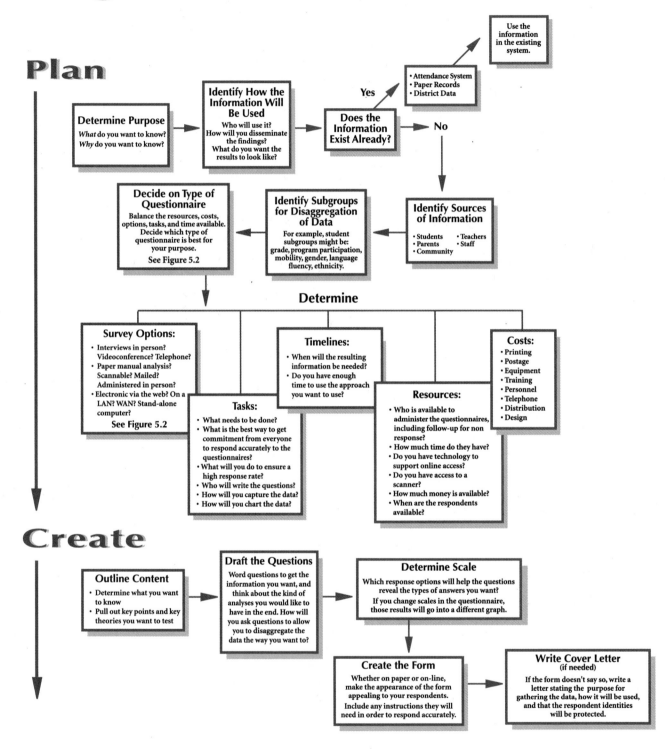

Figure 5.1 *(Continued)*

Begin With the End in Mind

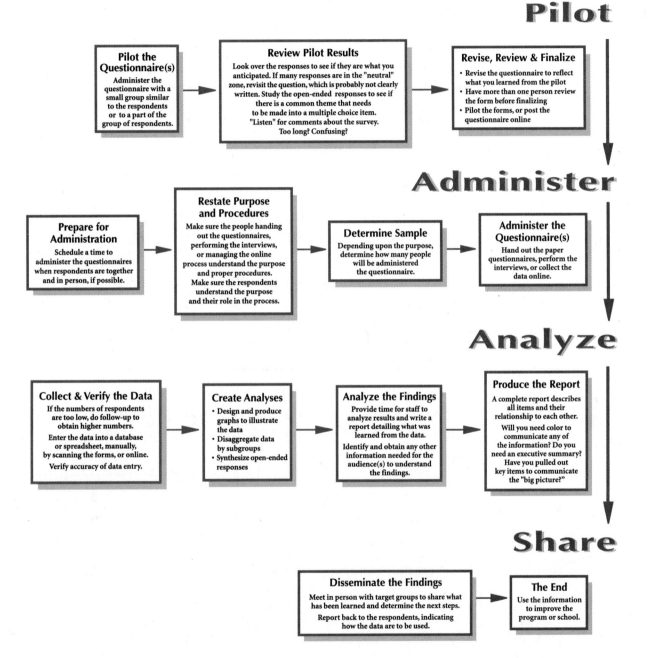

Pilot

Pilot the Questionnaire(s)
Administer the questionnaire with a small group similar to the respondents or to a part of the group of respondents.

Review Pilot Results
Look over the responses to see if they are what you anticipated. If many responses are in the "neutral" zone, revisit the question, which is probably not clearly written. Study the open-ended responses to see if there is a common theme that needs to be made into a multiple choice item. "Listen" for comments about the survey. Too long? Confusing?

Revise, Review & Finalize
• Revise the questionnaire to reflect what you learned from the pilot
• Have more than one person review the form before finalizing
• Pilot the forms, or post the questionnaire online

Administer

Prepare for Administration
Schedule a time to administer the questionnaires when respondents are together and in person, if possible.

Restate Purpose and Procedures
Make sure the people handing out the questionnaires, performing the interviews, or managing the online process understand the purpose and proper procedures. Make sure the respondents understand the purpose and their role in the process.

Determine Sample
Depending upon the purpose, determine how many people will be administered the questionnaire.

Administer the Questionnaire(s)
Hand out the paper questionnaires, perform the interviews, or collect the data online.

Analyze

Collect & Verify the Data
If the numbers of respondents are too low, do follow-up to obtain higher numbers.
Enter the data into a database or spreadsheet, manually, by scanning the forms, or online.
Verify accuracy of data entry.

Create Analyses
• Design and produce graphs to illustrate the data
• Disaggregate data by subgroups
• Synthesize open-ended responses

Analyze the Findings
Provide time for staff to analyze results and write a report detailing what was learned from the data.
Identify and obtain any other information needed for the audience(s) to understand the findings.

Produce the Report
A complete report describes all items and their relationship to each other.
Will you need color to communicate any of the information? Do you need an executive summary? Have you pulled out key items to communicate the "big picture?"

Share

Disseminate the Findings
Meet in person with target groups to share what has been learned and determine the next steps.
Report back to the respondents, indicating how the data are to be used.

The End
Use the information to improve the program or school.

can answer these questions? When at all possible, we want to go directly to the source, i.e., if we want to know what parents are thinking, we need to ask parents.

Education for the Future questionnaires are given anonymously. We want honest indicators of how the whole school is performing.

Identify Subgroups for the Disaggregation of Data

After you decide to whom you want to administer the questionnaire, it is advisable to think of ways you will want to use the information in the end. If you want to disaggregate the data, as mentioned in the previous chapter, think about the different subgroups you will want to split out for the analyses. For example, if you think there will be a difference in student responses by grade level and gender, you will want to ask students' grade level and gender on the questionnaire. This is information we cannot recapture after the questionnaire is administered. So, if you want to analyze your results in a certain way—ask it on the questionnaire. For *No Child Left Behind* (NCLB), you may want to disaggregate your questionnaire results by the same categories you will disaggregate your student achievement results—i.e., ethnicity/race, indicators of poverty, English language proficiency, and special education disabilities.

Decide on the Type of Questionnaire

There are many issues to consider when determining the type of questionnaire you will use, in addition to the ones already discussed. Think about the best way to get the information. Is it through interviews—either in-person, through videoconference, or by telephone—or would it be through a questionnaire that the respondents actually get to look at, feel, think about, and respond to on their own time? Or will it be a questionnaire that will require respondents to use technology? A lot of what will help you decide depends upon—

▼ your timeline

▼ the purpose for administering the questionnaire

▼ how much money you have available

▼ who is going to be completing the questionnaire and their availability

▼ who is going to be completing the questionnaire, their technological skills and availability of technology

Time considerations will definitely impact whether or not you want to mail out a questionnaire because you will need ample time to send out a follow-up for any non-responses (more on this topic later in this chapter). In addition, it takes time to put the questionnaire together, write the questions, create the form, get reviews, pilot the questionnaire, update it, and send it out. If you are planning to conduct in-person interviews, the questions need to be written very clearly and consistently, especially if more than one person is going to do the interviewing. In this case, you will also need precise instructions for interviewing and possibly training. How the questionnaire will be analyzed in the end is another planning and time consideration.

Figure 5.2 profiles advantages and disadvantages of different types of questionnaires.

Figure 5.2

Types of Questionnaires			
Types of Questionnaires	**Advantages**	**Disadvantages**	**Appropriate When—**
Interview *(Face-to-face)*	♦ Allows for in-depth person-to-person exchanges ♦ Might be the most appropriate way to get information from people with disabilities ♦ Can see evidence of change as well as hear about it	♦ Can be cost prohibitive; often need to pay interviewers and sometimes interviewees ♦ Requires extensive training and quality control to standardize ♦ Collating the responses is tedious, time consuming, and difficult ♦ Easy for the interviewers to change the questions	♦ You have a captive audience, such as students ♦ Physical changes are a result of the program ♦ Need to understand all aspects of change from the individuals ♦ Persons you seek to know about are physically or language impaired ♦ You have people trained to standardize questions ♦ The length of the questionnaire requires over an hour of a respondent's time
Telephone Interview *(Person-to-person)*	♦ Allows for the personal contact of face-to-face interviews, at a lower cost ♦ Can be done relatively cheaply ♦ Interviewers can enter responses into an electronic database as they interview ♦ Can hear individual perspective, while still using standardized questions ♦ People can usually be contacted faster by phone	♦ Requires extensive training and quality control ♦ Might require interviewers to be able to speak different languages ♦ People do not like to be called for questionnaire responses ♦ Easy for the interviewers to change the questions slightly or greatly ♦ Interviewees might not answer all questions before they hang up the telephone	♦ People do not speak or read English ♦ You use the interview as a win-win, and want to connect closer to the community, to get people talking, and add an element of public relations to your questions ♦ You have people trained to standardize questions ♦ You need fast results ♦ The technology is available ♦ Need less than 20 minutes of respondent's time (some say 10 minutes maximum)
Mailed	♦ Flexible ♦ Can gather a large number of responses ♦ Individuals can respond at their convenience ♦ Relatively inexpensive ♦ Respondents can look up information if necessary ♦ Can include visuals (e.g., pictures)	♦ It is sometimes difficult to get an adequate return rate ♦ Must be able to write a compelling cover letter/request to complete questionnaire ♦ Probably need to send twice ♦ Can be expensive ♦ Takes a long time to get to the point where you are ready to analyze results	♦ All perspective respondents are not present in one location at a particular time ♦ You need to ensure anonymity ♦ Respondents live out of the immediate area ♦ You have time ♦ You are not asking time-certain questions ♦ You can live with a small response rate

Figure 5.2 *(Continued)*

Types of Questionnaires	Advantages	Disadvantages	Appropriate When—
Paper	♦ Can give classes or groups oral instructions and guide them through the questionnaire ♦ Can be mailed ♦ Can easily include different types of questions and graphics to make it aesthetically appealing ♦ Responses can be scanned	♦ Requires knowledge about scanning, databases, and analysis of data to make easy analysis of responses ♦ Can be difficult and time-consuming to score if automation is not an option ♦ Cannot disaggregate easily if analyzing by hand ♦ Requires time to check the accuracy of the input procedure on every questionnaire response	♦ Documented comparisons of groups are desired ♦ Anonymity is desired ♦ Surveying large numbers of people ♦ Respondents are in many locations ♦ A large number of questions is required
Online	♦ Least expensive to administer and analyze of all methods ♦ It is still somewhat unique and has an element of appeal ♦ Students and adults like to complete questionnaires using computers ♦ Can do with computers networked to the Internet, in a lab, or on stand-alone computers ♦ Database can be automatically loaded as individuals submit responses ♦ Converts responses to numeric, electronic data immediately, removing that step that is present in other methods ♦ Do not have to type open-ended responses ♦ Easy to check for double submissions ♦ Fastest way to administer questionnaires	♦ It is not always possible to get parents and community to complete computer questionnaires (although not impossible) ♦ Not everyone has a computer at her/his disposal ♦ Still need to organize the administration as carefully as you would with any other data collection method ♦ It is difficult to complete in large schools with few computers—doable, just takes longer ♦ Need trained people to setup the questionnaire online	♦ School/organization has computer laboratories or a number of computers in each classroom ♦ Ever possible, since the advantages far outweigh the disadvantages ♦ You need quick return of responses ♦ You can get your respondents in person

Table title: **Types of Questionnaires** *(Continued)*

Data Collection Considerations

The approach decided on in the beginning will determine how the data can be analyzed in the end. If a questionnaire is set up for manual analysis—in other words, the completed questionnaires are not set up to be machine-scanned or entered directly into the computer by respondents—someone will have to figure out how to put the coded responses into a database or spreadsheet on the computer, or tally the responses by hand in order to get aggregated and disaggregated results. This process could take months to complete. We recommend that you not use this approach with over twenty respondents in a group. The exception would be if you can set up a database that looks like your questionnaire on the computer and someone can enter the written responses into the database quickly and accurately. The database will then take care of some of the analysis and data error issues.

Everyone has experienced fill-in-the-bubble kinds of questionnaires that can be read by a machine scanner. Many people are stunned to find out their scanner will not read a questionnaire they have administered. Every scanner can not read every bubble form. Many details must be taken into consideration when setting up a scannable form. First of all, you will want to ensure that the completed questionnaire can be scanned with the scanner you are going to use. Secondly, if at all possible, the questionnaire needs to be scanned into a database that will allow analyses to be done quickly and easily. If you have the appropriate software and equipment, you can set up your own scannable forms, print them on a laser printer, and scan them into a database. This requires knowledge of databases and time to understand both the scanner software and the scanning machine. It is wise to try out the questionnaires on the scanning machine to confirm their readability by the scanner and the database before administration of the questionnaire.

Using an online method of data collection is usually the most cost-effective in terms of time and personnel required to process the data, offers the best option for data accuracy, and fastest turnaround from administration to analysis. Considerations for collecting perceptions data are shown in Figure 5.3. Some of those considerations include time for design and production, number of respondents, age of respondents, literacy of respondents, availability of respondents, availability of equipment, and time for analysis and reporting. Figure 5.4 describes the different data collection trade-offs.

Figure 5.3

Data Collection Considerations for Perceptions Data

Considerations for Different Approaches to Collecting Perceptions Data

Time for Design and Production

Scannable questionnaires produced by a contracting firm will generally require six to eight weeks of production time after the questionnaire items have been identified. If the questionnaire needs to be administered in a very short period of time, it is best to go with an in-house form (either manual data entry or scannable) or an online questionnaire. Use scannable forms only when you cannot get respondents to use the computer.

Number of Respondents

Scannable questionnaires produced by a contracting firm or produced in-house and sent to a printer are only cost effective when more than 500 people are being surveyed, when the questionnaire will be administered again, or when you cannot get respondents to use the computer. For smaller numbers of respondents, questionnaire responses can be entered cost effectively using either manual or online data entry. Online data entry is most cost-effective, regardless of numbers.

Age of Respondents

Generally speaking, the younger the respondents, the more likely they will want to use a computer. Assistance should be provided to respondents who do not yet have mouse skills and are expected to complete online questionnaires.

Literacy of Respondents

Assistance should be provided to respondents who do not have the literacy skills required to understand the questions being asked of them, either by providing a written translation or an interpreter.

Availability of Respondents

Captive audiences—teachers and students—usually are best situated to complete questionnaires, written or online, at school. Community members may find it easier to take and complete a paper questionnaire at home, although a better response rate may be realized if the questionnaires are completed at parent-teacher conferences or open houses.

Availability of Equipment

Using an online questionnaire requires an adequate number of computers to service the number of respondents at each site. Using scannable forms requires the availability of a scanner. The use of either is helpful only if a computer with a database is available for analysis.

Time for Analysis and Reporting

If the time available from response to analysis is very short, try to go with an online or scannable option. If manual data entry is being used, administer a few and enter data for "test" questionnaires in order to predict the time required to enter the expected number of responses.

There are always trade-offs in terms of personnel and production costs. Figure 5.4 shows some of the pros and cons of the options presented.

Figure 5.4

Data Collection Trade-offs		
Data Collection Options	**Advantages**	**Disadvantages**
Manual Data Entry *(Non-scannable Forms)* Once the questionnaire items are finished, the questionnaire form is produced in word processing, database, or desktop publishing software and photocopied or printed. After the forms come back, the responses are manually entered into a database package such as *FileMakerPro* or *Access*, or into a spreadsheet program.	◆ This option requires the least technical expertise and equipment	◆ Time required for data entry and the possibility for human error during the data entry process ◆ If a database is not used, the ability to disaggregate results is essentially lost
In-House Produced Scannable Forms Scannable questionnaires can be produced in-house and printed on a laser printer or sent to a commercial printer for mass copying. This option requires the knowledge and use of a software package that will create a master digital file that is either sent out of the office (off-site) to be printed on an offset printing press or printed to an inhouse laser printer. (In-house printers are often not consistent enough. Not all commercial printers can print them correctly).	◆ Producing the form can be done faster than contracting the job out ◆ Can accommodate small groups on a cost-effective basis ◆ Scanning the forms is much faster than manual data entry	◆ Scannable questionnaire can be expensive to produce ◆ Technically challenging
Purchased Scannable Forms Companies such as Scantron and NCS offer scannable (bubble) forms for purchase. You need to add the questions. Some forms allow you to write the questions on the form. Others require the use of two sheets of paper—one for the questions and another sheet for the answers.	◆ Forms are readily available	◆ Somebody has to ensure that all the equipment used is compatible—one cannot just create a scannable form and expect it to work ◆ Resorting to two sheets is not brain-compatible ◆ Can be expensive
Contracted Scannable Forms Scannable questionnaires can be roughly designed and sent to companies like Scantron or NCS for final production. This option takes the most time; however, it is a good option on a per-unit basis when there is adequate lead time and large numbers of forms are needed.	◆ Contracting companies usually guarantee that all forms will scan properly ◆ No need for in-house expertise in publishing design ◆ Scanning the forms is much faster than manual data entry	◆ It generally takes from six to eight weeks to have the forms produced ◆ This is not a cost-effective option for small numbers of completed forms.
Digital Data Collection Collecting questionnaire responses online is the best option for speed, flexibility, and accuracy.	◆ No paper—no printing or distribution costs ◆ Questionnaires can be modified for different groups at minimal cost ◆ People tend to "write" more in response to open-ended questions ◆ Opportunities for human error in scanning or manual data entry are eliminated ◆ Data are available immediately ◆ Responses are automatically converted to electronic/ numeric data	◆ Expertise required in-house or contracted technical expertise and related equipment

If your school does not have the capacity to set up and analyze its own forms, bubble questionnaires can be sent to an outside contractor to set up for administration and analysis. With either approach, you must be very sure of the questions you want to have answered before a machine-scannable questionnaire is printed. If you want the outside contractor to do the analyses once the responses are returned, you must also be clear on the kinds of analyses you want as an end result. An approach between these two options would be to use a pre-printed scannable sheet in addition to a sheet with the questions. However, that would mean having respondents deal with two different pieces of paper, which may increase the chance of inaccurate responses.

The fastest, most cost-effective approach is to collect the data electronically—on a stand-alone computer, in a computer laboratory, or through online processes. Costs for printing, postage, and telephone are eliminated, and the accuracy is increased significantly. This approach, of course, requires that someone know how to work with databases and questionnaires in this manner. We highly recommend that, whenever possible, you gather your data electronically. The trade-offs of the different methods of data collection are described in Figure 5.4. *Education for the Future* has setup our nine most popular questionnaires online and has made these available to anyone via our website *(http://eff.csuchico.edu)*, and in any of our books that come with CD-Roms.

Create the Questionnaire

Creating the questionnaire can be an arduous task. Many people who want to design questionnaires often stop when it comes to writing the questions. It is definitely one of those tasks that looks much easier than it actually is.

Outline Content

Begin by thinking about what you want to know and by pulling out key points or key theories that you want to test through the questionnaire. For example, the *Education for the Future* student questionnaires in Appendix A were designed by teachers who wanted this questionnaire to ask questions related to what they wanted their students to be able to say by the time they had implemented their vision—that they feel safe at school, have freedom, fun, and like school—theories from William Glasser's *The Quality School* (1990). Once you determine what you want to know, outline the key points and jot down ideas in the outline.

Draft the Questions

Formulate questions that address issues based upon what you want to know. There are many different ways to ask questions. Figure 5.5 describes different types of questions, advantages and disadvantages for each type, and when it is appropriate to use a specific type of question. You can create forms that will allow you to use different types of questions; however, it is probably not wise to use more than two or three different types of questions in a form. The key is to make the questionnaire interesting and fast to complete.

The types of questions that might be appropriate for a school working toward building a quality learning organization and aligning parts to create a whole system are those related to whether or not these goals are being met. It would follow that student, parent, and teacher questions would focus on their perceptions of the learning organization, creating questions that are a part of the hypotheses of how the quality learning organization should look. Be sure to ask purposeful questions—don't just ask questions for the sake of asking questions; and make sure the questions will be interpreted the same way by many different people

Think about the impact of every question on your respondent. Will it offend anyone? Hints in developing the questions are summarized below.

Helpful hints include—

▼ Simple is best

▼ Keep items and the questions short (definitely less than 20 words)

▼ Eliminate all jargon and bureaucratic wording

▼ Be sure that phrasing does not suggest a response

▼ Use a logical sequence to asking questions (general to specific)

▼ Ask questions that everyone understands in the same way

▼ Ask all questions in the same way (e.g., all positive so double negatives are not possible)

▼ Make sure that, if necessary, your questions will allow you to disaggregate responses in your analyses

▼ List question first and response option second (left-to-right—it is brain-compatible)

Figure 5.5

Types of Questions			
Types of Questions	**Advantages**	**Disadvantages**	**Appropriate When—**
Written *(Open-ended)* Example: *What do you like about this school?* (Write your response in the space provided below.)	◆ Spontaneity of the response ◆ Can really understand what the respondent thinks ◆ Can get deep into the topic ◆ Can use to build multiple choice items ◆ Sometimes respondents provide quotable material ◆ Can ask all types of individuals, regardless of language differences	◆ Must pay for someone's time to transcribe and synthesize ◆ Takes time—on everyone's part ◆ Coding can be unreliable ◆ Cannot always read the response ◆ Some handicapped people might have difficulty responding ◆ Language translations are expensive ◆ Difficult to interpret ◆ Many people might have said the same thing with prompting ◆ Difficult to categorize when taking frequencies of types of responses	◆ Are not sure about what respondents are thinking and feeling about a topic ◆ Want to gain insight into the respondents' thinking ◆ Are in the process of designing closed-ended questions ◆ Want to supplement or better understand closed ended responses
Multiple Choice *(Nominal, Closed-ended)* Example: Suppose you are a school board member. On what one thing do you think the school should focus to ensure well-prepared students? (Circle the one response option below that best represents your position.) 1. Basic skills 2. Computers 3. Problem-solving skills 4. Lifelong learning 5. Flexibility	◆ Fast to complete ◆ Respondents do not need to write ◆ Relatively inexpensive ◆ Easy to administer ◆ Easy to score ◆ Can compare groups and disaggregate easily ◆ Responses can be scanned and interpreted easily	◆ Unless one has thought through how the items will be scored and has the capabilities of scoring items mechanically before sending out the questionnaires, it can be expensive to do, time-consuming, and easy to make mistakes ◆ Lose spontaneity ◆ Don't always know what you have as results ◆ Respondents are not always fond of these questionnaires ◆ Some respondents may resent the questioner's pre-selected choices ◆ Multiple-choice questions are more difficult to write than open-ended ◆ Can make the wrong assumption in analyzing the results when response options are not the same as what respondents are thinking	◆ Want to make group comparisons ◆ Know some of the responses that the sample is considering, and want to know which option they are leaning toward ◆ Have large samples ◆ Want to give respondents finite response choices
Ranking *(Ordinal, Closed-ended)* Example: *Why did you choose to enroll your child in this school?* (Mark a 1 by the most important reason, 2 by the second most important reason, etc.) ◆ It is our neighborhood school ◆ Reputation as a quality school ◆ Know someone else who attends ◆ I went there when I was in elementary school ◆ My child needs more challenge ◆ My child needs more personal help	◆ Allows understanding of all reasons in priority order	◆ More than seven response options will confuse respondents ◆ May leave out important item response options ◆ Relatively hard to analyze—you will know the number of respondents who rated item one as 1, etc.	◆ Want to know all responses in an order ◆ Are clear on common response options ◆ Do not want people to add to list

Figure 5.5 *(Continued)*

Types of Questions *(Continued)*			
Types of Questions	**Advantages**	**Disadvantages**	**Appropriate When—**
Rating *(Interval, Closed-ended)* Example: (Write your response in the space provided below.) *I feel like I belong at this school.* Strongly Disagree / Disagree / Neutral / Agree / Strongly Agree 1 2 3 4 5	◆ Allows you to see the passion behind respondents' feelings, i.e., *Strongly Agree/Strongly Disagree* ◆ Easy to administer ◆ Easy to score ◆ Can compare group responses ◆ If an ordinal scale is created similar to the 5-point example, one can average the results ◆ There are many ways one can analyze the results ◆ Since there are usually only five options, frequencies of each response can be taken, along with the mode to determine most popular response	◆ Do not always know if every respondent is reading the question and response options in the same way ◆ Do not always know what you have when *neutral* is circled—might be a bad question or the respondent doesn't care, or it might be a viable option ◆ Unless one has thought through how the items will be scored and has the capability of scoring items mechanically before sending out the questionnaires, it can be expensive to do, time-consuming, and easy to make mistakes ◆ Questions are more difficult to write than open-ended ◆ If charted together, questions must be written so the desired response all fall in the same direction (in other words—all written positively)	◆ Want respondents to rate or order choices, such as: *strongly disagree* to *strongly agree*, or show passion ◆ Want to make group comparisons ◆ Have large samples ◆ Want to understand where problems are in the organization
Yes – No *(Closed-ended)* Example: Yes No *I like this school* ☺ ☹	◆ Very young children can answer questions with these response options ◆ Very easy to score, analyze, and chart	◆ Not sure how meaningful the data are ◆ Responses do not give enough information	◆ Want all or nothing responses ◆ Have a sample that would have difficulty responding to more options

Nominal *(Categorical)*
 	
Example:
I am–
   Male   O
   Female O
	◆ Factual: have no values attached to the questions
	◆ Useful for disaggregating other question responses by groups
	◆ Lets you know if sample is representative of the total population
		◆ Some people will not respond to these types of questions
		◆ Some people could respond falsely to these questions
		◆ With small groups, one might be able to identify the respondent on an anonymous questionnaire because of the demographic information given
			◆ Want to disaggregate data by male/female, ethnicity, program
			◆ Want to know the impact of a program on different types of individuals
			◆ Want to know if respondents resemble the population

Avoid—

▼ Trying to assess a little bit of everything

▼ Conjunctions in questions (and, or)

▼ Adverbs such as "sometimes," "nearly," and "always" in the questions—let the response options discriminate responses

▼ Leading questions

▼ Jumping around content-wise

▼ Showing response options first and then the question—you are asking respondents to skip a part of the process and then come back to it—not efficient

▼ Asking the same question more than once

Determine scales

Questionnaires are collections of items intended to reveal levels of information not readily observable by direct means. We develop scales when we want to measure phenomena that we believe exist because of our theoretical understanding of the world, but which we cannot access directly.

Scales, or response options to questions in questionnaires, are developed to measure underlying constructs.

Most items have a stem (the question) and then a series of response options. How many response categories should an item have? The number of response options could be anywhere from two to a hundred. If we want to see discrimination in our analyses, we need to allow discrimination in our options. For example:

▼ How many response options does it take to discriminate meaningfully?

▼ How many response options will bore or confuse our respondents?

▼ Presented with many response options, will respondents use only those responses that are multiples of five, for instance, reducing the number of options anyway?

There are several kinds of response options. The response option chosen depends upon the purpose for considering the questionnaire and the types of questions desired. For the majority of questionnaires, five-point options are recommended. Possible labels include—

▼ *Endorsement:* strongly disagree, disagree, neutral, agree, strongly agree

- ▼ *Frequency:* never, almost never, sometimes, very often, always
- ▼ *Intensity:* really apprehensive, somewhat apprehensive, mixed feelings, somewhat excited, really excited
- ▼ *Influence:* big problem, moderate problem, small problem, very small problem, no problem
- ▼ *Comparison:* much less than others, less than others, about the same as others, more than others, much more than others; much worse than others, worse than others, no difference, better than others, much better than others

The scale you use is determined by personal preference. The example questionnaires provided in Appendix A utilize a five-point endorsement scale. Each item is presented as a declarative sentence, followed by response options that indicate varying degrees of agreement with the statement—from strongly disagree to strongly agree. The questionnaires go from strongly disagree to strongly agree because it is our opinion that this direction is left to right—the way our brains work. That is also why our response options are to the right of the questions.

People often ask about the center option. They worry that most individuals will just use the middle response option if it is made available. Our years of experience with thousands of questionnaires show that people will not automatically choose the middle response. If they commit to responding to the questionnaire, they will typically respond with precision. When responses on a questionnaire do appear in the middle, the questionnaire constructor needs to examine if it is the question causing indecision, if the response option and the statement do not go well together, or if, indeed, the respondent does not have a definite response to the question. One of the first things to check is whether there is a conjunction or an adverb in the statement that would cause people to say: *Well, I agree with this part of the question, and I disagree with that part of the question.* Researchers often add the middle response to give respondents a legitimate response option for opinions that are divided or neutral. If you prefer to force your respondents to make a decision, you can always use an even point scale that has no middle point. You will not be able to average the responses if you do this. We add that middle response option because we think it is a reasonable response option, and because it makes an interval scale with the possibility to average. We want to graph all the item averages together, to show relationships.

Other scales include nominal scales that give numbers to different categories, such as: 1=male, 2=female; ordinal scales provide information about direction and ranking; interval scales create meaning between the intervals; and ratio has an absolute zero point, such as GPA, time, age. Each scale implies how it can be analyzed. Interval ratio scales can be averaged. The others must be added or summed.

Do note that if more than one scale is used in a questionnaire, the results will need to be anlayzed separately—in other words, questions with different scales will probably need to be graphed separately.

An often-neglected but very important factor that must be taken into consideration when establishing a scale and format for the questionnaire is the age and attention span of the respondent. Young children do best with two or three response options—smiling faces versus frowning faces. Most adults will not finish a questionnaire that requires over 30 minutes of their time.

What about offering *don't know* or *not applicable* as a response option? Some researchers say that *don't know* does not affect the proportion of responses. Depending upon the question, a *not applicable* response might give you more information than getting no response. *Education for the Future* typically does not use either of these options because we want to average the results. We feel these options "mess-up" the scale.

Create the Form

Appearance and arrangement of the questionnaire frequently determine whether respondents will complete it. In fact, research shows that individuals determine within five seconds whether or not they will respond to a questionnaire. Think about what would get you to psychologically commit to completing a questionnaire, and build in those same considerations for your respondents. The good news is that once respondents take the effort to read and start a questionnaire, they make a psychological commitment to complete it.

Upon first glance, we definitely want the questionnaire to be appealing to the eye. We want to have white space. We want to keep the questionnaire consistent. Never split questions, instructions, or responses from the questions between pages. Use an easy-to-read, equally spaced font for the questions themselves. Avoid italics. Make the questionnaire look professional. We typically want to end the questionnaire by giving each respondent a chance to comment on the topic. Figure 5.6(a) offers tips to consider when creating the form. Figure 5.6(b) offers tips to consider when writing and placing open-ended questions in a questionnaire. Take the time to make the appearance pleasing and the instructions clear to the respondent. Also, take the time to make the questionnaire brain-compatible.

Figure 5.6 (a)

Design Considerations for Multiple Choice Questionnaires

The appearance and arrangement of the questionnaire frequently determine whether or not the respondents will complete it. Try to fit the questions and answers onto one page, if possible. You want the questionnaire to be quick to complete so that the respondent will answer all of the questions.

The majority of respondents read from left to right. If the layout of the questions and responses is consistent with this pattern, it will increase the accuracy, and will be easier and faster for respondents to complete.

Placing response options close to the questions decreases the chance of error due to respondents mismatching lines.

If the questions are worded so that the answers fit into one scale, it will be easier for the respondent to complete and for you to analyze and graph later.

Make it obvious where respondents should make their mark.

A clear label shows respondents for whom the questionnaire is intended.

Begin with more general questions and lead up to the more specific.

Write instructions that tell your respondents what you would like them to do.

Leaving white space makes the questionnaire easier to read.

Do not use questions that have conjunctions. Use two separate questions instead.

Ask questions to address the issues that are based on what you want to know, and that cannot be gathered from other sources.

For evidence of school improvement, ask questions that you want to ask over time to see growth.

Think about the impact of every question on your respondent. Make sure the questions will not offend anyone.

Make the questions simple, short, and free of jargon/bureaucratic words.

Avoid:
- trying to assess a little of everything
- leading questions
- jumping around content-wise
- double negatives

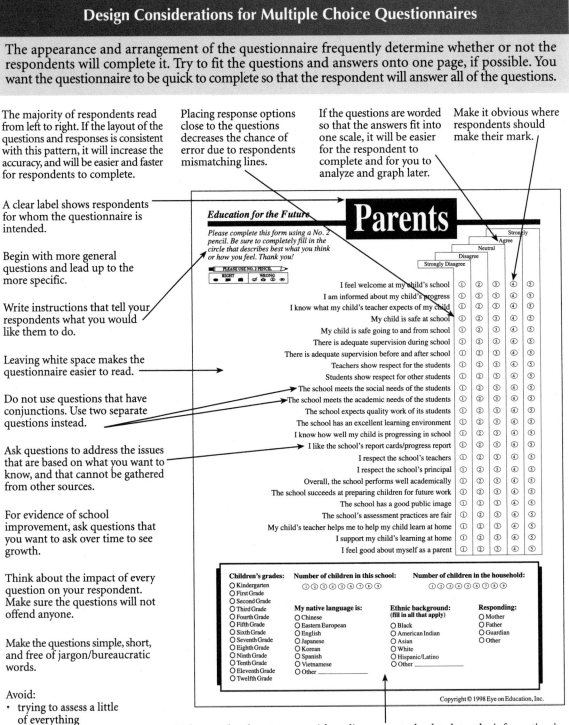

Make sure that, however you wish to disaggregate the data later, the information is captured on the form.

In other words, if you want to know the difference between males and females on their responses to particular questions, ask your respondents their gender on the questionnaire.

Figure 5.6 (b)

Design Considerations for Open-ended Questions

Ask only a few open-ended questions because of the length of time it takes respondents to reply and because of the difficulty of analyzing the responses. Open-ended questions usually appear at the end of the questionnaire. If all scannable items can be put on one page, place the open-ended on the back.

Place open-ended section at the end of the questionnaire.

Leave enough space for respondents to comment.

Do not use lines. Lines limit feedback.

What are the strengths of your child's school?

What needs to be strengthened at your child's school?

If you are planning to scan the questionnaire responses, you must begin by setting up the questionnaire so that it is scannable. One cannot expect to scan something that was not set up for scanning in the beginning.

Questionnaire constructors differ on where demographic information should be placed in a questionnaire. The majority feel that the personal information needs to go at the end. Demographic information is specific. Occasionally, if people see personal questions first, they may find these kinds of questions worrisome and might decide to not complete the questionnaire, or it might impact the way they respond to the questionnaire. Some people believe in putting the demographic questions first because they are easy to respond to. Respondents can answer them quickly, feel accomplished, and will, therefore, keep going. Wherever you decide to place these important questions, always group them together. *Education for the Future* usually places demographic questions at the end of a questionnaire because our experiences show us that personal information should be last.

Write a Cover Letter (if needed)

If you must mail or send home a questionnaire, it is important to include a cover letter. Most of the time when schools want questionnaires completed, there are ways to get them completed in person. You still need a letter to inform respondents, such as parents, that they are being asked to complete a questionnaire at the school. Student and teacher questionnaires can be administered during school hours or during a staff meeting. Parent questionnaires can be administered at parent-teacher conferences. It is ideal to administer the questionnaires when you can gather all responses in person and at the same time. The chances of getting a good response rate is tremendously increased when you administer a questionnaire in person. Plus, you know who came to the conference and can follow-up with those who were not there.

Just make sure that you receive most, if not all, responses from your target group. Small numbers of responses (less than 30%) not only give you unreliable results, if used, the small numbers could lead people to draw faulty conclusions.

Cover letters should include what the questionnaire is about, why the respondent's response is important, how long it will take to complete the questionnaire, and when the results can be seen. Don't forget to thank people for their help and cooperation. Figure 5.7 shows a sample letter that could be mailed or sent home with a questionnaire. Figure 5.8 shows a sample letter informing parents that a questionnaire will be administered during parent–teacher conferences.

Figure 5.7

ARCHER ELEMENTARY SCHOOL
PARK SCHOOL DISTRICT. PARK CITY. U.S.A.

Date

Name
Address
City, State Zip

Dear Parent:

The enclosed questionnaire has been developed to assist Archer Elementary School in examining its effectiveness for students. As a parent of an Archer student, your input about our effectiveness is important to us.

The questionnaire consists of 25 statements. After you read a statement, please fill in the bubble that represents the first response that comes to mind which is the closest to what you think or how you feel. Responses range from strongly disagree to strongly agree.

It takes approximately 15 minutes to complete the questionnaire. All of your responses are confidential and will be combined with other parent responses for reporting purposes.

Please return the completed questionnaire in the envelope provided as soon as you can, or no later than (date). If you have any questions, call (name) at (telephone number). The results of the questionnaire will be reported at Open House in May.

Thank you for your cooperation and valuable response.

Sincerely,

Name

Enclosures
 Questionnaire
 Return Envelope

Figure 5.8

ARCHER ELEMENTARY SCHOOL
PARK SCHOOL DISTRICT. PARK CITY. U.S.A.

Date

Name
Address
City, State Zip

Dear Parent:

I am happy to invite you to meet with me at 2:00 p.m. on Wednesday (date) to discuss (name of child's) progress. I would appreciate very much if you would please arrive at 1:30 p.m. to complete a questionnaire that will give our staff valued information that will help us improve our school.

One of our sixth-grade Technology Wizards will meet you in the lobby and escort you to the computer where you will take the questionnaire. (You may opt to take the questionnaire on paper.) She/he will assist as needed and will direct you to our conference when you have completed the questionnaire, which should take approximately 15 minutes to complete.

Thank you in advance for showing your support for (name of child's) learning and providing valuable information for our school's improvement.

We look forward to seeing you at 1:30, on Wednesday, (date).

Sincerely yours,

Name of Teacher

Pilot the Questionnaire

No matter how many times you go over the individual question, no matter how many times you look at the questions collectively, you won't know how the questions will actually perform until you administer them to a small number of respondents in your target group as a pilot test. We highly recommend piloting the questionnaire to be able to analyze the data to understand if you are asking questions that respondents understand questions that provide responses which lead to your purpose.

To pilot the questionnaire, you can use one of two approaches. One, organize a small group of respondents who are similar to the larger target group. Administer the questionnaire and analyze the results. Include questions on the pilot questionnaire to help you know if the pilot group understood everything on the questionnaire, if they thought the questions were relevant, if there are other questions they feel you should be asking, if they feel the questionnaire was easy to respond to, and to solicit their general overall comments. Another approach would be to administer one-on-one, to two to three people from each major demographic subgroup. Have each read each item aloud, offer responses, and tell you orally what she/he thinks it is asking, and what her/his responses mean. This is a very powerful information gatherer *and* quicker than traditional pilot tests.

Review Pilot Results

After the pilot responses come in, look over those responses to see if they are what you anticipated. Look at each of the questions with responses to see if each item was understandable. Look at the open-ended responses for clues to responses that you felt were not logical. Ask respondents, if they are available, to tell you why particular questions were hard to understand.

Revise, Review Again, and Finalize

After you study the responses from the pilot group, revise the questionnaire to reflect what you have learned. If you feel that the questions need to be piloted again, do so. It is much better to try out a questionnaire on a small group again than to administer a poor questionnaire to a large group.

Have several people review the questionnaire once it has been put into its final form to ensure there are no typographical errors and to ensure that the content flow is as you intend. When you feel that all of the bases have been covered, print the forms or post them online for the "real" questionnaire administration.

Administer the Questionnaire

Prepare for Administration

When at all possible, administer the questionnaire when people are together, in person. Schedule a convenient and efficient time for the administration. For example, administer the staff questionnaire during a faculty meeting. If you want all students in your school to complete the questionnaire, work with the teachers to have them administer the questionnaires to the students during first period or in periods when students are in the computer lab. State the purpose and procedures, making sure the people handing out the questionnaires, performing the interviews, or managing the online process understand clearly the purpose for giving the questionnaire and the proper procedures for administering and collecting the information. Also, make sure respondents understand the purpose and the importance of their roles in the process, and that their honest responses are desired and necessary.

Restate Purposes and Procedures

Teachers and administrators often ask how to get the students and teachers to take the questionnaire seriously. You must have a clear purpose for doing the questionnaire, clear instructions for completing it, and assurance that the information will be used to understand more about a program or its impact on students. It is the job of the person in charge to make sure that the people administering the questionnaire understand the purpose and can relay that purpose to the respondents.

Sometimes, providing input for continuously improving programs is incentive enough for people to respond to a questionnaire. Other times it is not enough. If you have a nice budget, you might want to offer a small gift or cash incentive.

In some elementary schools, students are encouraged to get their parents' responses to the questionnaire by offering them a pencil in return for a completed questionnaire. Response rates have improved from non-pencil days to pencil-incentive days, from 40% to 85% and 90%. Middle and high schools have offered raffle tickets for a $25 gift certificate to all students returning their completed parent questionnaires. Classes of high school students are awarded pizza parties for 100% return rates.

The downside of giving incentives is that you may have to keep giving incentives in the future to get responses.

Determine Sample

A common question about questionnaire administration is *to how many people do we need to send the questionnaire?* We usually include everyone because we want all participants to know their opinions were sought and will be considered. We also want the results to be used by staff. If you really cannot or do not want to get all participants, you could sample the overall group. A sample is a portion or subset of the larger group called a population. A good sample is a miniature version of the population—just like it, only smaller.

Let's think first about why we would sample. To whom you send your questionnaire has to be dependent upon your purpose for doing the questionnaire in the first place. If one reason is to find out what all of your parents are thinking about your school, you will want to send the questionnaire to every parent. There is nothing wrong with trying to look for the win-wins. You could receive parents' perceptions of the school and, at the same time, you could be informing them about things that are going on—building your public relations.

If your purpose leads you to sample instead of administer to the population, there are methods to use and references to study, some of which are listed in the reference section of this book. Although a lengthy discussion of sampling is beyond the scope of this book, methods of sampling are briefly described below.

A *stratified random sample* is one which divides the population into subgroups, and then a random sample is selected from each of the groups. You would use this approach when you want to make sure that you hear from all the groups of people you want to study. You might want to sample parents with low, medium, and high socioeconomic status; number of children in the household; or number of children at that school in order to feel that every condition of parenthood is heard.

A *simple sample* is a smaller version of the larger population that can be considered representative of the population. One classroom of students can be a simple sample, or one school in the district. This is typically used when administering a very large questionnaire.

One might use a *split questionnaire* design if you have a very large sample and a very long questionnaire. It is possible to split the questionnaire and to give one part to one group and another part to another group.

Convenience sampling is done when you want to survey people who are ready and available, and not hassle with trying to get everyone in the population ready and willing to complete the questionnaire.

Snowball sampling relies on members of one group completing the questionnaire to identify other members of the population to complete the questionnaire.

Quota sampling divides the population being studied into subgroups such as male and female, or young, middle, and old, to ensure that you set a quota of responses.

One important question to answer before sampling is *will the people who are supposed to use the questionnaire results accept a sample?* We hardly ever sample because of this issue. If all students, parents, and teachers are questioned, the results are compelling. Students and staff are easy to get. It takes a lot of effort to get all parents, however. If you get 80% response rate, you can feel pretty sure that you have heard from your group. Also, by the time you have created your sample, you might end up with most of your population anyhow, so you may as well survey all.

Administer the Questionnaire

Hand out the paper questionnaire, perform the interviews, or collect the data online. It is very important that the people assisting with the administration of the questionnaire take their jobs seriously and do a professional job of explaining the questionnaire's importance.

Analyze the Questionnaire

Collect and Verify the Data

Consider the number of people who were given the questionnaire and the number of responses received. If the number of responses is low—for example, a response of 60%—look to see if the responses are representative of the total population. If not, do a follow-up to get more responses. A response rate of 60% may or may not be low. For instance, if the questionnaire was administered to students during school, 60% is low. If it was mailed to parents, and is representative of the parent population, 60% could be high. If your parent questionnaire was given at parent–teacher conferences and only 60% of your parents attended, you could use another format to get additional responses from the parents who did not attend. Only with in-person administration procedures can you know who took an anonymous questionnaire. You could send the questionnaire to those who did not attend. In other circumstances, when you do not know who took the questionnaire, you would have to resend to everyone.

For each of the approaches to gathering questionnaire data, you will need to verify the accuracy of the data entry. In other words, you want to make sure that each of the dots were scanned into the right location in your database (if you are using a scannable form with a database), or entered into the correct location, if they are manually tallied. If the numbers were analyzed manually, every number must be verified for accuracy by preferably more than one person. For electronic gathering of questionnaire data, you will want to make sure there are no duplicate responses.

It is best to set up a database that will handle the questionnaire responses early in the process—preferably when you check your scanning process. It is an excellent double-check for your questionnaire and questions.

Create Analyses

After you are 100% confident that the data you are going to analyze are accurate and representative of the population you want to assess, begin using whatever software program you choose to design the analyses. Look at the total group and subgroup responses, synthesize the open-ended responses, and design and produce graphs to illustrate the data (see examples at the end of this chapter).

Analysis of questionnaires depends upon what you want to know and why you are doing the questionnaire in the first place.

One of the first things you might want to do is take a look at the average responses, by item, for students who took the questionnaire, as long as an interval scale was used. *Education for the Future* graphs our questionnaire results to show the group average to each item, which helps us get a big picture of the results, as shown in the examples at the end of this chapter.

If you diligently set up the variables by which to disaggregate questionnaire results, graphs can also display disaggregated information. In Chapter 9, Figures 9.6 and 9.7 show how disaggregating information can lead deeper and deeper into the issues. One caution is to make sure subgroup numbers do not drop below ten; otherwise, it is easy to identify individuals. Overall, small n's must be dealt with cautiously. Small response rates have more to do with carelessness in administration, than anything else.

Many people who conduct analysis of questionnaire results often feel they do not know enough about statistics. They have a perception that statistical significance must be calculated. Our belief is that descriptive statistics are very powerful for what we want to know about a school. We want to know how students are doing, and if different groups are responding to the processes in the same or different ways. Statistical significance tells very little about what you need to do differently in order to improve your program. What we really want to know is how we can better do what we do for students. Descriptive statistics can help us understand that.

How to Analyze Open-ended Responses

Open-ended questions should not be overlooked when assessing perceptions of the learning environment. While open-ended responses to questions are very time-consuming to compile or aggregate, one can get a complete sense of the learning environment by asking students, for example, two questions:

▼ *What do you like about this school?*

▼ *What do you wish was different?*

Or, ask students, staff, and parents these two questions—

▼ *What are the strengths of this school?*

▼ *What would make the school better?*

Sample student responses:

▼ *What I like most about this school are the teachers. I like the way they have fun making us learn.*

▼ *What I wish was different is, I wish we didn't ever have to leave this school.*

Sample staff and parent responses:

▼ *One of our school's strengths is the good relationship/ collaboration between grade-level teachers.*

▼ *Using positive reinforcement in the classroom would make the school better.*

There is no fast or automated way to analyze open-ended responses. The best way to analyze open-ended responses is to type the list of open-ended responses (if they were not typed via the online administration route). Review the responses and add up the number of times students said the same thing. Place the number, in parentheses, after the statement, eliminate the duplicates, and revise your list. You will need to make judgment calls about how to collapse the items when parts of the responses are different. Figure 5.9, *Aggregating Open-ended Responses*, shows the open-ended response list in the left-hand column. The other two columns show how the list can be condensed. Use one of these

Figure 5.9

Aggregating Open-ended Responses

All Responses	Eliminate Duplicates	Add Descriptors
I like the caring teachers and the friendly school	The teachers (8)	The teachers (8) (e.g., nice, 2; respect/fair, 2; caring, 1; good, 1; way of learning, 1)
I like that our school is new and the teachers are nice	The principal (2)	The school (3) (e.g., friendly, 1; new, 1; nice, 1)
I really like our new principal and my friends	My friends (3)	The principal (2)
I have a good teacher and friends who treat me nice	The school (3)	My friends (3) (e.g., treat me nice, 1)
I like the way teachers make us learn things	My classes (2)	My classes (2)
I feel safe and treated with respect from teachers	Recess (2)	Recess (2) (e.g., playground equipment, 1)
I like my teacher and the principal	Social Studies (1)	I feel safe
My teacher treats me with respect	P.E. (1)	Social Studies
I like recess, social studies, P.E., and music	Playground equipment (1)	P.E.
I like my friends and my nice teacher	Music (2)	Math
I like recess and the slide and the swings	Reading (1)	Not too much homework
We have a nice school	Math (1)	Music (2)
I like reading and music and math	I feel safe (1)	Reading
Not too much homework	Not too much homework (1)	

approaches—not two or three. The middle column, labeled "Eliminate Duplicates," shows the number of times students wrote teachers—the main thought—and so forth. The right-hand column, labeled "Add Descriptors," shows the number of times teachers were mentioned and in parentheses indicates the descriptions and the number of times the descriptors were mentioned, which gives a better understanding of the aggregated responses. For example:

▼ Teachers (6) (caring, 3; nice, 2; good, 1)

The approach you use is not important. What is important is to capture the feelings of the respondents. Open-ended responses are very helpful in painting the picture of your school and in understanding the multiple choice responses.

Analyze the Findings

Someone has to analyze the graphs and write a report that explains what the data say. It is very important to be able to read words that relate to graphs while viewing the graphs. Additional information might be taken into consideration in order for your audience to understand the responses. If some of the questions relate to specific issues that aren't mentioned in the questionnaire, you need to discuss that issue in the report and discuss how the questionnaire information relates to the issue. Figures 9.9 and 9.10 in Chapter 9 are examples of graph interpretation and sample analyses.

Produce the Report

It is very important to graph results so everyone can see the same picture. It is equally important to document the findings and to list next steps that come out of the analyses. There is something psychological about documentation that keeps groups from repeating what they have already done. The documentation of where they are right now often helps staffs plan for and begin next steps.

A complete report describes all items and their relationship to each other and to the overall questionnaire purpose.

In reporting questionnaire results, the following are important to include:

▼ Why the questionnaire was done

▼ The setting in which it was administered

▼ Unique features of the questionnaire

▼ Type of questionnaire

▼ Number of respondents (total and sample populations)

▼ Response rate

▼ How long the questionnaire took to complete

▼ General content of questionnaire

▼ Analysis and graphs

▼ Results

▼ Recommendations/next steps

Share

Disseminate the Findings

Once the report is written, you will need to determine the best way in which to get a summary of the analyzed results to the respondents and other interested parties. You may need to meet in person with target groups to share what was learned and to discuss next steps together. Think about what was promised when the questionnaire was administered—follow through on your word.

Graphs, as previously mentioned, can set the stage for discussion, convey a message, or reinforce a central point. Graphs must display the data, be concise in conveying the information, and be easily digestible to all readers.

The power of graphs comes from their ability to convey data directly to the viewer. Viewers use spatial intelligence to retrieve data from a graph—a source different from the language-based intelligence of prose and verbal presentations. Data become more credible and more convincing when the audience has direct interaction with the data. The communication process becomes more direct and immediate through graphic displays.

Just as important as getting the questionnaire constructed and analyzed appropriately is the use of the questionnaire results. It is important never to use one piece of data in isolation from the numerous other pieces of data available to schools. It is also important, whenever in doubt of what the results say, to ask respondents to clarify meaning.

Whether the meaning of the results is analyzed by a small group or by the entire staff, the results must be distributed back to staff with agreed upon next steps.

As you think through all the steps in setting up and completing a questionnaire, remember this—you are taking an individual's time and energy, as well as your own time and energy, to put a questionnaire together and to analyze it. Think through all the steps, research the topics, and think about the people involved before you begin. Treat each questionnaire as a scientific instrument, not as just a list of questions to ask people.

Congratulations! You have now completely thought through your questionnaire administration and analysis.

Our Example Schools

Figure 5.10 shows three years of staff questionnaire results for Archer Elementary. Because of their lack of attention to details in administration each year, they received a different number of responses. Unfortunately, it is hard to know what these data tell us because we do not know how the questionnaire was administered and who completed it.

Figure 5.10

Archer Elementary School Staff Responses
By Year, May 2001, May 2002, and May 2003

	5 Strongly Agree	4	3	2	1 Strongly Disagree	

I feel like I belong at this school

I feel that the staff cares about me

I feel that learning can be fun

I feel that learning is fun at this school

I feel recognized for good work

I feel intrinsically rewarded for doing my job well

I work with people who treat me with respect

I work with people who listen if I have ideas about doing things better

My administrator treats me with respect

My administrator is an effective instructional leader

My administrator facilitates communication effectively

My administrator supports me in my work with students

My administrator supports shared decision making

My administrator allows me to be an effective instructional leader

My administrator is effective in helping us reach our vision

I have the opportunity to develop my skills

I have the opportunity to think for myself, not just carry out instructions

I love working at this school

I love seeing the results of my work with students

I work effectively with special education students

I work effectively with English Learners

I work effectively with an ethnically/racially diverse population of students

I work effectively with heterogeneously grouped classes

I work effectively with low-achieving students

I believe every student can learn

I BELIEVE STUDENT ACHIEVEMENT CAN INCREASE THROUGH: "hands-on learning"

effective professional development related to our vision

integrating instruction across the curriculum

thematic instruction

— ● — Total Survey Respondents May 2001 (*n*=61)

— ■ — Total Survey Respondents May 2002 (*n*=25)

— △ — Total Survey Respondents May 2003 (*n*=37)

Figure 5.10 *(Continued)*

Archer Elementary School Staff Responses
By Year, May 2001, May 2002, and May 2003

5 Strongly Agree	4	3	2	Strongly Disagree 1	

I BELIEVE STUDENT ACHIEVEMENT CAN INCREASE THROUGH: cooperative learning

multi-age classrooms

student self-assessment

authentic assessment

the use of computers

the use of varied technologies

providing a threat-free environment

close personal relationships between students and teachers

addressing student learning styles

effective parent involvement

partnerships with business

teacher use of student achievement data

The instructional program at this school is challenging

This school provides an atmosphere where every student can succeed

Quality work is expected of all students at this school

Quality work is expected of me

Quality work is expected of all the adults working at this school

The vision for this school is clear

The vision for this school is shared

We have an action plan in place which can get us to our vision

This school has a good public image

I think it is important to communicate often with parents

I communicate with parents often about their child's progress

I communicate with parents often about class activities

MORALE IS HIGH ON THE PART OF: teachers

students

support staff

administrators

I am clear about what my job is at this school

I feel that others are clear about what my job is at this school

— ● — Total Survey Respondents May 2001 (*n*=61)

— ■ — Total Survey Respondents May 2002 (*n*=25)

— △ — Total Survey Respondents May 2003 (*n*=37)

Figure 5.10 *(Continued)*

**Archer Elementary School Staff
Items for Teachers and Instructional Assistants by Year
May 2001, May 2002, and May 2003**

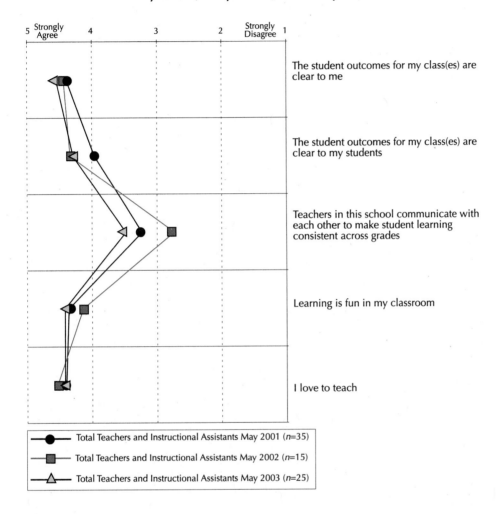

Figure 5.11 shows Majestic High School's student questionnaire responses disaggregated by year in high school. One can clearly see that the longer students were at this school, the less positive they are about the learning environment.

Figure 5.11

**Majestic High School Student Responses
By Grade Level, February 2003**

Total Survey Respondents (N=210)	Freshman (n=66)
Sophomore (n=55)	Junior (n=51)
Senior (n=33)	

Figure 5.11 *(Continued)*

Majestic High School Student Responses
By Grade Level, February 2003

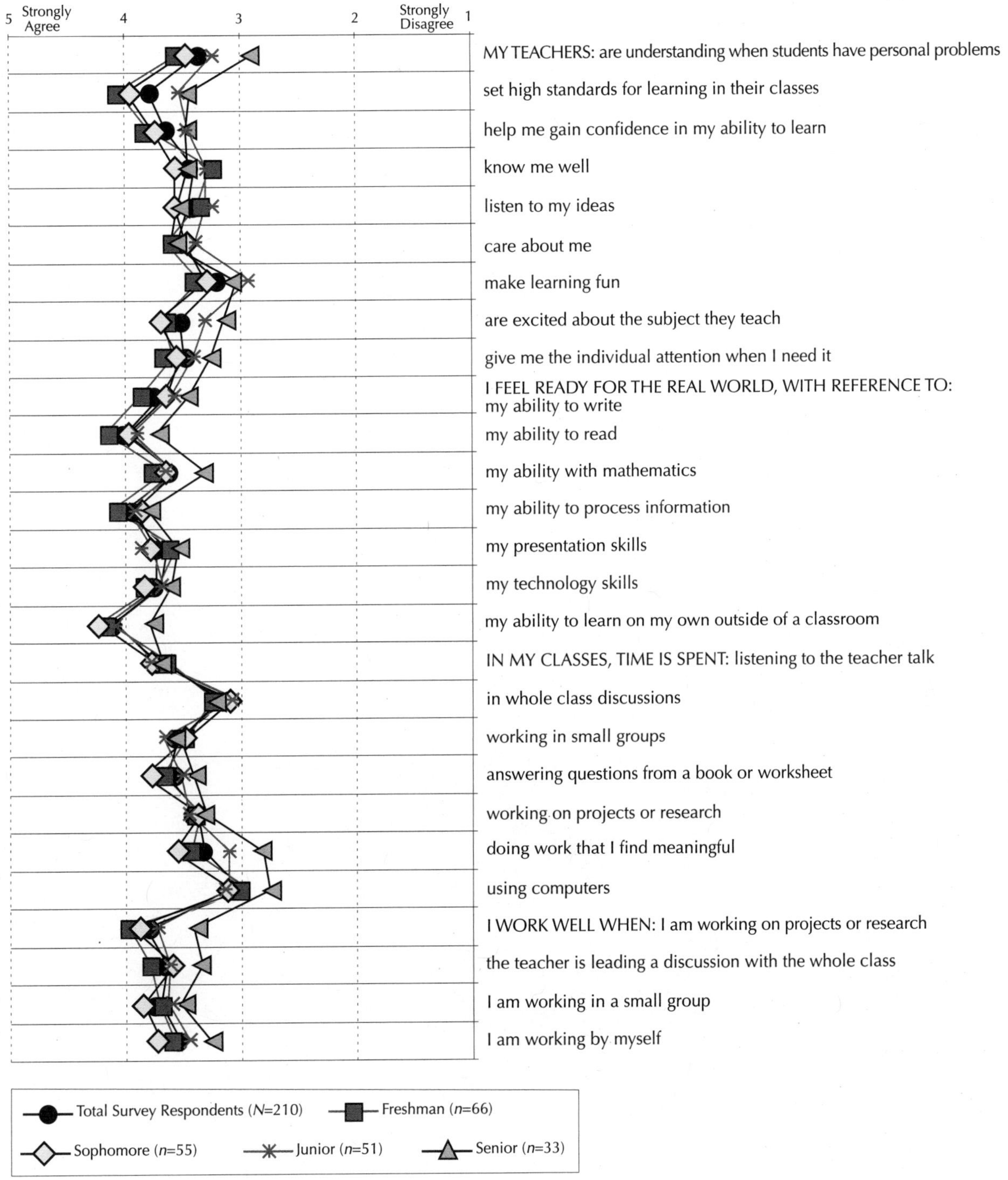

Study Questions for Perceptions

Think about the questionnaires that you want to design, administer, analyze, and use. What information do you want to glean from the questionnaires? Please review Figure 5.1, *Begin with the End in Mind,* before you begin. The questions below can also help you get started.

• What is the purpose for administering the questionnaire? What information do you want to collect?

• To whom do you need to give the questionnaire in order to get this information?

• How will you administer the questionnaires?

• How do you want the results displayed (i.e., charts, graphs, tables, averages, distributions, percentages, comparisons)?

• By what categories will you want to disaggregate the responses?

• How will you get the information from the questionnaires into some form, such as a database, that will allow you to graph the results?

• Who is going to do the work?

Summary

As you think through all the steps in setting up and completing a questionnaire, remember this—you are taking an individual's time and energy, as well as your own time and energy, to put a questionnaire together and to analyze it. Think through all the steps, research the topics, and think about the people involved before you begin. Treat each questionnaire as a scientific instrument, not just as a list of questions to ask people.

Also remember that *Education for the Future* has proven questionnaires, processes, and tools for administering, analyzing, and using perception results. Visit the *Education for the Future* website *(http://eff.csuchico.edu)* for more information.

STUDENT LEARNING

Chapter 6

Most school improvement efforts focus on increasing the learning of all students. Measures of student learning help us understand how students are performing and what students know as a result of instruction. Before thinking about how to measure student learning, however, schools must be clear on why they are assessing student learning. Only then can they gain the congruence needed in an assessment program to achieve those student learning increases.

The most commonly stated reasons schools give for measuring student learning include knowing—

- ▼ if students have particular skills and knowledge
- ▼ if students have attained a level of proficiency/competence/mastery
- ▼ if instructional strategies are making a difference for all students
- ▼ the effectiveness of instructional strategies and curricula
- ▼ how to improve instructional strategies
- ▼ how to classify students into instructional groups
- ▼ that students are ready to graduate or proceed to the next level of instruction
- ▼ if school processes are making the intended progress

Unfortunately, student learning results are not always used in these ways. Most of the time it is because school personnel struggle with the way student learning is measured. How to analyze and display the results of this learning may also be a struggle.

Ways to Measure Student Learning

A student assessment program that truly meets the needs of every student must be congruent with its purposes, uses, and practices. The program can then begin to predict not only student needs, but also the approaches required to meet those needs.

While we know that student learning measures must be interpreted in context, student learning has been traditionally measured by one or more of the approaches listed below:

- ▼ standardized tests
- ▼ norm-referenced tests
- ▼ criterion-referenced measures
- ▼ authentic assessments
- ▼ teacher-made tests
- ▼ teacher-assigned grades
- ▼ performance assessments
- ▼ standards-based assessments

Analyses of all types of student learning measures used in the school can help one know if all students are learning and if true learning can be detected better with one measure than another. Looking across measures, teachers can determine how the different measures contrast in performance and if students perform differently on one type of test versus another. Comparing results on different measures gives teachers insight into what teaching strategies, as well as testing strategies, work best with different students.

Standardized Tests

Standardized tests are assessments that have uniformity in content, administration, and scoring. They can be used for comparing results across students, classrooms, schools, school districts, and states. Norm-referenced, criterion-referenced, and diagnostic tests are the most commonly used standardized tests. Arguments *for* and *against* standardized testing appear in Figure 6.1.

Figure 6.1

Arguments For and Against Standardized Testing

Arguments For Standardized Testing

- Standardized testing can be designed to measure performance, thinking, problem solving, and communication skills.
- The process students use to solve a problem can be tested, rather than just the result.
- Standardized tests can be developed to match state standards.
- Standardized tests can help drive the curriculum standards that are supposed to be taught.
- Ways need to be developed to determine if students have the skills to succeed in society; standardized tests can ensure all students, across a state or the entire country, have essential skills.
- Employers and the public need to know if students are able to apply skills and knowledge to everyday life; standardized testing can help with that assurance.
- Standardized testing may be helping to raise the bar of expectations for students in public schools— especially the lowest performing schools.
- Many schools, districts, and states have seen achievement levels rise in recent years which they attribute to higher expectations of students because of standardized tests.
- Standardized tests provide data that show which skills students are lacking, giving educators the information necessary to tailor classes and instructional strategies to student needs.
- Standardized tests can tell how the school or student is doing in comparison to a norming group, which is supposed to represent the typical students in the country.
- With most standardized tests, one can follow the same students over time.

Arguments Against Standardized Testing

- Standardized testing often narrows student learning to what is tested; what is tested is usually only a sample of what students should know.
- Standardized tests typically focus on what is easy to measure, not the critical thinking skills students need to develop.
- Standardized tests do not always match the state standards.
- To make standardized tests align to the state standards requires expertise and can be costly.
- The quality of standardized tests is a concern.
- Standardized tests are better at measuring rote learning than evaluating thinking skills.
- Too much instructional time is used to prepare students for multiple-choice tests, to the detriment of other uses of instructional time.
- Standardized tests could be culturally biased, drawing primarily upon the experiences of one socio-economic group.
- Decisions are sometimes made about a student's promotion from grade to grade or graduation based solely on one multiple-choice test.
- It is not fair to hold students accountable on one test when the schools might not be providing students with quality teachers, curricula, and time to master concepts.
- Students are not always provided with time to master what is expected on the standardized tests.
- There is a concern with standardized tests over getting the right answers.
- Standardized tests sometimes measure only what students know, not what they understand.
- Standardized testing is expensive.
- Testing is costly in teaching time and student time.

Norm-referenced Tests

Norm-referenced tests are also standardized tests. Norm-referenced test scores create meaning through comparing the test performance of a school, group, or individual with the performance of a norming group. A norming group is a representative group of students whose results on a norm-referenced test help create the scoring scales with which others compare their performance. Norming groups' results are professed to look like the normal curve, shown in Figure 6.2 below.

Figure 6.2

The Normal Curve and Scores

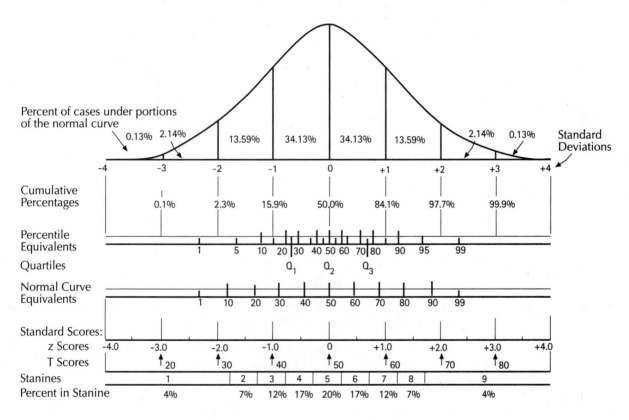

The normal curve is a distribution of scores or other measures that in graphic form has a distinctive bell-shaped appearance. In a normal distribution, the measures are distributed symmetrically about the mean, or average, score. Most results are near the mean and decrease in frequency the farther one departs from the mean. Stated another way— the theory of the normal curve basically says that when test publishers give a test to a representative sample of students, most students score around the mean with very few students scoring very high or very low. Using this theory, test publishers are able to create scales that are useful for schools to compare their scores with the norming group.

National Percentile Ranks. The two most commonly used and useful normed scales, or score types, are national percentile ranks and normal curve equivalents. The national percentile rank (NPR), also known as the national percentile equivalent, ranges from 1 to 99, with a midscore of 50. The NPR is one of the most used scales; it is also misused the most. The misuse of this scale stems from the fact that it is an unequal interval scale, which *prohibits* adding, subtracting, multiplying, and dividing the scores. *One should not look at gains, losses, or averages with percentile ranks.* Median scores, or the middle scores, are the most appropriate means of describing a whole school's typical performance.

Normal Curve Equivalent Scores. Normal curve equivalent (NCE) scores were created by educational researchers to alleviate the problem of unequal interval scales. This equal interval scale has a mean of 50, and range of 1 to 99, just like the NPR. A standard deviation of 21.06 was used to ensure that NCE and percentile ranks have equivalent scores at the 1st, 50th, and 99th percentiles. NCEs have the same meaning across students, subtests, grade levels, classrooms, schools, and school districts. Fifty (50) is what one would expect for an average year's growth, or put another way, 50 is grade level—always the national average for the grade and month the test is taken. You can look at how close your scores are to expected performance, averages, gains, losses, highest, and lowest scores. NCEs are excellent for looking at scores over time.

If you need to convert percentile ranks to NCEs, or NCEs to percentiles, use the tables in Figures 6.3 and 6.4. Note how the conversion can be more exact going from NCE scores to percentiles. A conversion in the opposite direct uses an average NCE.

Figure 6.3

NCE to Percentile Conversion							
NCE Range	Percentile Rank	NCE Range	Percentile Rank	NCE Range	Percentile Rank	NCE Range	Percentile Rank
1.0 – 4.0	1	36.1–36.7	26	50.3–50.7	51	64.6–65.1	76
4.1 – 8.5	2	36.8–37.3	27	50.8–51.2	52	65.2–65.8	77
8.6–11.7	3	37.4–38.0	28	51.3–51.8	53	65.9–66.5	78
11.8–14.1	4	38.1–38.6	29	51.9–52.3	54	66.6–67.3	79
14.2–16.2	5	38.7–39.2	30	52.4–52.8	55	67.4–68.0	80
16.3–18.0	6	39.3–39.8	31	52.9–53.4	56	68.1–68.6	81
18.1–19.6	7	39.9–40.4	32	53.5–53.9	57	68.7–69.6	82
19.7–21.0	8	40.5–40.9	33	54.0–54.4	58	69.7–70.4	83
21.1–22.3	9	41.0–41.5	34	54.5–55.0	59	70.5–71.3	84
22.4–23.5	10	41.6–42.1	35	55.1–55.5	60	71.4–72.2	85
23.6–24.6	11	42.2–42.7	36	55.6–56.1	61	72.3–73.1	86
24.7–25.7	12	42.8–43.2	37	56.2–56.6	62	73.2–74.1	87
25.8–26.7	13	43.3–43.8	38	56.7–57.2	63	74.2–75.2	88
26.8–27.6	14	43.9–44.3	39	57.3–57.8	64	75.3–76.3	89
27.7–28.5	15	44.4–44.9	40	57.9–58.3	65	76.4–77.5	90
28.6–29.4	16	45.0–45.4	41	58.4–58.9	66	77.6–78.8	91
29.5–30.2	17	45.5–45.9	42	59.0–59.5	67	78.9–80.2	92
30.3–31.0	18	46.0–46.5	43	59.6–60.1	68	80.3–81.7	93
31.1–31.8	19	46.6–47.0	44	60.2–60.7	69	81.8–83.5	94
31.9–32.6	20	47.1–47.5	45	60.8–61.3	70	83.6–85.5	95
32.7–33.3	21	47.6–48.1	46	61.4–61.9	71	85.6–88.0	96
33.4–34.0	22	48.2–48.6	47	62.0–62.5	72	88.1–91.0	97
34.1–34.7	23	48.7–49.1	48	62.6–63.1	73	91.1–96.4	98
34.8–35.4	24	49.2–49.6	49	63.2–63.8	74	96.5–99.0	99
35.5–36.0	25	49.7–50.2	50	63.9–64.5	75		

Stanford Achievement Test: Eighth Edition. Copyright © 1989 by The Psychological Corporation. Reproduced by permission. All rights reserved.

Figure 6.4

Percentile to NCE Conversion

Percentile Rank	NCE	Percentile Rank	NCE	Percentile Rank	NCE	Percentile Rank	NCE
1	1.0	26	36.5	51	50.5	76	64.9
2	6.7	27	37.1	52	51.1	77	65.6
3	10.4	28	37.7	53	51.6	78	66.3
4	13.1	29	38.3	54	52.1	79	67.0
5	15.4	30	39.0	55	52.6	80	67.7
6	17.3	31	39.6	56	53.2	81	68.5
7	18.9	32	40.1	57	53.7	82	69.3
8	20.4	33	40.7	58	54.2	83	70.1
9	21.8	34	41.3	59	54.8	84	70.9
10	23.0	35	41.9	60	55.3	85	71.8
11	24.2	36	42.5	61	55.9	86	72.8
12	25.3	37	43.0	62	56.4	87	73.7
13	26.3	38	43.6	63	57.0	88	74.7
14	27.2	39	44.1	64	57.5	89	75.8
15	28.2	40	44.7	65	58.1	90	77.0
16	29.1	41	45.2	66	58.7	91	78.2
17	29.9	42	45.8	67	59.3	92	79.6
18	30.7	43	46.3	68	59.9	93	81.1
19	31.5	44	46.8	69	60.4	94	82.7
20	32.3	45	47.4	70	61.0	95	84.6
21	33.0	46	47.9	71	61.7	96	86.9
22	33.7	47	48.4	72	62.3	97	89.6
23	34.4	48	48.9	73	62.9	98	93.3
24	35.1	49	49.5	74	63.5	99	99.0
25	35.8	50	50.0	75	64.2		

When displaying NCE results, many schools show results for grade levels over time as shown in Figure 6.5. While one can make few comparisons within grade levels over time because the students are not the same, one usually can see that the scores are fairly stable, unless something very different happens, such as new teaching strategies or new teachers. Grades three and four illustrate the type of increases we would like to see every year.

NCE scores can be used for comparisons because they:

▼ have equal intervals

▼ can be aggregated, disaggregated, and averaged

▼ have a derived average of 50 and a standard deviation of 21.06

▼ can be compared from one grade to another

▼ can be used to calculate gain scores

▼ match percentiles of 1 to 99

▼ can be converted to percentiles after analysis

Figure 6.5

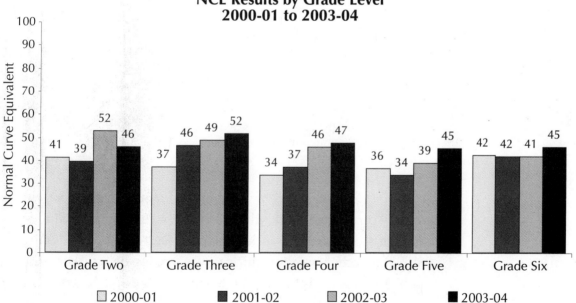

**NCE Results by Grade Level
2000-01 to 2003-04**

Figure 6.6 shows how to reorganize a grade level over time graph to follow the same group of students. This type of graph is called a *cohort* graph. The cohorts can be *matched* (following the same students over time), or *unmatched* (following the same groups over time).

Figure 6.6

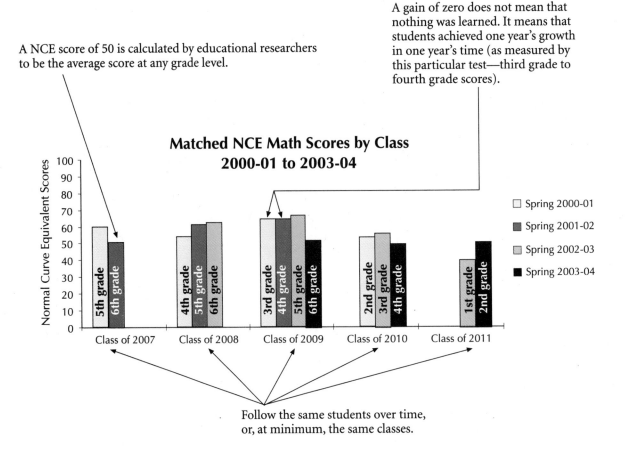

A NCE score of 50 is calculated by educational researchers to be the average score at any grade level.

A gain of zero does not mean that nothing was learned. It means that students achieved one year's growth in one year's time (as measured by this particular test—third grade to fourth grade scores).

Follow the same students over time, or, at minimum, the same classes.

Grade-level Equivalent Scores. Grade-level equivalents represent yet another score type used with norm-referenced tests. Grade-level equivalent scores result in an interesting scale that shows the grade and month of the school year for which a given score is the actual or estimated average. Its meaning is that the student obtained the same score that one would expect average x^{th} grade students in their x^{th} month to score if they took the xth grade test. Based on a ten-month school year, scores would be noted as 3.1 for third grade, first month, or 5.10 for fifth grade, tenth month. For example, if a third grader scored a 5.8 on a subtest, that does not mean that she/he should be doing fifth grade, eighth-month work. It only means that the student obtained the same score that one would expect average fifth grade students to score if they took the same third-grade test during the eighth month of grade five. Grade-level equivalent scores are okay for a snapshot in time, but they should not be averaged or taken literally.

Standard Scores. Standard scores, or scaled scores, refer to scores that have been transformed for reasons of convenience, comparability, and ease of interpretation. Ranges vary depending upon the test, and sometimes even the subtest. The best uses of standard scores are averages calculated over time-allowing for the study of change. These scores are good to use for calculations because of their equal intervals and their easy conversions to other score types. The downsides are that, with the various ranges, it is difficult to look across subtests, grade levels, and years. It is often hard for laypeople to create meaning from these scores. The normal curve is needed to interpret the results with respect to other scores and people.

Anticipated Achievement/Cognitive Abilities Scores. Occasionally, norm-referenced tests provide indicators of ability, such as anticipated achievement scores, cognitive abilities, or cognitive skills indexes. The anticipated achievement score is an estimate of the average score for students of a similar age, grade, and academic aptitude. It can be computed in grade-level equivalents, normal curve equivalents, standard scores, and national percentiles. The higher the student scores on sequences, analogies, memory, and verbal reasoning tests, the higher the student is expected to score on standardized tests.

A cognitive abilities or cognitive skills index is also created from the same four tests mentioned above. The index assesses the student's academic aptitude. The range of this scale is 58 to 141, with a mean of 100. Two-thirds of the scores will fall between 84 and 118. Anticipated Achievement/Cognitive Abilities scores can tell teachers if they are teaching to students' potential.

Criterion-referenced Tests

Criterion-referenced tests compare an individual's performance to a specific learning objective or performance standard and not to the performance of other test takers. Criterion-referenced assessments tell us how well students are performing on specific criteria, goals, or standards. For school level analyses, criterion-referenced tests are usually scored in terms of the number or percentage of students meeting the standard or criterion, or the number or percentage of students falling in typical descriptive categories, such as *far below basic, below basic, basic, proficient,* and *advanced.* Criterion-referenced tests can be standardized or not, and they can also have norming groups.

Diagnostic Tests

Diagnostic tests, usually standardized and normed, are given before instruction begins to help the instructor(s) understand student learning needs. Diagnostic tests can help teachers know the nature of students' difficulties, but not the cause of the difficulty. Many different score types are used with diagnostic tests.

These tests, score types, and other frequently used terms are defined in Figure 6.7, along with a description of most effective uses and cautions for use.

Figure 6.7

Standardized Test Score Terms, Their Most Effective Uses, and Cautions for Their Uses			
Score	**Definition**	**Most Effective Uses**	**Cautions**
Anticipated Achievement Scores	A student's anticipated achievement score is an estimate of the average score for students of similar ages, grade levels, and academic aptitude. It is an estimate of what we would expect the student to score on an achievement test.	Anticipated achievement scores can be used to see if a student is scoring "above" or "below" an expected score, indicating whether or not she/he is being challenged enough, or if her/his needs are being met.	It is easy to think of these scores as "IQ" scores. They are just achievement indicators on a standardized test.
Cognitive Abilities or Skills Index	The cognitive skills index is an age-dependent normalized standard score based on a student's performance on a cognitive skills test with a mean of 100 and standard deviation of 16. The score indicates a student's overall cognitive ability or academic aptitude relative to students of similar age, without regard to grade level.	Cognitive skills index scores can be used to see if a student is scoring "above" or "below" an expected score, indicating whether or not she/he is being challenged enough, or if her/his needs are being met.	It is easy to think of these scores as "IQ" scores. They are just achievement indicators on a standardized test.
Criterion-referenced Tests	Tests that judge how well a test-taker does on an explicit objective relative to a predetermined performance level.	Tell us how well students are performing on specific criteria, goals, or standards.	CRTs test only what was taught, or planned to be taught. CRTs can not give a broad estimate of knowledge.
Deciles	Deciles divide a distribution into ten equal parts: 1–10; 11–20; 21–30; 31–40; 41–50; 51–60; 61–70; 71–80; 81–90; 91–99. Just about any scale can be used to show deciles.	Deciles allow schools to show how all students scored throughout the distribution. One would expect a school's distribution to resemble a normal curve. Watching the distribution move to the right, over time, could imply that all students in the distribution are making progress.	One must dig deeper to understand if all students and all groups of students are moving forward.
Diagnostic Tests	Diagnostic tests, usually standardized and normed, are given before instruction begins to help the instructor(s) understand student learning needs. Many different score types are used with diagnostic tests.	Help teachers know the nature of students' difficulties, but not the cause of the difficulty.	Make sure the diagnostic test is measuring what you want it to measure and that it can be compared to formative and summative assessments used.

Figure 6.7 *(Continued)*

Standardized Test Score Terms, Their Most Effective Uses, and Cautions for Their Uses			
Score	**Definition**	**Most Effective Uses**	**Cautions**
Grade-level Equivalents	Grade-level equivalents indicate the grade and month of the school year for which a given score is the actual or estimated average. Based on a ten-month school year, scores would be noted as 3.1 for third grade, first month, or 5.10 for fifth grade, tenth month.	Grade-level equivalents are most effectively used as a snapshot in time. Scores are comparable across subtests.	These scores should not be taken literally. If a third grader scored a 5.8 on a subtest, that does not mean that she/he should be doing fifth grade, eighth-month work. It only means that the student obtained the same score that one would expect average fifth-grade students in their eighth month of school to score if they took the third-grade test.
Latent-trait Scale	A latent-trait scale is a scaled score obtained through one of several mathematical approaches collectively known as Latent-Trait Procedures or Item Response Theory. The particular numerical values used in the scale are arbitrary, but higher scores indicate more knowledgeable students or more difficult items.	Latent-trait scales have equal intervals allowing comparisons over time.	These are scores set up by testing professionals. Laypeople typically have difficulty understanding their meaning.
NCE (National or Local)	Normal Curve Equivalent (NCE) scores are standard scores with a mean of 50, a standard deviation of 21.06, and a range of 1 to 99. The term National would indicate that the norming group was national; local usually implies a state or district norming group.	NCEs have equal intervals so they can be used to study gains over time. The scores have the same meaning across subtests, grade levels, and years. A 50 is what one would expect in an average year's growth.	This score, just like all scores related to norm-referenced tests, cannot be taken literally. The score simply shows relative performance of a student group or of students to a norming group.
Percent Passing	Percent passing is a calculated score implying the percentage of the student group meeting and exceeding some number, usually a cut score, proficiency/mastery level, or a standard.	With standards-based accountability, it is beneficial to know the percentage of the population meeting and exceeding a standard and to compare a year's percentages with the previous year(s) to understand progress being made.	This is a very simple statistic, and its interpretation should be simple as well. Total numbers (n=) of students included in the percentage must always be noted with the percentage to assist with the understanding.

Figure 6.7 *(Continued)*

Standardized Test Score Terms, Their Most Effective Uses, and Cautions for Their Uses			
Score	**Definition**	**Most Effective Uses**	**Cautions**
Percentile / Percentile Rank (PR) (National or Local)	Percentile ranks indicate the percentage of students in a norm group (e.g., national or local) whose scores fall below a given score. The range is from 1 to 99. 50th percentile ranking would mean that 50 percent of the scores in the norming group fall below a specific score. The term National would indicate that the norming group was national; local usually implies a state or district norming group.	One-year comparison to the norming group. Schools can see the relative standing of a student or group in the same grade to the norm group who took the test at a comparable time.	Percentile rank is not a score to use over time to look for gains because of unequal intervals, unless the calculations are made with equal interval scores and then converted to percentile ranks. One cannot calculate averages using NPR because of the unequal intervals. Medians are the most appropriate statistic to use.
Quartiles	There are three quartiles— Q1, Q2, Q3 — that divide a distribution into four equal groups: Q1=25th percentile Q2=50th percentile (Median) Q3=75th percentile	Quartiles allow schools to see the distribution of scores for any grade level, for instance. Over time, schools trying to increase student achievement would want to monitor the distribution to ensure that all students are making progress.	With quartiles, one cannot tell if the scores are at the top of a quartile or the bottom. There could be "real" changes taking place within a quartile that would not be evident.
Raw Scores	Raw scores are the number of questions answered correctly on a test or subtest. A raw score is simply calculated by adding the number of questions answered correctly. The raw score is a person's observed score.	The raw score provides information about the number of questions answered correctly. To get a perspective on performance, raw scores must be used with the average score for the group and/or the total number of questions. Alone, it has no meaning.	Raw scores do not provide information related to other students taking the test or to other subtests. One needs to keep perspective by knowing the total number possible. Raw scores should never be used to make comparisons between performances on different tests unless other information about the characteristics of the tests are known and identical.
RIT Scale Scores	RIT scores, named for George Rasch who developed the theory of this type of measurement, are scaled scores that come from a series of tests created by the Northwest Evaluation Association (NWEA). The tests, which draw from an item bank, are aligned with local curriculum and state/local standards.	RIT scores provide ongoing measurement of curriculum standards and a way for students to see progress in their knowledge. The scores can also be shown as percentiles to know performance related to other students of similar ages and/or grades. You will most probably see gains each time a measurement is taken with a group of students.	RIT scores are great as long as the test was carefully designed to measure standards.

Figure 6.7 *(Continued)*

Standardized Test Score Terms, Their Most Effective Uses, and Cautions for Their Uses			
Score	**Definition**	**Most Effective Uses**	**Cautions**
Scaled Scores	A scaled score is a mathematical transformation of a raw score.	The best uses of scaled scores are averages and averages calculated over time allowing for the study of change. These scores are good to use for calculations because of equal intervals. The scores can be applied across subtests on most tests. Scaled scores facilitate conversions to other score types.	Ranges vary, depending upon the test. Watch for the minimum and maximum values. It is sometimes hard for laypeople to create meaning from these scores. The normal curve is needed to interpret the results with respect to other scores and people.
Standard Scores	Standard score is a general term referring to scores that have been "transformed" for reasons of convenience, comparability, ease of interpretation, etc. z-scores and T-scores are standard scores.	The best uses of standard scores are averages and averages calculated over time, allowing for the study of change. These scores are good to use for calculations because of equal intervals. The scores can be applied across subtests on most tests. Scaled scores facilitate conversions to other score types.	Ranges vary, depending upon the test. Watch for the minimum and maximum values. It is sometimes hard for laypeople to create meaning from these scores. The normal curve is needed to interpret results with respect to other scores and people.
Standards-based Assessments	Standards-based assessments measure students' progress toward mastering local, state, and/or national content standards.	The way standards-based assessments are analyzed depends upon the scales used. The most effective uses are in revealing the percentage of students achieving a standard.	One has to adhere to the cautions of whatever test or score type used. It is important to know how far from mastering the standard the students were when they did not meet the standard.
Stanines	Stanines are a nine-point standard score scale. Stanines divide the normal curve into nine equal points: 1 to 9.	Stanines, like quartiles, allow schools to see the distribution of scores for any grade level, for instance. Over time, schools trying to increase student achievement would want to monitor the distribution to ensure that all student scores are improving.	Often, the first three stanines are interpreted as "below average," the next three as "average," and the top three as "above average." This can be misleading. As with quartiles, one cannot tell if the scores are at the top of a stanine or the bottom. There could be "real" changes taking place within a stanine that would not be evident.

Figure 6.7 *(Continued)*

Standardized Test Score Terms, Their Most Effective Uses, and Cautions for Their Uses			
Score	**Definition**	**Most Effective Uses**	**Cautions**
T-scores	A T-score is a standard score with a mean of 50 and a standard deviation of 10. T-scores are obtained by the following formula: $T = 10z + 50$	The most effective uses of T-scores are averages and averages calculated over time. T-scores are good to use for calculations because of their equal intervals. T-scores can be applied across subtests on most tests because of the forced mean and standard deviation.	T-scores are rarely used because of the lack of understanding on the part of most test users.
z-scores	A z-score is a standard score with a mean of zero and a standard deviation of one. z-scores are obtained by the following formula: $z = \dfrac{\text{raw score (x)} - \text{mean}}{\text{standard deviation (sd)}}$	z-scores can tell one how many standard deviations a score is away from the mean. z-scores are most useful, perhaps, as the first step in computing other types of standard scores.	z-scores are rarely used by the lay public because of the difficulty in understanding the score.

Performance Assessments

The term performance assessment refers to assessments that measure skills, knowledge, and ability directly—such as through performance. In other words, if you want students to learn to write, you assess their ability on a writing activity. One must find a way to score these results and make sense for individual students and groups of students. Some of the arguments for and against performance assessments are listed in Figure 6.8. (See References for sources.)

115

Figure 6.8

Arguments For and Against Performance Assessments

Arguments For Performance Assessments

- Performance assessments can be designed to measure performance, thinking, problem solving, and communication skills.
- Performance assessments can be used to measure the process students use to solve problems.
- Performance assessments can be developed to match state standards.
- Many schools, districts, and states have seen achievement levels rise in recent years, which they attribute to higher expectations of students and what they can do, attributed to the use of performance assessments.
- Performance assessments provide data that show what students are lacking, giving educators the information necessary to tailor classes and instructional strategies to student needs.
- Students can learn during a performance task.
- Some teachers believe that when students participate in developing a rubric for evaluating their performance, they come to appreciate high-quality work.
- Performance assessments provide opportunities for students to reflect on their own work.
- Performance assessments can allow students to work until standards are met—to ensure quality work from all students.
- Performance assessments can help the teacher improve instructional strategies.
- Performance assessments allow students to perform in the learning style that suits them best.

Arguments Against Performance Assessments

- Designing good performance assessments that accurately measure performance, thinking, problem solving, and communication skills is difficult.
- Designing good performance assessments that accurately measure performance, thinking, problem solving, and communication skills is very costly.
- Some performance tasks require long periods of time to complete, such as graduation or end-of-course exhibitions.
- To be effective, skills and performances being assessed should be taught in the same way they are measured.
- The quality of performance assessments is a concern.
- It is not fair to hold students accountable on one test when the schools might not be providing students with quality teachers, curricula, and time to master concepts.
- Scoring criteria requires analyzing performance into its components, such as breaking out the craft of writing into developmental elements.
- Many scoring criteria are no different from giving grades or norm-referenced scoring.
- Good scoring criteria could take a long time to develop.
- It is very difficult to design performance assessments that can be compared across grade levels in other than descriptive terms.

Grades

Teachers use number or letter grades to judge the quality of a student's performance on a task, unit, or during a period of time. Grades are most often given as A, B, C, D, F, with pluses and minuses given by some teachers for the first four to distinguish among students. Grades mean different things to different teachers. Needless to say, grades can be subjective. "It appears that teachers consider grading to be a private activity, thus 'guarding practices with the same passion with which one might guard an unedited diary' (Kain, 1996, p. 569)" (O'Connor, 2000, p. 11). Some of the arguments for and against teacher grading are shown in Figure 6.9.

Figure 6.9

Arguments For and Against Teacher Grading

Arguments For Teacher Grading

- Grades can be designed to reflect performance, thinking, problem solving, and communication skills.
- Teachers can grade the process students use to solve a problem, rather than just the result.
- Grades can communicate to students, parents, and administrators the student's level of performance.
- Grading can allow teachers to be very flexible in their approaches to assessing student performance.
- Grades can match teaching.
- Grades can be given for team work and not just individual work.
- Grades can be effective if students are aware of expectations.
- Grades can cover multiple standards.
- Certain teacher-developed tests can be graded quickly.
- Most people believe they know what grades mean.

Arguments Against Teacher Grading

- It is difficult to convert activities, such as performance, thinking, and problem solving, into numbers or letters and have them hold true for all students in a class.
- Grading can be very subjective.
- Grading can be distorted by effort, extra credit, attendance, behavior, etc.
- To be beneficial, students must trust the grader and the grading process, have time to practice and complete an assessment, and have choices in how they are assessed—all of which make it time-consuming for teachers to do this type of assessment well.
- To be beneficial, grading assessments must be meaningful and promote learning.
- Grades must include a variety of assessment techniques to get to all areas of student understanding and performance.
- Often parents, students, and teachers focus on grades and not on learning.
- Grading is not reflective of instructional strategies.
- Grades are not always motivators; in fact, they can demoralize students on the low end, and on the high end.
- Grades tell little about student strengths and areas for improvement.
- Grading can mean many different things within a grade level, across grade levels by teacher, subject area, and school.
- Some teachers' highest priorities with grading are to use techniques where the grades can be calculated quickly.
- Grading is not always compatible with all instructional strategies.
- Grades often are given for more than achievement.
- Grading is not essential for learning.

Analyzing the Results, Descriptively

Descriptive statistics (i.e., mean, median, percent correct) can give schools very powerful information. It is imperative that the appropriate analyses be used for the specific score type. Figure 6.10 summarizes terms of analyses, their definitions, their most effective uses, and cautions for their uses in analyzing student achievement scores descriptively. Descriptive statistics are used in the examples in this chapter largely because they can show a school how its students are doing, and because anyone can do the calculations.

Descriptive statistics summarize the basic characteristics of a particular distribution, without making any inferences about population parameters. Graphing the information can also be considered descriptive.

Figure 6.10

Terms Related to Analyzing Student Achievement Results, Descriptively, Their Most Effective Uses, and Cautions for Their Uses			
Term	**Definition**	**Most Effective Uses**	**Cautions**
Disaggregate	Disaggregation is breaking a total score into groups for purposes of seeing how subgroups performed. One disaggregates data to make sure all subgroups of students are learning.	Disaggregating student achievement scores by gender, ethnicity, backgrounds, etc., can show how different subgroups performed.	Disaggregations are for helping schools understand how to meet the needs of all students, not to say, "This group always does worse than the other group and always will." We must exercise caution in reporting disaggregations with small numbers in a subgroup.
Gain	Gain scores are the change or difference between two administrations of the same test. Gain scores are calculated by subtracting the previous score from the most recent score. One can have negative gains, which are actually losses.	One calculates gains to understand improvements in learning for groups of students and for individual students.	Gain scores should not be calculated using unequal interval scores, such as percentiles. The quality of gain score results is dependent upon the quality of the assessment instrument; the less reliable the assessment tool, the less meaningful the results. One needs to make sure the comparisons are appropriate, e.g., same students, same score types.
Maximum	A maximum is the highest score achieved, or the highest possible score on a test.	Maximum possible scores and highest received scores are important for understanding the relative performance of any group or individual, especially when using scaled or standard scores.	A maximum can tell either the highest score possible or the highest score received by a test-taker. One needs to understand which maximum is being used in the analysis. It is best to use both.
Mean	A mean is the average score in a set of scores. One calculates the mean, or average, by summing all the scores and dividing by the total number of scores.	A mean can be calculated to provide an overall average for the group, and/or student, taking a specific test. One can use any equal interval score to get a mean.	Means should not be used with unequal interval scores, such as percentile ranks. Means are more sensitive to extreme results when the size of the group is small.
Median	A median is the score that splits a distribution in half: 50 percent of the scores fall above and 50 percent of the scores fall below the median. If the number of scores is odd, the median is the middle score. If the number of scores is even, one must add the two middle scores and divide by two to calculate the median.	Medians are the way to get a midpoint for scores with unequal intervals, such as percentile ranks. The median splits all scores into two equal parts. Medians are not sensitive to outliers, like means are.	Medians are relative. Medians are most effectively interpreted when reported with the possible and actual maximum and minimum.
Minimum	A minimum is the lowest score achieved, or the lowest possible score on the test.	Minimum possible scores and lowest received scores are important for understanding the relative performance of any group or individual.	A minimum tells either the lowest score possible or the lowest score received by a test-taker. One needs to understand which minimum is being used. It is best to use both.

Figure 6.10 *(Continued)*

Term	Definition	Most Effective Uses	Cautions
Mode	The mode is the score that occurs most frequently in a scoring distribution.	The mode basically tells which score or scores appear most often.	There may be more than one mode. The mode ignores other scores.
Percent Correct	Percent correct is a calculated score implying the percentage of students meeting and exceeding some number, usually a cut score, or a standard.	This calculated score can quickly tell educators how well the students are doing with respect to a specific set of items. It can also tell educators how many students need additional work to become proficient.	Percent correct is a calculated statistic, based on the number of items given. When the number of items given is small, the percent correct can be deceptively high or low.
Percent Proficient *Percent Passing* *Percent Mastery*	Percent proficient, passing, or mastery represent the percentage of students who passed a particular test at a "proficient," "passing," or "mastery" level, as defined by the test creators or the test interpreters.	With standards-based accountability, it is beneficial to know the percentage of the population meeting and exceeding the standard and to compare a year's percentage with the previous year(s) to understand progress being made.	This is a very simple statistic, and its interpretation should be simple as well. Total numbers (N=) of students included in the percentage must always be noted with the percentage to assist in understanding the results. Ninety percent passing means something very different for 10 or 100 test-takers.
Range	Range is a measure of the spread between the lowest and the highest scores in a distribution. Calculate the range of scores by subtracting the lowest score from the highest score. Range is often described as end points also, such as the range of percentile ranks is 1 and 99.	Ranges tell us the width of the distribution of scores. Educators working on continuous improvement will want to watch the range, of actual scores, decrease over time.	If there are outliers present, the range can give a misleading impression of dispersion.
Raw Scores	Raw scores refer to the number of questions answered correctly on a test or subtest. A raw score is simply calculated by adding the number of questions answered correctly. The raw score is a person's observed score.	The raw score provides information only about the number of questions answered correctly. To get a perspective on performance, raw scores must be used with the average score for the group and the total number of questions. Alone, raw scores have little meaning.	Raw scores do not provide information related to other students taking the test or to other subtests or scores. One needs to keep perspective by knowing the total number possible. Raw scores should never be used to make comparisons between performances on different tests unless other information about the characteristics of the tests are known and identical.

Figure 6.10 *(Continued)*

Terms Related to Analyzing Student Achievement Results, Descriptively, Their Most Effective Uses, and Cautions for Their Uses			
Term	**Definition**	**Most Effective Uses**	**Cautions**
Relationships	Relationships refer to looking at two or more sets of analyses to understand what they mean to each other without using extensive statistical techniques.	Descriptive statistics lend themselves to looking at the relationships of different analyses to each other; for instance, student learning results disaggregated by ethnicity, compared to student questionnaire results disaggregated by ethnicity.	This type of analysis is general and the results should be considered general as well. This is not a "correlation."
Rubric	A rubric is a scoring tool that rates performance according to clearly stated levels of criteria. The scales can be numeric or descriptive, or both	Rubrics are used to give teachers, parents, and students an idea of where they started, where they want to be with respect to growth, and where they are right now.	Students need to know what the rubrics contain or, even better, help with the development of the rubrics.
Standard Deviation	The standard deviation is a measure of variability in a set of scores. The standard deviation indicates how far away scores are from the mean. The standard deviation is the square root of the variance. Unlike the variance, the standard deviation is stated in the original units of the variable. Approximately 68 percent of the scores in a normal distribution lie between plus one and minus one standard deviation of the mean. The more scores cluster around the mean, the smaller the variance.	Tells us about the variability of scores. Standard deviations indicate how spread-out the scores are without looking at the entire distribution. A low standard deviation would indicate that the scores of a group are close together. A high standard deviation would imply that the range of scores is wide.	Often this is a confusing statistic for laypeople to understand. There are more descriptive ways to describe and show the variability of student scores, such as with a decile graph. Standard deviations only make sense with scores that are distributed normally.
Triangulation	Triangulation is a term used for combining three or more measures to get a more complete picture of student achievement.	If students are to be retained based on standards proficiency, educators must have more than one way of knowing if the students are proficient or not. Some students perform well on standardized measures and not on other measures, while others do not do well with standardized measures. Triangulation allows students to display what they know on three different measures.	It is sometimes very complicated to combine different measures to understand proficiency. When proficiency standards change, triangulation calculations will need to be revised. Therefore, all the calculations must be documented so they can be recalculated when necessary.

Analyzing the Results, Inferentially

Many school administrators and teachers have taken statistics courses that taught them that it is important to have control groups, experimental designs, and to test for significant differences. These terms fall in the category of inferential statistics. Inferential statistics are concerned with measuring a sample from a population, and then making estimates, or inferences, about the population from which the sample was taken. Inferential statistics help generalize the results of data analysis when one is not using the entire population in the analysis.

The *main* purpose of this book is to model analyses that school personnel can perform without the assistance of statisticians. Descriptive analyses provide helpful and useful information and can be understood by a majority of people. When using the entire school population in your analyses, there is no need to generalize to a larger population—you have the whole population. There is no need for inferential statistics.

Inferential statistical methods, such as analyses of variance, correlations[1], and regression analyses are complex and require someone who knows statistics to meet the conditions of the analyses. Since there are times when a statistician is available to perform inferential statistics, some of the terms the statistician might use with tests include those listed in Figure 6.11.

---

[1]Correlation does not have to be inferential, but it is often used that way. If it is used inferentially, then assumptions of population-parameters need to be met.

Figure 6.11

Terms Related to Analyzing Student Achievement Results, Inferentially, Their Most Effective Uses, and Cautions for Their Uses

Term	Definition	Most Effective Uses	Cautions
Analysis of Variance (ANOVA)	Analysis of variance is a general term applied to the study of differences in the application of approaches, as opposed to the relationship of different levels of approaches to the result. With ANOVAs, we are testing the differences of the means of at least two different distributions.	ANOVAs can be used to determine if there is a difference in student achievement scores between one school and another, keeping all other variables equal. It cannot tell you what the differences are, per se, but one can compute confidence intervals to estimate these differences.	Very seldom are the conditions available to study differences in education in this manner. Too many complex variables get in the way, and ethics may be involved. There are well-defined procedures for conducting ANOVAs to which we must adhere.
Correlation Analyses	Correlation is a statistical analysis that helps one understand the relationship of scores in one distribution to scores in another distribution. Correlations show magnitude and direction. Magnitude indicates the degree of the relationship. Correlation coefficients have a range of -1.0 to +1.0. A correlation of around zero would indicate little relationship. Correlations of .8 and higher, or -.8 and lower would indicate a strong relationship. When the high scores in one distribution are also high in the comparing distribution, the direction is positive. When the high scores in one distribution are related to the low scores in the other distribution, the result is a negative correlational direction.	Correlations can be used to understand the relationship of different variables to each other, e.g., attendance and performance on a standardized test; .40 to .70 are considered moderate correlations. Above .70 is considered to be high correlations.	It is wise to plot the scores to understand if the relationship is linear or not. One could misinterpret results if the scores are not linear. Pearson correlation coefficient requires linear relationships. Also, a few outliers could skew the results and oppositely skewed distributions can limit how high a Pearson coefficient can be. Also, one must remember that correlation does not suggest causation.
Regression Analyses	Regression analysis results in an equation that describes the nature of the relationship between variables. Simple regression predicts an object's value on a response variable when given its value on one predictor variable. Multiple regression predicts an object's value on a response variable when given its value on each of several predictor variables. Correlation tells you strength and direction of relationship. Regression goes one step further and allows you to predict.	A regression equation can be used to predict student achievement results, for example. Regression can determine if there is a relationship between two or more variables (such as attendance and student background) and the nature of those relation-ships. This analysis helps us predict and prevent student failure, and predict and ensure student successes.	One needs to truly understand the statistical assumptions that need to be in place in order to perform a regression analysis. This is not an analysis to perform through trial and error.

Figure 6.11 *(Continued)*

Terms Related to Analyzing Student Achievement Results, Inferentially, Their Most Effective Uses, and Cautions for Their Uses			
Term	**Definition**	**Most Effective Uses**	**Cautions**
Control Groups	During an experiment, the control group is studied the same as the experimental group, except that it does not receive the treatment of interest.	Control groups serve as a baseline in making comparisons with treatment groups. Control groups are necessary when the general effectiveness of a treatment is unknown.	It may not be ethical to hold back from students some method of learning that we believe would be useful.
Experimental Design	Experimental design is the detailed planning of an experiment, made beforehand, to ensure that the data collected are appropriate and obtained in a way that will lead to an objective analysis, with valid inferences.	Experimental designs can maximize the amount of information gained, given the amount of effort expended.	Sometimes it takes statistical expertise to establish an experimental design properly.
Tests of Significance	Tests of significance use samples to test claims about population parameters.	Tests of significance can estimate a population parameter, with a certain amount of confidence, from a sample.	Often laypeople do not know what *statistically significant* really means.

A Note About *Scientifically-based Research.* With the passage of the *No Child Left Behind (NCLB) Act of 2001,* which reauthorized the *Elementary and Secondary Education Act of 1965,* school districts and schools are required to gather, analyze, and use data to ensure adequate yearly progress or continuous school improvement. While increased accountability is just one part of NCLB, all schools must gather data and overcome the barriers to analyzing and using the data.

The term *scientifically-based research* (Title IX, General Provisions, Part A, Section 9101, Definitions) means (A) research that involves the application of rigorous, systematic, and objective procedures to obtain reliable and valid knowledge relevant to education activities and programs; and (B) includes research that:

▼ employs systematic, empirical methods that draw on observation or experiment

▼ involves rigorous data analyses that are adequate to test the stated hypotheses and justify the general conclusions drawn

▼ relies on measurements or observational methods that provide reliable and valid data across evaluators and observers, across multiple measurements and observations, and across studies by the same or different investigators

▼ is evaluated using experimental or quasi-experimental designs in which individuals, entities, programs, or activities are assigned to different conditions and with appropriate controls to evaluate the effects of the condition of interest, with a preference for random-assignment experiments, or other designs to the extent that condition controls

▼ ensures that experimental studies are presented in sufficient detail and clarity to allow for replication or, at a minimum, offer the opportunity to build systematically on their findings

▼ has been accepted by a peer-reviewed journal or approved by a panel of independent experts through a comparably rigorous, objective, and scientific review

The bottom line: schools are required to use research-based instructional strategies and to be able to justify their use.

Measurement Error

All measurement, by definition, contains some error. However, that error can be measured.

We often hear people talk about sample sizes being too small to make any conclusions. Typically, what this means is that the larger the number of students in a sample, the more confidence we have that the score is an accurate reflection of that sample group's abilities. We also want to know if the increases showing up in a testing program in any year are because of "true" increases in learning. In order to understand a "true" gain resulting from an instructional program, we construct confidence bands that give each score a range as opposed to a single number. This range provides flexibility in understanding what the score would be if there were "errors" in the test. The table that follows (Figure 6.11) gives the calculated standard error of measure for normal NCEs.

To construct a confidence band, consider that a group of five students had an average score of 40 on a reading test. We need to look at Figure 6.12, the *Give and Take Table,* to see that the error of measurement associated with the five students in this group is 4.5—the smaller the number of students, the more likely it is that the average represents a chance occurrence or error. The confidence band would then be formed from 35.5 to 44.5 (i.e., 40 - 4.5 = 35.5; 40 + 4.5 = 44.5). The interpretation: We can feel confident (68 percent of the time—one standard deviation) that the average true score of these students would be somewhere between 35.5 and 44.5. We can feel 95 percent confident that the average true score would be between 31 and 49 (double the size of the band—two standard deviations—2 x 4.5 = 9) (i.e., 40 - 9 = 31; 40 + 9 = 49).

Figure 6.12

Give and Take Table			
Number of Students	Error (NCEs)	Number of Students	Error (NCEs)
1	10.1	20	2.3
2	7.1	25	2.0
3	5.8	30	1.8
4	5.1	35	1.7
5	4.5	40	1.6
6	4.1	45	1.5
7	3.8	50	1.4
8	3.6	75	1.2
9	3.4	100	1.0
10	3.2	200	0.7
15	2.6	300	0.6

Looking Across Student Learning Measures

Even though one should not put more than one kind of measurement scale into one graph, graphs of different measures can be generally compared, as shown in Figure 6.13. By looking at these graphs, we can see different distributions and begin to understand student motivation and learning styles.

Figure 6.13

Multiple Measures of Student Learning

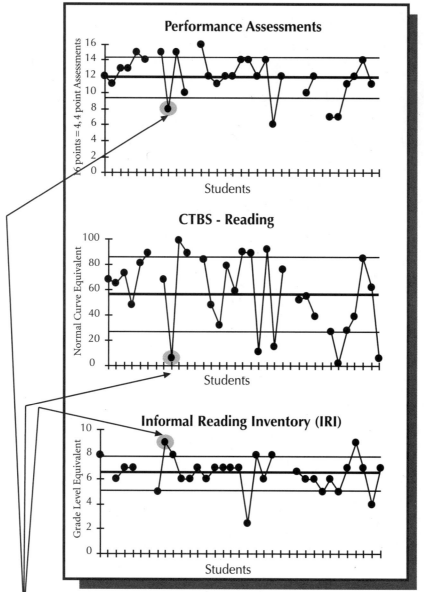

Teachers could ask the following questions:

- Of all the sixth graders having difficulty reading, how did they perform on each of these measures?

- Are there characteristics of non-readers that we can identify at the sixth grade level?

- Can we identify similar characteristics at the fifth, fourth, third, second, and first grade levels?

- Are there interventions we can use with these identified characteristics to prevent non-reading?

Looking at individual student measures gives teachers valuable information about how the different measures perform, the learning styles and motivation of individual students, and begins to show teachers whether a continuum of learning for students is in place or not.

To answer some of the questions posed in Figure 6.13, let's just look a little closer at the example. Mrs. Jones, the sixth grade teacher, interviewed every student about her/his scores on the three measures. What the students told Mrs. Jones was very insightful. Student number 9, to which the arrows are pointing, told Mrs. Jones that he had no reason to do well on the performance assessments (8 out of 16) because they were not graded. He obviously did not understand what performance assessments were all about.

Concerning his score of 2 on the CTBS, student number 9 responded that he had no reason to do well on that test. He heard teachers talking about how it didn't help the students and that it took valuable time out of classroom, so he made patterns with the bubbles on the answer sheet. Almost afraid to ask, Mrs. Jones asked student number 9 why he did so well on the Informal Reading Inventory. Number 9 stated that he did not know it was a test. He went to a quiet space to read with the Reading Specialist. He loved it and wanted to do it more often.

Needless to say the teachers had a lot to discuss after Mrs. Jones told them what she did to better understand her class' performance on different measures. She also discussed what she was going to do differently, so she could ensure different results.

Other Common Testing Terms

Other common terms associated with testing are defined below. Please see the References and Resources section at the end of this book for further information about these terms.

Validity

The validity of a test or assessment refers to whether it provides the type of information desired. Validity can be enhanced by asking appropriate questions that get to what you want to know.

Different types of validity include the following:

- ▼ *Content validity* relates to the appropriateness of the items with respect to the content, instruction, or the curriculum being measured.

- ▼ *Predictive validity* refers to a test's ability to predict future performance in the area that the instrument is measuring.

- ▼ *Face validity* relates to the appearance that the test measures what it claims to measure.

▼ *Construct validity* refers to the degree to which the test actually measures the particular construct (trait or aptitude) in question.

▼ *Concurrent validity* refers to the scores on a test being related to currently existing measures of the same content or behavior.

Reliability

The reliability of a test or assessment relates to the consistency with which knowledge is measured. Reliability tells us that if students were to take the test more than once, they would get the same (or nearly the same) score.

Reliability is impacted by—

▼ asking appropriate questions that would get to what you want to know (cannot be reliable if not valid)

▼ the length of the test (with other things being equal)

▼ the range of item difficulty (more variation of item difficulty tends to lower reliability)

▼ the consistency of the testing environment among test sites

A test may be reliable without being valid, but it cannot be valid without being reliable.

Our Example Schools

The following examples show different ways to summary student achievement data. The Archer Elementary School example (Figure 6.14) shows the number and percentage of students scoring at five different proficiency levels for Communication Arts, over time, for grade three and by gender, ethnicity, and free/reduced lunch status, as required by NCLB.

Figure 6.14

Summary of Archer Elementary School
Student Proficiency Results, 2001-02 to 2003-04

Grade Three Communication Arts

Grade 3	Year	Step 1		Progressing		Nearing Proficient		Proficient		Advanced		Totals
		Number	Percent	Number	Percent	Number	Percent	Number	Percent	Number	Percent	
Grade 3	2001-02	10	14%	16	22%	33	46%	12	17%	1	1%	72
	2002-03	9	13%	33	48%	16	23%	11	16%			69
	2003-04	17	21%	26	32%	25	31%	12	15%	1	1%	81

Gender	Year	Step 1		Progressing		Nearing Proficient		Proficient		Advanced		Totals
		Number	Percent	Number	Percent	Number	Percent	Number	Percent	Number	Percent	
Females	2001-02	7	19%	11	30%	12	32%	6	16%	1	3%	37
	2002-03	5	11%	20	45%	10	23%	9	21%			44
	2003-04	10	24%	11	26%	15	36%	6	14%			42
Males	2001-02	3	9%	5	14%	21	60%	6	17%			35
	2002-03	4	16%	13	52%	6	24%	2	8%			25
	2003-04	7	18%	15	38%	10	26%	6	15%	1	3%	39

Ethnicity	Year	Step 1		Progressing		Nearing Proficient		Proficient		Advanced		Totals
		Number	Percent	Number	Percent	Number	Percent	Number	Percent	Number	Percent	
Black	2001-02	5	19%	12	46%	8	31%	1	4%			26
	2002-03	6	19%	20	65%	4	13%	1	3%			31
	2003-04	13	30%	19	44%	9	21%	1	2%			43
American Indian	2002-03					1	100%					1
Asian	2002-03							1	100%			1
	2003-04			1	100%							1
White	2001-02	5	11%	4	9%	24	53%	11	24%	1	2%	45
	2002-03	3	9%	13	38%	9	26%	9	26%	1	3%	34
	2003-04	3	8%	6	16%	16	43%	11	30%	1	3%	37
Hispanic/Latino	2001-02					1	100%					1
	2002-03					2	100%					2

Lunch Status	Year	Step 1		Progressing		Nearing Proficient		Proficient		Advanced		Totals
		Number	Percent	Number	Percent	Number	Percent	Number	Percent	Number	Percent	
Free/Reduced	2001-02	6	15%	13	32%	16	39%	5	12%	1	2%	41
	2002-03	7	16%	25	57%	10	23%	2	5%			44
	2003-04	14	27%	23	44%	11	21%	4	8%			52
Not Free/Reduced	2001-02	4	13%	3	10%	17	55%	7	23%			31
	2002-03	2	8%	8	32%	6	24%	9	36%			25
	2003-04	2	7%	3	10%	15	52%	8	28%	1	3%	29

Figure 6.15 shows grouped National Percentile Ranking scores for Majestic High School students on their state assessment for grades 9, 10, and 11.

Figure 6.15

Summary of Majestic High School
National Percentile Rank (NPR) Scores by Grade Level, 2003-04

Grade	NPR Score Level	Total Reading		Total Math		Language		Science		Social Science	
		Number	Percent	Number	Percent	Number	Percent	Number	Percent	Number	Percent
Grade Nine (*n*=58)	Above 75	4	7%	25	43%	35	60%	9	16%	8	14%
	Above 50	23	40%	41	71%	17	29%	25	43%	33	57%
	Above 25	44	76%	52	90%	36	62%	51	88%	47	81%
Grade Ten (*n*=52)	Above 75	6	12%	14	27%	4	8%	8	17%	13	25%
	Above 50	16	31%	29	56%	19	37%	9	48%	22	42%
	Above 25	32	62%	45	87%	35	67%	40	77%	27	52%
Grade Eleven (*n*=50)	Above 75	6	12%	10	20%	9	18%	13	26%	16	32%
	Above 50	13	26%	25	50%	21	42%	22	44%	28	56%
	Above 25	27	54%	43	86%	40	80%	39	78%	40	80%

Study Questions for Student Learning

Think through your student learning assessment program and how it can be aligned. The following questions provide a guide for your thinking.

Questions	Current Status	Desired Status
Why do you measure student learning in your school?		
How is student learning measured in your school?		
How are student learning results used?		
How are student learning results disaggregated?		
How and to whom are student learning results reported?		

Summary

School personnel typically think about data analysis as being only about student achievement results. These alone can give schools information with which to improve; but as you can see from the examples, schools must assess the same measures, grades, and students, over time, in order to use the information in a comprehensive fashion.

Used with other measures, these scores will become invaluable to school personnel in understanding what needs to change to get different results. Intersections of student learning and other measures will be explored in succeeding chapters.

SCHOOL PROCESSES

Chapter 7

Where outcomes are evaluated without knowledge of implementation, the results seldom provide a direction for action because the decision maker lacks information about what produced the observed outcomes (or lack of outcomes).

Michael Quinn Patten

Of the four measures discussed in this book, school processes are the only measures that we actually have control over in the educational setting. Public schools cannot control who the students are, where they come from, or why they think the way they do. They can only control a portion of the student learning results—through their processes (i.e., programs, practices, and instructional strategies).

School processes are important to continuous school improvement because they are what produce school and classroom results. If different results are desired, processes must be changed. To change these processes, teachers must—

▼ be clear on what is being implemented

▼ study the results of these processes over time

▼ understand the relationship between the processes, results, mission/purpose, and actions

▼ study the research on effective processes

▼ build hypotheses and action plans to achieve different results

These hypotheses and understandings of the literature on student learning are crucial in the prediction of the types of processes schools will need to implement in order to get the results they want in the future. Analyzing the data is only one piece of the puzzle. It helps teachers see what results they are getting, based upon what they are doing, but it neither gives solutions nor designs new programs/processes.

School processes refer to the educational and psychological events at the school and classroom level; i.e., the way schools "do" business. Work with school processes can be analyzed descriptively, qualitatively, and quantitatively. Processes are often mapped, sometimes in the form of a flow chart. Schoolwide and classroom rubrics or questionnaires can assist with the qualitative assessment of where the school is with respect to the implementation of processes. Additionally, some of the data gathered in the category of demographics can be used to understand processes, such as number of discipline referrals, and numbers of students by background in special education or advanced placement classes.

School Level Processes

When studying the school's processes for improvement, teachers need to think about what they ask students to do, and how these requests align with the purpose and vision of the school. Administrators need to think about how the system is set-up for success. School processes are what administrators and teachers do to achieve that purpose—the vision. School processes are also those things that teachers do by habit, by custom, or inadvertently, and those things that may help or hinder progress.

Guiding questions that help create theoretical school processes are listed below:

- ▼ What do teachers want students to know and be able to do?
- ▼ How are teachers enabling students to learn, in terms of—
  - ◆ instructional strategies
  - ◆ learning strategies
  - ◆ instructional time
  - ◆ instructional location
  - ◆ student-teacher ratio
  - ◆ organization of instructional components
  - ◆ assessment
  - ◆ philosophies and strategies of classroom management
  - ◆ personal relationships, among students, and among students and teachers
- ▼ How will teachers know if any given approach helps all students learn what they want them to learn?
- ▼ What will teachers do with the students who do not learn this way?
- ▼ What is the responsibility of all members of the school staff?
- ▼ What is the job of each member of the school staff?
- ▼ How will all parts of the curriculum relate?
- ▼ What learning strategies do successful learners use?
- ▼ What learning strategies have "unsuccessful" learners used in the past, successfully, that could be used again?

Collecting data about a work process has little meaning to us until we use this data to predict and draw conclusions about the future, based on the past performance of this process. Data is value added only to the extent that it allows us to predict and draw conclusions about the future.

Neil Paulsen
Intel Corporation

Not everything that is faced can be changed, but nothing can be changed until it is faced.

James Baldwin

School processes impact the success of classroom processes. These broader school processes could include many of the items described and counted in the demographic section, such as:

▼ Scheduling

▼ Class size

▼ Discipline strategies and results

▼ Student groupings

▼ Policies and procedures

▼ Enrollment in different courses/programs/program offerings

▼ Retentions

▼ Dropout rates

▼ Graduation rates

▼ Teacher demographics

▼ Teacher assignments

▼ Teacher turnover rates

▼ Leadership turnover rates

▼ Number of support personnel

Processes can also be described through other categories of data including:

▼ Perceptions of the learning environment

▼ Perceptions of program or process implementation

▼ Student work

▼ Staff development

▼ Leadership

▼ Partnerships

▼ Use of technology

▼ *Education for the Future Continuous Improvement Continuums*

The structure of any of these processes helps determine the outcomes of a school and students' lives.

Classroom Level Processes

In working with schools, we have learned that articulating any given school process seems very hard for teachers. Processes are complex, and not something that is often rigorously described—either philosophically or actually.

At the classroom level, teachers can be much more effective if they are able to describe the processes they are implementing—from their perspective and from the perspective of their students.

The first step in defining classroom processes is to identify what processes you want to use—the more specific, the more helpful in the end. The next step is to describe what gets implemented in the classroom. It is then important to understand the discrepancies between actual and desired, and to determine what has to change to get the desired results for students. Flow charts and curriculum mapping approaches (see References and Resources) are helpful for describing processes used in classrooms. In many cases, processes vary widely from one classroom to another, and many depend as much upon an individual teacher's own educational experiences as a schoolwide philosophy. Examining and describing what actually exists helps everyone become clear on the processes that are and are not making a difference, which helps everyone become clear on what change to implement.

School and Classroom Level Processes
Working Together

Our ultimate goal is to build instructional congruence—a continuum of learning that makes sense for all students—one that builds upon itself through all classrooms, and across the years, to create the cumulative effect we want for all students.

Understanding school processes is the first step to understanding if a school is achieving its goals, and if instructional congruence exists. Understanding the cumulative effect of the entire system, including classroom processes, is necessary for determining what needs to change for students.

Charting School Processes

A flow chart can help describe and visualize a process or procedures. Using flow charting tools can help everyone see a process in the same way. A flow chart allows everyone to see the major steps in a process, in sequence, and then evaluate the difference between the theoretical and actual—first by describing what teachers would like to be doing, and then by describing what teachers are really doing, or vice-versa.

Typical symbols used in flow charting follow:

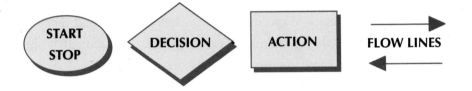

A flow chart is a visualization of a process—a process everyone can see and understand in the same way.

Steps in establishing flow charts follow:

1. *Define* the beginning and the end of the process being charted.

2. *Decide* on the level of detail to be used.

3. *Determine* the major steps in the process and their sequence.

4. *Label* each symbol/step in the process.

5. *Verify* the flow chart. Is it clear?

6. *Evaluate.* Compare the charted version of the process to the "perfect" flow.

Figure 7.1 shows an example flow chart of reading program placement.

Figure 7.1

Example Reading Programs Placement

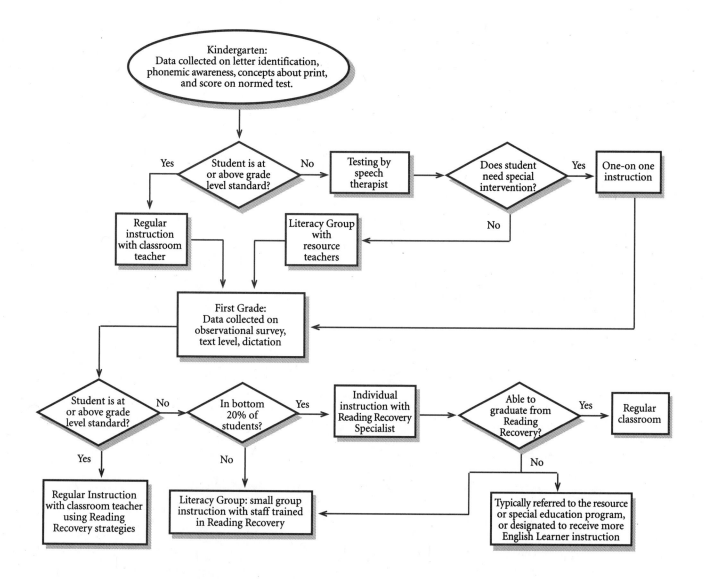

Another type of flow chart is called the top-down flow chart. This is probably the easiest and fastest way to chart processes/procedures. In a top-down flow chart, one simply follows the primary steps of the process being analyzed and under each primary process writes in the secondary steps, and so on. There should be no more than five-to-seven primary or secondary steps, or the process has not been identified enough. A top-down flow chart framework is shown in Figure 7.2. One benefit of looking at processes or procedures in some type of flow chart is that one can almost always determine that something needs to change.

Figure 7.2

Title: Processes for Teaching Reading—Grade 1

1a	Instructional Strategies	2a	Assessment Strategies	3a	Groupings
1b	If reading at or above grade level—regular instruction with classroom teacher using Reading Recovery strategies.	2b	All students assessed at the beginning of first grade level using an observational survey. All students assessed using the Text Level and Dictation subtests mid-year and at the end of the year.	3b	Regular students are grouped in the classroom by ability and by Family Learning Teams.
1c	If below grade level and in the bottom 20% of the class—individual instruction with resource staff as part of the formal Reading Recovery program.	2c	Same as above.	3c	Reading Recovery students are grouped in the classroom by ability and by Family Learning Teams.
1d	If below grade level and not in bottom 20% of the class—Literacy Group instruction using Reading Recovery strategies with resource staff.	2d	Same as above.	3d	Literacy Group students are grouped in the classroom by ability and by Family Learning Teams.
1e	If not able to graduate from Reading Recovery program into Literacy Group or regular classroom—referred to the resource or special education program staff for additional assessment, or to receive additional English Learner instruction.	2e	Same as above.	3e	Students grouped by program.

Assessing School Processes

What is done in the name of processes in a school describes how a school gets its results. If schools are not getting the results they want, they need to consider their processes, or how they are getting their results. If they want different results, they must change the processes that create the results.

One approach to assessing the impact of school processes is to study the resulting flow charts and note the discrepancies between theoretical and actual implementation. Another approach might be the use of rubrics or continuums that give schools an idea of where they started, where they want to be with respect to *Approach, Implementation,* and *Outcomes,* and where they are right now, such as with the *Education for the Future* Continuous Improvement Continuums (CIC), as described in *The School Portfolio: A Comprehensive Framework for School Improvement, Second Edition* (Bernhardt, 1999). These continuums help schools assess their processes in seven categories which, when working together, have proven to lead to systemic change. The Continuums for schools appear in Appendix B. The *Education for the Future* Continuous Improvement Continuums for districts appear in Appendix C. The Continuums are broad and seem over-arching. However, to move up a continuum, one must improve many internal processes.

Self-assessments, like the CICs, help build the discussion base for staff to know what they need to do to move ahead. These are assessments staff will want to conduct over time to monitor progress. A Continuous Improvement Continuums assessment is shown in the Majestic High School example at the end of this chapter.

A key factor in moving implementation forward is identifying who is doing the assessment of school processes. Since teachers have the ultimate responsibility for implementing change at the classroom level, their assessment of school and classroom processes is crucial. A problem arises because many teachers tend to view the entire school in terms of their own classroom; they rarely get into other rooms. Giving teachers the opportunity to observe each other allows them to develop a schoolwide view of implementation and to understand their role in moving the school forward. It also has the added benefit of allowing teachers to learn from their colleagues. Using continuums to assess where the school is on implementation, and establishing next steps, is far more meaningful if

Why bother doing it right if we're not sure we're doing the right thing?

Peter Drucker

teachers are able to see their colleagues in their classroom settings. To understand whether instructional strategies are being implemented, some schools send a teacher or a "critical friend" to take pictures of children working in their classrooms, gather samples of student work, and observe their colleagues teaching. Together, the colleagues analyze the information to understand whether the actual classroom strategies and work required of students are in line with the intended school processes. Only when schools know how well their processes have actually been implemented can they answer the question, *Does this process work for our students?*

Students' perceptions of school processes should not be ignored. When items on student questionnaires reflect the vision of the school, student responses give powerful information about their view of implementation. The results of the student questionnaire can indicate to teachers the realities of student experiences, which may be different from teachers' understandings.

Our Example Schools

The flow chart is an excellent way to graph how a process flows. Our example schools show two other approaches. Archer Elementary School gave a questionnaire to staff related to standards implementation A part of that questionnaire is shown in Figure 7.3. Figure 7.4 shows Majestic High School's assessment on its Continuous Improvement Continuums.

Figure 7.3

Archer Elementary School Standards Assessment
Summary of Results

In March 2003, *Education for the Future* piloted a standards assessment questionnaire with Archer Elementary School teachers. The questionnaire contained a total of nine questions, asking how well teachers know the state content standards and to what degree they are implementing the standards. (The items on this questionnaire are a part of the staff questionnaire in Appendix A.)

A summary of the results follows:

The black dots shown in the graphs below indicate the average responses to the questions. Elementary teachers were asked to respond to items using a five-point scale: 1=just know they exist; 2=have skimmed; 3=have read at least once; 4=have read in-depth; and, 5=am very knowledgeable. The following indicates the average response attributed to each content item, in descending order.

1. Archer Elementary teachers were asked how well they know the state content standards for their grade level(s) in each of the subject areas they teach. Average teacher responses were: Mathematics, 3.52; English/Language Arts, 3.47; Science, 2.50; Social Studies, 2.48; Technology, 2.44; The Arts, 1.61; Foreign Language, 1.52.

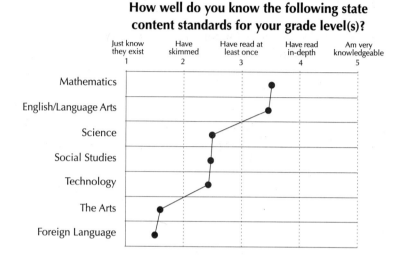

2. Archer Elementary teachers were asked how well they know the state content standards that precede their grade level(s) in each of the subject areas they teach. Averaged teacher responses were: English/Language Arts, 2.88; Mathematics, 2.84; Science, 2.23; Social Studies, 2.13; Technology, 1.97; The Arts, 1.63; Foreign Language, 1.47.

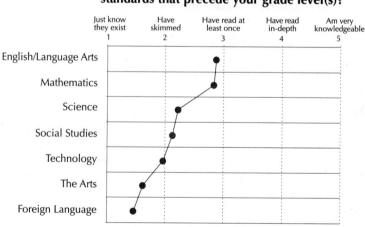

3. Archer Elementary teachers were asked how well they know the state content standards that follow their grade level(s) in each of the subject areas they teach. Averaged teacher responses were: English/Language Arts, 2.79; Mathematics, 2.76; Science, 2.13; Social Studies, 2.06; Technology, 1.91; The Arts, 1.55; Foreign Language, 1.52.

How well do you know the following state content standards that follow your grade level(s)?

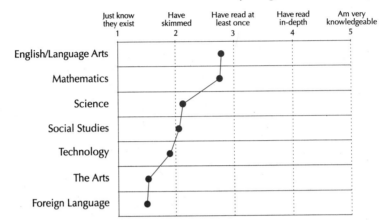

4. Archer Elementary teachers were asked how much of the time they implement the standards in their classroom. Averaged teacher responses were: English/Language Arts, 3.64; Mathematics, 3.55; Science, 2.50; Social Studies, 2.48; Technology, 2.06; The Arts, 1.71; Foreign Language, 1.17.

How much of the time are you implementing the following standards in your classroom?

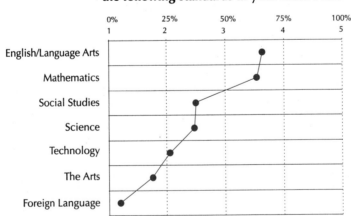

The bars shown in the graphs below indicate the average percent response attributed to each content item, in descending order.

5. Archer Elementary teachers were asked what would help them to better know the standards. They were told to check all responses that apply. Teacher responses were, in descending order: Cross-grade-level meetings about standards, 57%; Grade-level meetings about standards, 46%; Professional development, 37%; Demonstration lessons, 34%; Schoolwide meetings about standards, 29%; Peer coaching, 23%; Other, 3%.

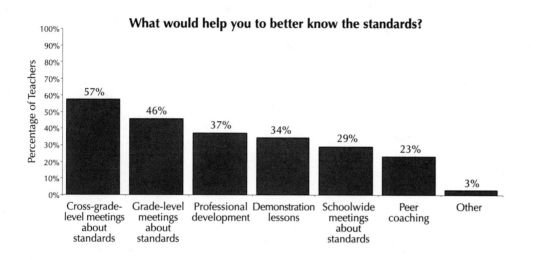

6. Archer Elementary teachers were asked how well they know what it would look like, sound like, and feel like if they were teaching to the standards 100% of the time. No teacher responded *Not at all*. Twelve percent responded *Little bit*; 56% *Getting there*; 18% *Well*; 15% *Extremely well*.

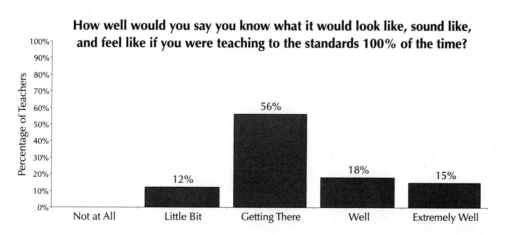

7. Archer Elementary teachers were asked which statements best describe how they use standards to design instruction. One hundred percent of responding teachers agreed with the statement, I teach the curriculum and instructional strategies our school/district has adopted.

Which of the following statements best describes how you use standards to design instruction?

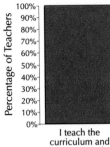

I teach the curriculum and instructional strategies our school/district has adopted	I follow the textbooks, and I believe they are aligned to the state standards	I am pretty sure my instructional strategies are already aligned to the state standards	I take my existing instructional plans and indicate where the standards are being taught	I study the standards and create instruction to take students from where they are to where the standards say they should be by the end of the year	I study the standards, determine outcomes related to the standards, frequently assess where students are with respect to the standards, and adapt my lesson plans to create instruction to take students to where they need to be by the end of the year	I teach the standards through ongoing assessments

8. When asked to check all the response options that apply to describe what they do when their students do not learn, the majority of Archer teachers (74%) stated they reteach the content in different ways. Fifty-seven percent stated they adapt their instructional strategies to the learning styles of individual students; 54% stated that after reteaching, they assess the students in different ways; 43% stated they reteach the content; 43% stated they get help from others in the school, such as colleagues and/or specialists; 9% stated they cannot make a student learn; 3% stated they move on to make sure the curriculum gets covered.

What do you do when your students do not learn the standards?

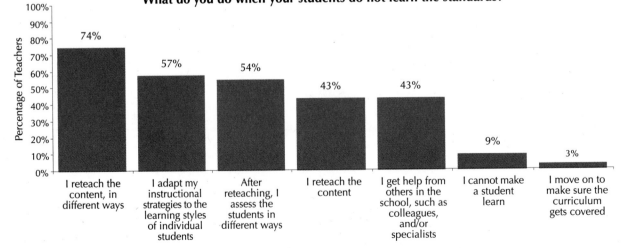

9. Archer Elementary teachers were asked how much support they feel from their learning organization to ensure they are teaching to the standards, that students are learning the standards, that all teachers at their grade level/content area are teaching to the same standards, and across grade levels. They were also asked how much support they feel they were getting to ensure that teachers across grade levels are building a continuum of learning that makes sense for all students, and that teachers are using formative assessments.

The majority of Archer teachers indicated they feel there is a system for support from their learning organization for all the statements. Average teacher responses were as follows: Your students are learning the standards, 3.59; All teachers at your grade level are teaching to the same standards, 3.53; You are teaching to the standards, 3.50; Teachers across grade levels are teaching to standards, 3.45; Teachers are using formative assessments, 3.33; Teachers across grade levels are building a continuum of learning that makes sense for all students, 3.26.

How much support do you feel from your learning organization to ensure that:

Figure 7.4

Majestic High School Continuous Improvement Continuum
Baseline Results

In May 2003, staff members of the Majestic High School staff conducted their baseline assessment of where the school is on the *Education for the Future* Continuous Improvement Continuums. Staff members discussed why they thought their school is where they rated it. The staff then came to consensus on a number that represented where the school is for each element. The ratings and brief discussions for each Continuum follow.

Information and Analysis

Majestic High School staff rated their school 2s in *Approach, Implementation,* and *Outcome* with respect to *Information and Analysis.* Staff agreed that the process of data gathering and use is not systematic.

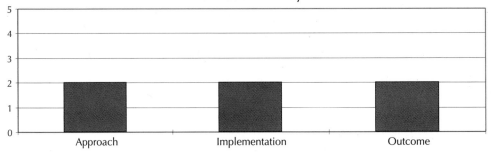

Next Steps:

Staff agreed:

- ▼ We need student achievement data available to all teachers.
- ▼ Our data need to be organized and communicated to students, teachers, and parents.
- ▼ We need to revisit our data on a regular basis.
- ▼ We need to get our state assessment test results back for individual students.
- ▼ We need to learn more about how our graduates are performing in college and careers.
- ▼ The data results must be presented back in a clear fashion so everyone understands what they say.
- ▼ We need to track student achievement data in a standardized fashion.
- ▼ We need to balance standardized test results with teacher assessments.

Student Achievement

Majestic High School staff rated their school 2s in *Approach, Implementation,* and *Outcome* with respect to *Student Achievement.* According to staff, student learning standards need to be consistently implemented, and learning gaps used to direct improvement throughout the school.

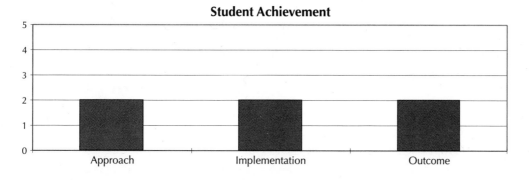

Next Steps:

Staff agreed:

- ▼ We need to collaborate with each other in a formalized manner.
- ▼ We need more planning time to talk about the vision and what we are doing for students, perhaps more minimum days.
- ▼ We need to clarify the continuum of learning for students so they know what they need to take next.
- ▼ The master schedule needs to be reviewed.
- ▼ We need to consider adding student-led parent conferences.

Quality Planning

Majestic staff rated their school 2s in *Approach* and *Implementation,* and a 3 in *Outcome* with respect to *Quality Planning.* Teachers say they understand the importance of having a vision and a plan. Teachers indicate that there is evidence that the school plan is being implemented in some areas of the school. However, improvements are neither systematic nor integrated schoolwide.

Next Steps:

Staff agreed:

▼ We need to revisit and reevaluate our school plan.

▼ We need to have ongoing department and cross-curricular meetings.

Professional Development

Majestic School staff assessed their school on *Professional Development* as a 2 in *Approach,* 2 in *Implementation,* and 3 in *Outcome.* Teachers agreed that the school plan and student needs need to be used to target appropriate professional development for all employees.

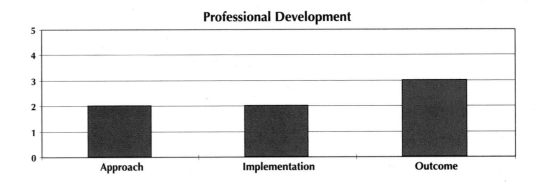

Next Steps:

Staff agreed:

▼ We need to have cross-curricular meetings and professional development.

▼ Our professional development needs to be more systematic and related to the vision.

▼ We need professional development in assessment.

Leadership

Majestic staff rated their school a 3 in *Approach,* 2 in *Implementation,* and 3 in *Outcome* with respect to *Leadership.* According to staff, most decisions are focused on solving problems and are reactive. Leaders are seen as committed to planning and quality improvement.

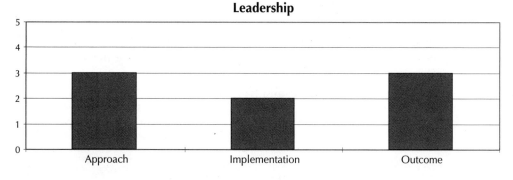

Next Steps:

Staff agreed:

▼ We need to clarify a leadership structure for the school that is congruent with our vision and mission.

▼ We need to link our learning standards and our improvement plan.

▼ We need to review progress toward achieving our goals on a continuous basis.

Partnership Development

Majestic school staff rated their school 3s in *Approach, Implementation,* and *Outcome* with respect to *Partnership Development.* Teachers say that the school has knowledge of why partnerships are important and want to seek more business and parent partnerships to help with the achievement of student learning standards for increased student achievement. Involvement of business, community, and parents is taking place in a way to utilize their expertise schoolwide. Some gains are achieved in implementing partnerships, and teachers believe that some student achievement increases can be attributed to this involvement.

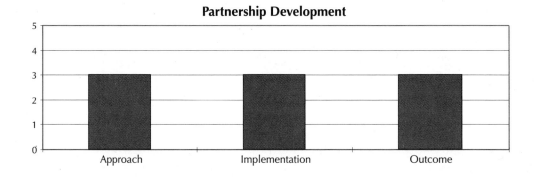

Next Steps:

Staff agreed:

▼ We need an overall plan to connect to partnerships schoolwide and to build on our successes and strengths, such as senior projects. It would be beneficial to have freshmen involved in something like a senior project.

▼ We need to get an organized approach to work experiences and tie them back to the standards.

▼ We need to understand how to get more parent involvement and input.

Continuous Improvement and Evaluation

With respect to the big picture, *Continuous Improvement and Evaluation,* staff rated their school 2s in *Approach, Implementation,* and *Outcome.* A plan for evaluation and continuous improvement does not exist at this point.

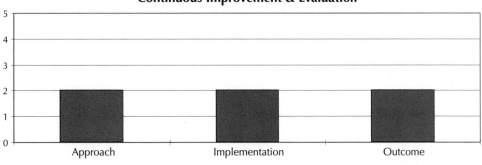

Continuous Improvement & Evaluation

Next Steps:

Staff agreed:

- ▼ We need comprehensive analyses done in an ongoing fashion.
- ▼ Our school staff must meet as a team on a continuous basis to talk about continuous improvement and evaluation.
- ▼ We need to incorporate continuous improvement and evaluation into the school plan.
- ▼ We need to improve our assessment literacy and knowledge.
- ▼ We need to continue this process and measure again in six months.

Study Questions for School Processes

Think about the processes your school is using to achieve its purpose. Choose a process/program that might not be getting the results you want. Pick a specific teaching concept or procedure within the program. Use one of the tools (i.e., flow chart, top-down flow chart, curriculum mapping, rubrics) to chart how you teach the concept.

Summary

School processes might be the most important measure in understanding what needs to be done to improve student learning results in school organizations. If we want different results, we have to change the processes that create the results.

When schools understand their school processes, especially in relationship to the results they are getting, they can know exactly what they need to do differently to get different results.

INTERSECTIONS AND ANALYSES

Chapter **8**

Intersection analysis helps us understand what is going on in all parts of a program, and helps us assess the impact of our actions on the people we serve.

Victoria L. Bernhardt

Up to this point, we have taken *Multiple Measures,* Figure 1, found in Chapter 3, and explored each of the four major *measures—demographics, perceptions, student learning,* and *school processes.* We have defined them, and we have given examples of what each measure looks like in a snapshot, and over time.

This chapter takes the four major measures and intersects each with one to three other measures for more complex analyses. On the next page is a table (Figure 8.1) of possible two-way and three-way intersections across measures, and the all-important four-way intersection that gives us the ability to predict what we need to do to meet the learning needs of all students in the school. Each intersection shown is illustrated with an example of what the intersection of the measures can tell us. There are, of course, other possibilities for intersecting these measures. As you read the table, keep in mind that complex intersections can mean different things depending upon the perspective from which one looks at them—and what it is one wants to know.

These intersections become insights for use in continuous school improvement processes.

Intersection Analyses

Intersection analyses allow us to look closely and understand each piece of information we gather about a school. The first levels are easy to understand, as shown in Chapters 4 through 7. Figure 8.1 demonstrates how much more information two and three measures together can provide than a single measure alone.

Change is the law of life and those who look only to the past or present are certain to miss the future.

John F. Kennedy

You can see from the examples throughout this book that as the analyses get more sophisticated, answers to evaluation questions become evident. A caution as one starts these analyses: *Stay clear on the purposes for your analyses.* It is easy to keep gathering and analyzing and forget the purposes one is striving to answer. If you keep sight of the purpose, you'll know when to stop. A two-way intersection might answer the question just as well as a three-way.

Figure 8.1

Summary of Data Intersections

Intersections	Can tell us —
Two-way Intersections	
◆ Demographics by student learning	◆ If subgroups of students perform differently on student learning measures
◆ Demographics by perceptions	◆ If subgroups of students are experiencing school differently
◆ Demographics by school processes	◆ If all subgroups of students are represented in the different programs offered by the school
◆ Student learning by school processes	◆ If different programs are achieving similar student learning results
◆ Student learning by perceptions	◆ If student perceptions of the learning environment have an impact on their learning results
◆ Perceptions by school processes	◆ If people are perceiving programs and processes differently
Three-way Intersections	
◆ Demographics by student learning by perceptions	◆ The impact demographic factors and attitudes about the learning environment have on student learning
◆ Demographics by student learning by school processes	◆ The impact of specific programs on different subgroups of students, as measured by subgroup learning results
◆ Demographics by perceptions by school processes	◆ What programs different students like best, or the impact different programs have on student attitudes
◆ Student learning by school processes by perceptions	◆ The relationship between the processes students prefer and learning results
Four-way Intersections	
◆ Demographics by student learning by perceptions by school processes	◆ What processes or programs have the greatest impact on different subgroups of students' learning, according to student perceptions, and as measured by student learning results

In the beginning you think. In the end you act. In-between you negotiate the possibilities. Some people move from complexity to simplicity and on into catastrophe. Others move from simplicity to complexity and onward into full-scale confusion. Simplification makes action possible in the face of overwhelming complexity. It also increases the odds of being wrong. The trick is to let a sense of simplicity inform our thinking, a sense of complexity inform our actions, and a sense of humility inform our judgments....

Michael Quinn Patten

Going back to Chapter 2, most often the purposes for conducting data analyses are to—

▼ improve instruction

▼ provide students with feedback on their performance—make sure all students are proficient

▼ gain a common understanding of what quality performance is and how close we are to achieving it

▼ measure program success and effectiveness

▼ understand if what we are doing is making a difference

▼ make sure students do not "fall through the cracks"

▼ know which programs are getting the results we want

▼ get to the root causes of problems

▼ guide curriculum development and revision

▼ promote or measure accountability

▼ meet district, state, and federal requirements

The analyses that have been described throughout this book are not new, unique, or particularly difficult to perform. We have merely begun at the lowest level of analysis, and built upon each level to produce meaningful data that can be used for decision making and continuous school improvement. These data are used for gap and root cause analyses, and can also be used within the context of commonly known analytical frameworks, such as needs assessment, program evaluation, and research.

How do intersection analyses relate to gap and root cause analyses, and to more traditional methods of analysis, such as program evaluation, needs assessment, and research? How do they all relate to comprehensive schoolwide improvement?

Gaps are the differences between where the school wants to be and where the school is right now. Where the school wants to be can be defined through the school's vision and goals.

A *vision* is what the school would look like, sound like, and feel like when it is carrying out its purpose. To be effective in getting all staff members implementing the same concepts, a vision must be spelled-out in specific terms that everyone can understand in the same way. (*The School Portfolio Toolkit: A Planning, Implementation, and Evaluation Guide for Continuous School Improvement* [Bernhardt, 2002], Chapter 5, beginning on page 97.)

Goals are the outcomes of the vision. Goals are stated in broad, general, abstract, and measurable terms. (*Objectives* are much more specific.) Schools often want to attempt many goals, and very few get implemented. There should be only two to three school goals that reflect the results the school wants to achieve by implementing the vision.

Where the school is right now are the results—specifically what all the data say about strengths, challenges, and areas for improvement. To uncover gaps, one must review the data and dig deeper. Just looking at one level of analysis could be misleading. One must dig deeper to uncover those students not meeting the standards and where they rank on the scoring scale. The reason for digging deeper is that a large gap may not seem as large as a smaller gap when one discovers that the students in the area with the largest gap scored only one or two points away from mastery. However, the students not mastering the subtest with the smallest gap could be on the very bottom of the distribution—a long way from mastery.

Once school personnel see the gaps, they typically want to start implementing solutions without discovering the root causes.

Root causes are real reasons that problems or challenges exist. Schools must uncover the root causes of their undesirable results to alleviate the problem or to get desirable results that will last over time. If they do not understand the root causes, schools could be merely treating a symptom and never get to the real reason for the results.

Most of the time in education, staff want to rush their thinking as they endeavor to solve problems. It is worthwhile, however, to first think through what they know about the problem; think about the data that can assist with a better understanding of the problem; understand all that the data reveal; and, clarify goals and desired outcomes before identifying solutions. (Preuss, 2003)

> *Root cause—the deepest underlying cause, or causes, of positive or negative symptoms within any process that, if dissolved, would result in elimination, or substantial reduction, of the symptom.*
>
> Paul Preuss

Problem-solving Cycle

Problem identification and analysis help us think through the big picture and locate the root causes of problems. Steps in solving problems are shown in Figure 8.2 and are described in the text that follows the figure.

Today's problems are
yesterday's solutions.

Peter Senge

Figure 8.2

Steps in Solving a Problem

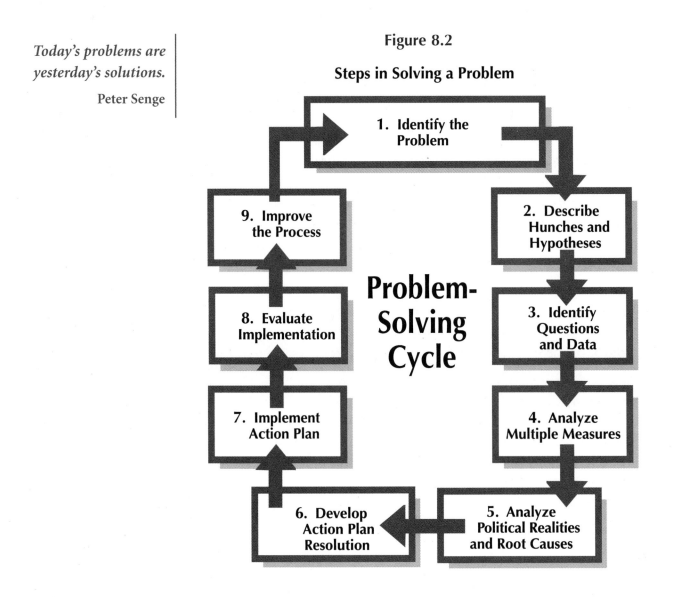

Working with Problem-analysis Teams

When working with a team on "solving problems," getting to root causes of problems, and looking for solutions to problems, established ground rules can keep purposes clear and the time focused on the issues at hand. It is smart to—

▼ start with guidelines or ground rules of acceptable and unacceptable individual and team behavior

▼ determine how ground rules will be monitored

▼ determine how decisions will be made (e.g., by consensus or majority rule)

▼ identify a leader and roles for participation; how the process will be led

▼ make sure a "safe" room is established to enable threat-free, honest, open discussion

As the team works together, keep track of the agreements by writing down the points of agreement as they occur throughout the meeting. Because of a lack of personal involvement with the issues, sometimes an outside facilitator can help keep the interaction positive and productive, while managing conflicts that may arise out of the group's discussion.

Participation techniques are useless in the absence of leadership and purposeful goals.

Marvin Weisbord

1. Identify the Problem

Identifying the problem helps focus the data analysis. A problem might be the discrepancy between actual or desired results, or it might be a goal for improvement. Decide as you start if you are going to use neutral, positive, negative, or solution-oriented questions or statements. An example problem presented in two different ways:

All students are not reading on grade level by grade three.

(Negative statement)

How can we get all students reading on grade level by grade three?

(Solution-oriented statement)

2. Describe Hunches and Hypotheses about the Problem

Brainstorm at least 20 hunches and hypotheses about the problem before looking at all the data. Brainstorming allows staff to think about all aspects of the issue and to see things they might otherwise miss. Often the 20th hunch is very close to the root cause.

Cause and Effect Analysis

Another approach to laying out hunches and hypotheses is the cause and effect analysis. Also known as the fishbone analysis (named for the shape that results), the Cause and Effect Diagram (Figure 8.3) shows the relationship and the complexities between an effect or problem and all the possible causes. It is good for staff to be able to describe what they think are possible causes of the problem before looking at what the data tell them. This approach helps staff sort out the issues that get in the way of achieving the ideal situation. These approaches are sometimes needed in order for some staff to get away from what they think are the causes when the data do not support the cause.

Figure 8.3

Cause and Effect Diagram Built on Teacher Brainstorming

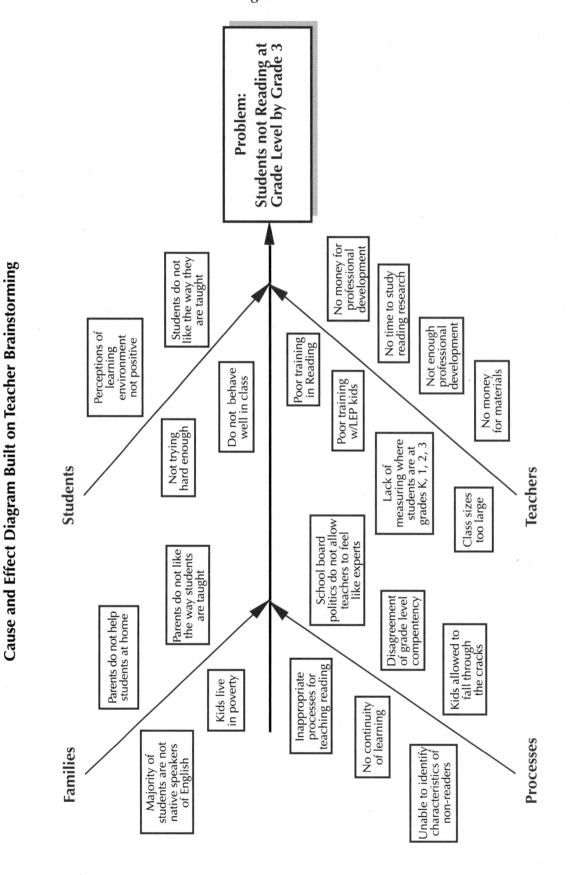

Steps in constructing a cause and effect diagram include:

- ▼ Identify the problem on the right-hand side of the diagram.

- ▼ Brainstorm the possible major causes of the problem (might want to use the affinity analysis described in the next section) to identify the causes and the headings that result. You can use any categories that emerge to get people thinking creatively.

- ▼ Place the causes in the boxes around the spine of the fish.

- ▼ For each cause, ask, *Why does this happen?* and list the responses as branches of the major causes (could also create header cards from brainstormed causes).

- ▼ To find the most basic causes of the problem, look for the causes that appear repeatedly, or as noted by Paul Preuss (2003). "Ammerman (1998) has identified three criteria to determine if each identified cause is a root cause or if it is a contributing cause. They are:

  - ◆ Would the problem have occurred if the cause had not been present? If *no,* then it is a root cause. If *yes,* then it is a contributing cause.

  - ◆ Will the problem reoccur as the result of the same cause if the cause is corrected or dissolved? If *no,* then it is a root cause. If *yes,* then it is a contributing cause.

  - ◆ Will correction or dissolution of the cause lead to similar events? If *no,* then it is a root cause. If *yes,* then it is a contributing cause."

Preuss suggests other indicators that you have found the root cause could include:

- ▼ You run into a dead end asking what caused the proposed root cause.

- ▼ Everyone agrees that this is a root cause.

- ▼ The cause is logical, makes sense, and provides clarity to the problem.

- ▼ The cause is something that you can influence and control.

- ▼ If the cause is dissolved, there is realistic hope that the problem can be reduced or prevented in the future.

*The evil is half-cured
whose cause we know.*

William Shakespeare

The Affinity Diagram

The Affinity Diagram can be used in nearly all cycles of problem-identification and problem-solving processes. This tool is used when groups need a non-judgmental process for collecting ideas in a short period of time. It encourages creativity on everyone's part. It allows for comprehensive thinking concerning issues, encourages non-traditional connections among ideas, often gets people talking about issues they normally might not, and allows breakthroughs to emerge naturally. The affinity diagram encourages ownership of the results that emerge to help overcome resistance to dealing with problems.

Steps in building affinity diagrams include:

▼ Clearly identify the problem.
Problem: *All students are not reading on grade level by grade 3*

▼ Brainstorm hunches and hypotheses.
Strive to capture the essence of *all* ideas. Record each idea on a self-adhesive note using at least a noun and a verb. Avoid using single words. Shortcuts here can greatly reduce the effectiveness of the final affinity diagram. Make sure staff identifies at least twenty hunches. The twentieth hunch is often important. The process will take about ten minutes.

Some of the issues that might surface include the following:

♦ Inappropriate processes for teaching reading are being used

♦ Students' perceptions of the learning environment are not positive

♦ There is a lack of measurement concerning students at grades K, 1, 2, 3

♦ Students don't like the way they are taught

♦ Parents don't like the way the students are taught

♦ Parents do not help students at home

♦ Lots of kids are living in poverty

♦ Students don't behave in class

♦ School board desires

♦ The majority of students are not native speakers of English

♦ Class sizes are too large

♦ There is disagreement on grade level definition

♦ There is no time to study reading research

- ◆ There is not enough professional development for teachers
- ◆ Teacher abilities are not up to snuff
- ◆ There is no money for professional development
- ◆ There is no money for materials
- ◆ Not all teachers are teaching to the standards
- ◆ Not all teachers know how to teach to the standards
- ◆ Teachers do not measure student progress on the standards

▼ Without discussion, the group sorts the items into classifications. It is okay for some notes to stand alone. They might be as important as all the others that naturally fit into groups. If there is an idea that goes under more than one grouping, you might want to decide as a group to duplicate the idea.

▼ For each grouping, create a header and agree on a concise identifier that combines the grouping's central idea.

▼ Divide large groupings into subgroups, if needed, and create subheadings.

▼ Draw the final affinity diagram connecting ideas to the header cards.

Figure 8.4 is an example of a typical affinity diagram that was built from the group brainstorm. The headings that emerged were Processes, Families, Students, and Teachers. The group lined up its brainstorming ideas under the header cards. This group was surprised that the majority of comments fell under two headers—Processes and Teachers. They also had a difficult time determining if the comments fell under the category of Processes or Teachers, which was quite informative to them. These teachers began to see that the standards—consistently teaching and assessing them—could be near the root cause of the problem of students not reading at grade level by grade three.

Figure 8.4

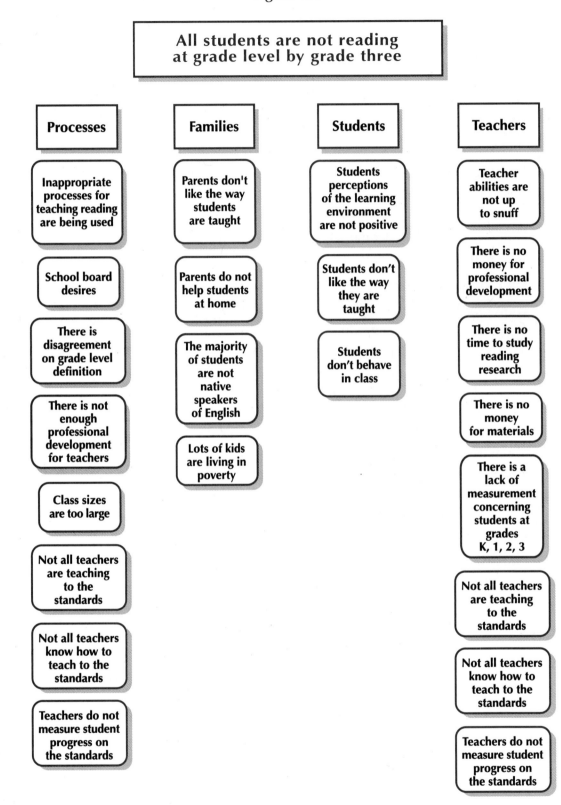

3. Identify Questions and Data

Once the hunches and hypotheses are identified, staff can brainstorm a list of questions they might want to ask to determine if the hunches are fact or fiction. These questions and the list of data required to answer the questions flow logically from the hunches, like the sample in Figure 8.5.

Figure 8.5

Questions About Hunches and Problem	Data
1. How do we define grade level reading for grades K through 3?	1. Staff Discussion
2. How have students performed in reading in the past 3, or more, years?	2. Student achievement data, by grade level, over time
3. What are the characteristics of the students who are performing below grade level at any grade level?	3. Student achievement data, by grade level, over time, by gender and ethnicity
4. What are the students' perceptions of the way reading is taught?	4. Student questionnaire results, disaggregated by gender, ethnicity, and grade level
5. What are parents' perceptions of the way reading is taught, and how their child is learning at our school?	5. Parent questionnaire
6. How are we teaching reading in the different grades?	6. Teacher report/process flow chart
7. How are these data related?	7. Student learning by perceptions by demographics by processes

Nine times out of ten, the data analysis can be designed through the data list. At this point in the problem-solving cycle, teachers usually express shock at how much data are required to "problem solve." It is then that they realize that they have been acting on hunches to this point. Their options are to continue doing the same things and get the same results, or to gather the data and find out what the problem really is.

The Flow Chart

The flow chart was described earlier (Chapter 7) as a means of mapping school processes. The flow chart is also useful when thinking through the questions and the data that can answer the questions—a means of mapping out a data analysis plan, if you will.

Start with the focus of your data analysis. It might be a problem, or it might be the purpose of the school. For example, related to the problem of *students not reading on grade level by grade three,* Figure 8.6 shows a flow chart of thinking through the questions and data analyses.

Figure 8.6

Thinking Through the Data Analysis Process Flowchart
Problem: *Not all Children are Reading on Grade Level by Grade Three*

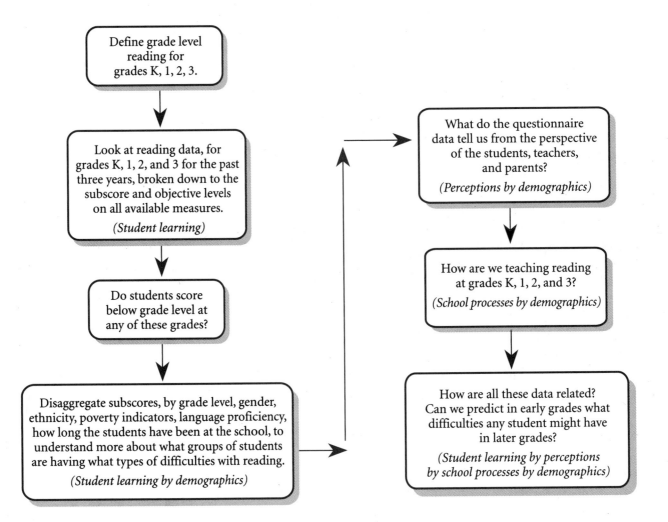

The flow chart starts with a definition of grade level reading for grades K, 1, 2, and 3, and then moves to an understanding of how the students have been doing on student learning measures for the past three years, or more. Looking at the data, one can determine if there are subscores below grade level at the different grade levels. Those scores are disaggregated by what is thought to make a difference with student results, the demographics (e.g., gender, level of poverty, ethnicity, English language proficiency, and length of time at the school). At the same time, data from the students' perspectives can be obtained via student questionnaires and disaggregated in similar ways. School personnel need to think about what they are doing to teach reading at each of the different levels. Are they seeing a difference in scores based upon a difference in teaching approach? Other questions begin to emerge, such as—

- ▼ Are there differences in how reading is taught at the different grade levels and in different classrooms?

- ▼ What student characteristics can be identified that will help predict the lack of reading at the third grade level?

- ▼ Which students did not meet end-of-year expectations?

- ▼ What methods need to be changed, based upon what was learned from this analysis?

- ▼ What will it look like when a new approach is implemented?

- ▼ How will the impact of a new approach be measured?

A flow chart can guide group processes that are focused on looking at the root causes of a problem. Similar flow charts can be used to uncover the problem. One could also use the process flow chart to focus data questions, or to simply list the questions and data. It is important to understand that these processes do not have the *solutions*, per se. Teachers must conduct research and study different approaches to implement. Without new knowledge of processes, the same mistakes can be made again and again.

Seek first to understand and then to be understood.

Stephen R. Covey

4. Analyze Multiple Measures of Data

Everyone on staff needs to understand and be able to use the data that are gathered about the school. There are many approaches to using group processes to this end. One approach to getting everyone to "own" the data is to get everyone involved in a systematic group discussion focused on the data.

▼ Give everyone an opportunity to get familiar with each piece of data gathered about the school.

▼ Focus the group on a piece of data, e.g., disaggregated questionnaire graph.

▼ Systematically go around the room and have each person say what they see in the graph that should be noted. With groups larger than 30, consider pairing people to examine the data first and note important observations. Then use a *fish bowl* approach in which the reporters sit in an inner circle surrounded by listeners who may move to an empty seat in the inside circle if they have observations that others are not reporting.

▼ Record observations related to the data on chart paper.

▼ Keep going around the room, encouraging participants to look deeper and for connections with the previously observed data. Individuals should pass if they have nothing new to add.

▼ Looking at the chart paper, the group looks for and classifies related issues.

▼ Using the same process, the group determines, *What else do we need to know?* Other disaggregations of the data that the group may want to see are then recorded.

▼ The process continues with other pieces of data, e.g., disaggregated student achievement scores.

▼ Eventually, the group looks at the relationship of the results of all the pieces of data and begins to brainstorm meanings and solutions.

Figure 8.7 below shows the brainstorming of multiple measures placed in an affinity diagram. The data analyzed are used as headings, and the teachers' brainstormings are listed under the appropriate heading.

Figure 8.7

Problem: All Students Are Not Reading at Grade Level by Grade Three

Student Learning by Demographics	Perceptions about Student Learning	Processes by Perceptions	Processes by Student Learning	Perceptions by Demographics	Perceptions by Processes by Student Learning by Demographics
Hmong students are not performing as well as other ethnicities.	Mien students feel responsible.	Students in the Reading Recovery Program feel that teachers care about them.	Most students are able to meet the standards for reading after Reading Recovery.	Mien students feel less positive than others that other children are nice to them.	Students who feel they can do the work, and that teachers feel they can do the work, meet the standards.
A greater percentage of Hmong students are not meeting the standard than other groups.	Fewer Mien students than others feel that school work is challenging.	Students in the Reading Recovery Program feel they can do the work.	Supportive teachers' classrooms have the best success after Reading Recovery.	Fewer Mien students than others like coming to school.	Students who do not reach a level 8 on Reading Recovery in grade one will not read at grade level by grade three.
Hmong and Mien children have not been exposed to American customs.	Fewer Mien students than others feel that they know how to solve problems.		Teachers must assist students in understanding the meanings of words to which students have not been exposed.	Mien students feel less positive than others that they are treated with respect.	Students who do well on Reading Recovery still must be supported by the classroom teacher.
Many students did not meet the standards.	Most students, regardless of ethnicity, feel that their families expect them to do well in school.			All American Indian students strongly agree that grown-ups treat them with respect.	
More students meet the standards when following cohorts.	American Indian students are bored with school.			All American Indian students strongly agree that their teacher thinks they can do well in school.	
All ethnicities are improving.					

Using the headings of the intersection analyses, we substitute the question in step 4 with this question, *What do the data tell us about this heading?* The data analysis diagram in Figure 8.8, built as a variation of a cause and effect, or fishbone, diagram, shows how data from different sources interact to solve problems. We find it useful to place the negative results on one side and the positive results on the other side of the bones. We also move the problem statement to the left because the data can lead to the solution; we have the arrows lead to a solution.

Figure 8.8

Cause and Effect Diagram Built on Data Analysis Results

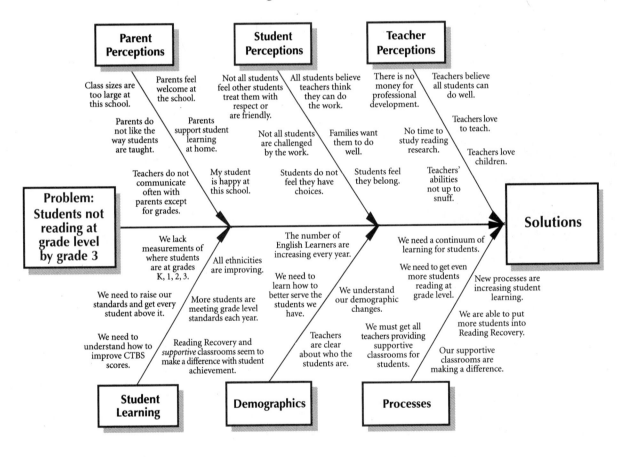

5. Analyze Political Realities and Root Causes

With all the analyses completed, we can use a force field analysis to understand the driving forces that can be strengthened and the restraining forces that can be deleted, or at least lessened.

Force Field Analysis

Force field analysis is a way to think through all aspects of a situation so that solutions can be easily considered. Like the affinity diagram process, force field analysis forces people to think together about problems and desired changes, encourages honest reflection on the real underlying root causes of a problem and its solutions, and encourages people to agree on the factors. Force field analysis presents the positives and the negatives of a situation, so they can readily be compared. It is another excellent way of looking at the big picture. Steps in a force field analysis follow:

▼ Write the ideal state at the top of a flip chart or a piece of paper.

▼ Brainstorm the forces that are *driving* toward this ideal state on the left.

▼ Brainstorm the forces that are *restraining* movement from the ideal state on the right.

Figure 8.9 shows the brainstormed driving and restraining forces effecting the ideal state of all students reading at grade level by grade three.

Figure 8.9

Ideal State — All Students Reading at Grade Level by Grade Three

Driving Forces	Restraining Forces
Fits with priorities	Our research does not support this possibility
What teachers want for kids	Class sizes are too large
Fits with the purpose of the school	Not enough money to incorporate the programs that are necessary
School board desires	No systematic measurements to know how we are doing
Reading Recovery can help	Reading specialist is needed
Parents do not like the way students are being taught	Families do not help with homework
We need better processes for teaching reading	Students are not native English speakers
Students like to go to school here	No agreement on what constitutes reading at grade level
Teachers want to improve	Kids are living in poverty
We need strong measurements	Students do not behave
Teachers need to create a continuum of learning that makes sense for students	Time
	No money for professional development
	No measurement of where students are with respect to reading at grades K, 1, 2, 3

The idea is to start gnawing away at the restraining forces, while strengthening the driving forces. Figure 8.10 shows Figure 8.9 reordered.

Figure 8.10

Ideal State — All Students Reading at Grade Level by Grade Three

Driving Forces	Restraining Forces
What teachers want for kids	Families do not help with homework
We need better processes for teaching reading	Students are not native English speakers
Teachers want to improve	No agreement on what constitutes reading at grade level
We need strong measurements	
School board desires	
Fits with priorities	
Fits with the purpose of the school	

When reordering Figure 8.9, staff started planning for immediate action. They determined that because they wanted all students to read at grade level by grade three, this had to become their highest priority. This desire was directly related to the purpose of the school and the vision—if all students weren't reading at grade level by grade three, they would have limited options in life. With reading as their priority, there was no reason to not agree on what constitutes reading at grade level—this became an action item for their next staff meeting. It was no longer a restraining force.

One of the reasons teachers had not agreed up to this point was the lack of a rigorous look at past data. When past data are used, everyone can see what is possible and establish the standard together. A group of teachers worked with an outside consultant to get past data together for the staff meeting. They committed to continue conducting rigorous measurements in order to assess their progress with new processes. Teachers, working with administration, determined that professional development and teachers' abilities would no longer be restraining forces. If reading at grade level by grade three is really the school priority, money cannot be an issue. Money has to be allocated first to the priorities that help everyone implement the vision. Time to prepare and learn about reading can no longer be an issue either. Time must be reallocated to the top priority issue. From this point forward, it was agreed that staff meetings would focus on this issue, and other items that tend to take up staff meeting time would be dealt with via electronic mail or memorandum. Staff determined that, with reading as a priority, every time teachers meet together, they must be working to that end.

As one can see, this group of teachers started sorting out what was really doable. By thinking through the pieces together, they began changing their thinking about the situation. They began to see that the way they were thinking about their processes and the children was at the root of the problem. The next important step would be for them to build a solid plan to ensure that everyone understands and implements the agreed upon action.

One reason force field analysis works is that teams select the targets for change. They are able to see those things that are changeable. Not all things can be changed, which brings up the difference between a *problem* and a *condition*. A problem is something we can do something about, so we can focus time and energy in that direction. A condition is something that we cannot do anything about—we acknowledge it and go around it, but we do not waste time trying to change it. In most common situations, restraining forces would probably be reordered from condition to problem. In this case, families not helping with homework and students' home language are conditions; whereas, students not reading at grade level by grade three is a problem.

Many people view change as a struggle between forces that seek to upset the status quo. We can build on the *driving forces* to implement change if we can remove *restraining forces*. When the opposing forces are equal, or the restraining forces are too strong to allow movement, there is no change.

Force field analysis can also be used to align what the data show are the driving forces and the restraining forces. In other words, if you know what the interaction analyses show, those results can be ordered as driving and restraining results, just like the other items above.

> A "problem" is something we can do something about, so we can focus time and energy in that direction. A "condition" is something that we cannot do anything about—we acknowledge it and go around it, but we do not waste time trying to change it.

Make no little plans. They have no magic to stir men's blood and probably themselves will not be realized. Make big plans. Aim high in hope and work. Remembering that a noble, logical diagram once recorded will not die.

Daniel H. Burnham

6. Develop an Action Plan

After analyzing for root causes of problems and looking for solutions, the team must plan to put the solutions to dissolve the root causes into action by first asking—

▼ Are our solutions congruent with the purpose of the school, and what are we trying to do ultimately for all students?

▼ Does our plan include a way to measure change?

▼ Does our plan include specific dates for implementation and review?

▼ Do our budget priorities line up with planned priorities?

▼ Does our plan truly represent an objective, analytical look at the root causes of problems and solutions?

Action plans include what is to be done, who is responsible for making sure that it gets done, cost considerations, and timelines (i.e., by when the work will be done). An outline of an action plan is shown as Figure 8.11. Do not be dismayed if the problem analysis leads to the need to gather more data. (See *The School Portfolio Toolkit* [Bernhardt, 2002] for more information and tools related to action planning.)

7. Implement the Action Plan

After the quality action plan for implementing the solutions is developed, a commitment to implementation needs to be made by all staff members. Teachers must commit to adjusting their instructional and assessment strategies to meet the needs of their students, and they must be able to assess the impact of their actions on students. Leaders must do everything they can do, at all times, to make sure that the plan is implemented. The plan will need to be implemented in ways that reflect grade levels and subject areas, and it must be congruent with the vision and overall strategic plan. A structure might need to be established to coordinate, implement, and support the plan.

8. Evaluate the Implementation

All parts of the implementation need to be evaluated, using multiple measures, on an ongoing basis. A continuously improving learning organization uses evaluation to understand the impact and effectiveness of its actions; to ensure the congruence and synergy of the elements of its vision; and to determine how well new strategies have been implemented.

Figure 8.11

Action Plan Outline

Goal: _____

**Baseline Proficiency
2003-04:**

Grade Three		Grade Four		Grade Five		Grade Six	
Language Arts:	%	Language Arts:	%	Language Arts:	%	Language Arts:	%
Science:	%	Science:	%	Science:	%	Science:	%
Mathematics:	%	Mathematics:	%	Mathematics:	%	Mathematics:	%
Social Studies:	%	Social Studies:	%	Social Studies:	%	Social Studies:	%

Measurable Objectives:
-
-
-

STRATEGY / ACTION	Person Responsible	Measurement	Resources	Due Date	TIMELINE
					Aug Sept Oct Nov Dec Jan Feb Mar Apr May Jun Jul

The overall desire is to improve processes, products, and procedures on an ongoing basis. To create an overall evaluation plan, take the *Measurement* column out of your plan, collapse like elements, and expand the measurement until it feels all encompassing.

9. Improve the Process

Understanding the impact each element has upon the other determines what to change. When evaluating on an ongoing basis, one can know what is working and what is not working. Improvements can and ought to be made, as they are necessary.

Traditional Analyses

Traditional analyses such as needs assessment, program evaluation, and research have distinct roles to play in continuous school improvement—some are more valuable than others.

▼ *Needs assessment* shows the discrepancies between the actual and the desired. What is our current status? What would we like it to be?

▼ *Formative program evaluation* asks questions about the current program. What is being done? Is it doing what it is intended to do?

▼ *Summative program evaluation* addresses questions at the end of the program or year. What was done? What was it worth?

▼ *Research* answers questions of curiosity: Does Group A perform better than Group B?

Schools often conduct one or the other of these analyses when they should be conducting a combination of analyses. For instance, without program evaluation, needs assessment becomes *problem* assessment, pointing to deficiencies without giving guidance to intervention strategies. Similarly, program evaluation depends upon needs assessment. If the worth of a program is to be judged, the needs of participants must be gauged. Without needs assessment, programs cannot really be evaluated; they can only be described. Research without elements of needs assessment and program evaluation is a "so what." It can be conducted by anyone, including people with only partial knowledge of the program.

Needs Assessment

Needs assessment helps decision making by clarifying what, and how important, the needs are. Within an educational setting, identifying needs requires uses of multiple measures—a knowledge of the population *(demographics);* values of the people to be served *(perceptions);* an idea of the success of the program or process in question *(student learning);* and the services available to the population *(school processes).*

Needs assessment is sometimes described as the feedback process that enables us to learn about, and adapt to, the needs of our "clients." These assessments usually move beyond the identification of needs to solution identification. The key to doing that well is ensuring that comprehensive data have been gathered so that the solution is appropriate and that schools are not only dealing with a symptom.

Common steps in needs assessments are described below.

▼ *Identify the uses of the needs assessment*
   Why are we conducting the assessment?

▼ *Describe the target population*
   Demographics

▼ *Identify needs*
   Define the discrepancy between expectations (what we expect students to know and be able to do) and current results (evidence of student learning) to define the problem. Your knowledge of student and teacher values (perceptions) and possible solutions (adaptation of existing or adoption of new school processes) may become obvious as a likely route to success.

▼ *Assess the importance of the needs*
   Which are the most important and relate most to the purpose of the school?

▼ *Communicate results*
   Measurements can be transformed to reflect the values, interests, or purposes of those who make decisions.

Program Evaluation

There are many approaches to program evaluation. Just like any data analysis that we conduct, the type of evaluation depends upon the purpose. There are many purposes for conducting an evaluation within a school or school district. The most common are to—

▼ understand how students are doing within the educational system the school/district is providing

▼ identify problems needing intervention

▼ understand cost benefits or cost effectiveness

▼ assess impact or monitor the program for improvement

The most often-heard terms associated with program evaluation are formative and summative. Formative simply refers to measuring how the program is doing while it is operating. Summative refers to assessments of overall program effectiveness, and usually takes place at the end of the year or program.

> *Evaluating a program is like shooting at a moving target—it's hard as hell to hit and requires precise anticipation. The rare bull's eye brings uncommon satisfaction. Improving your aim means lots of practice and careful study of the non-random movements of the target.*
>
> Michael Quinn Patten

An evaluation that begins with an experimental design denies to program staff what it needs most: Information that can be used to make judgments about the program while it is in its dynamic stages of growth.... We recognize that comparisons (of those receiving treatment versus those who didn't) have never been productive, nor have they facilitated corrective action. The overwhelming number of evaluations conducted in this way show no significant differences between "experimental" and "control" groups.

Malcom Provus

Typical steps in program evaluation are very similar to needs assessment. The steps, which follow, are focused a little differently.

▼ *Identify the purpose for the evaluation*
Why are we conducting the analysis?

▼ *Identify the audience*
Whom do you want to use the results?

▼ *Identify sources of information*
They could be from all four multiple measures of data.

▼ *Conduct the assessment*
It might be similar to intersection analyses, but it is usually focused on questions of effectiveness.

▼ *Communicate results*
Communicate in a manner that targeted groups will understand and use.

Research

Researchers study different phenomenon to make discoveries or to acquire information. Research relies on experimental designs, control groups, pure experimental designs, and significant differences. This may not be useful in education. For example, researchers studying the impact of technology might want some children to have technology and others to not have technology to serve as a control group. Although there could be occasions when circumstances exist that allow this type of research, we would never want to deliberately keep children from having the opportunity to work with something that we think would increase student learning. Schools use their best judgment to implement what they think is best for children. Never could we, in good conscience, deny children opportunities we think will make a difference simply for the sake of methodological research purity.

When selecting an analysis to use to determine whether or not an approach is working, school personnel often want to design an experiment. They believe that if there is no control group or tests of significance, the results are not valuable. Statistical significance of a result is the probability that the observed relationship in a sample occurred by pure chance. We want to use statistical significance only when it makes sense. In the analyses that we are conducting, statistical significance is not as important to us because we are not trying to generalize for the total population of learners or school. Instead, we are looking for analyses that are educationally significant.

I firmly believe that there is a place for applied research in education and in analyzing data for improving schools; however, the *use* of research as a data analysis strategy is probably our least effective approach for comprehensive schoolwide improvement. Looking at the research in the literature is beneficial. Conducting your own experimental research is probably beyond the scope of most school systems.

Pulling it Altogether

School personnel ask me all the time, *What does it look like when the data analysis is put altogether?* Answering that question is difficult. Part of it looks like a school profile (see Bernhardt's *Using Data to Improve Student Learning* series). It is important to gather data related to the four multiple measures of data to understand where the school is right now, and over time, to understand how the demographics, student learning, perceptions, and school processes have changed. It is also important to cross these measures in meaningful ways to answer evaluative questions; NCLB requires the disaggregation of student achievement results by demographics. It would follow that analyses disaggregating perceptions by these same demographics would make sense.

Figure 4.1 (Chapter 4) shows all the data a school needs to pull it all together. I personally believe documentation of profiles and graphs, similar to those shown in the book and stored in a school portfolio, updated over time, is the most powerful approach.

Study Questions for Intersections and Analyses from Using Data

Think about the school improvement questions that you identified in Chapter 3. What intersections would give you information related to the questions?

Intersections	Questions	What data do you have or need to answer the questions?
Demographics by Student Learning	*Is there a relationship between attendance and standardized achievement results?*	*Number of days attended and state standardized test results for each student.*
Demographics by School Processes	*Is participation in the pre-school program representative of all students?*	*Pre-school enrollment by gender and ethnicity.*

Intersections	Questions	What data do you have or need to answer the questions?
Perceptions by Demographics	*Are all students perceiving the learning environment in the same way?*	*Student questionnaire results disaggregated by gender, by ethnicity, and/or by grade level.*
Perceptions by Student Learning	*Are the students who are getting the best grades the happiest with the learning environment?*	*Student grades by student perceptions.*
Perceptions by School Processes	*Are there differences in how students perceive the learning environment, based on whom they have as teachers?*	*Student perceptions disaggregated by teacher.*

Intersections	Questions	What data do you have or need to answer the questions?
Student Learning by School Processes	*Is there a difference in student achievement results by program participation?*	*Student achievement test results by program.*
Demographics by Perceptions by Student Learning	*Are the differences in student learning results based on whom we have as students and how they perceive the learning environment?*	*Student achievement test results disaggregated by gender and ethnicity, compared to student questionnaire results disaggregated by gender and ethnicity.*
Perceptions by Demographics by School Processes	*Are the students most satisfied with school being taught differently from students not satisfied with school, and who are they?*	*Student questionnaires disaggregated by gender, ethnicity, grade level, and program participation.*

Intersections	Questions	What data do you have or need to answer the questions?
Perceptions by Student Learning by School Processes	*What are the differences in student achievement results because of attitudes related to whom students have as teachers?*	*Student achievement results disaggregated by teacher, compared to student questionnaire results disaggregated by teacher.*
Demographics by Student Learning by School Processes	*What are the differences in student learning results based on who the students are and how they are taught to read?*	*Student achievement results, disaggregated by gender and ethnicity, and sorted by what program they are in and whom they have as a teacher.*
Student Learning by Demographics by Perceptions by School Processes	*What are the differences in the results we are getting, based on whom we have as students and how they are being taught? How would they prefer to learn?*	*Student achievement results, disaggregated by gender, ethnicity, grade level, and program, compared to student questionnaire results, disaggregated by gender, ethnicity, grade level, and program.*

Summary

The analysis you choose depends upon the purpose for doing it in the first place. Think about the questions you have that are related to the purpose of your school, and consider what you want to know related to continuous school improvement. You might choose different approaches to answer different questions. You will most probably use gap analysis and root cause analysis. You might use elements of needs assessment, program evaluation, and research which can also be accomplished by simply looking at the intersections of the four major measures. Think through your questions logically. Most importantly, keep your focus on the purpose.

Intersection analyses allow one to understand data at an incremental level, and to see that one can create an analysis for any question. Intersection analyses are analyses that teachers and school personnel can do fairly quickly and easily. They can tell us different things depending upon the perspective and complexity of intersections. The information gained from these analyses is crucial for continuous school improvement.

COMMUNICATING THE RESULTS

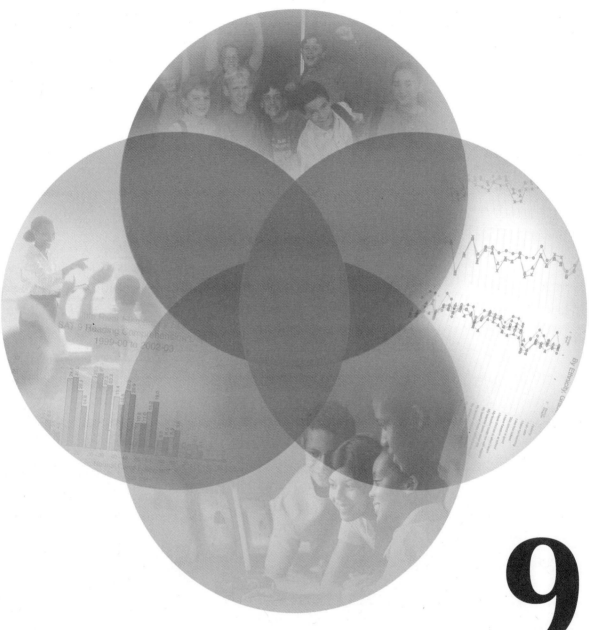

Chapter **9**

Analysis procedures that are employed should be appropriate to the data collected and analyses should always be done in a way that recognizes the evaluator's obligation to communicate to potential users. This communication should be in forms that are meaningful and likely to enhance the possibility of use. The evaluator's job is not to dazzle or to impress with sophisticated expertise, but rather to communicate.

Marvin Alkin

Communicating the purpose and results of data analysis are critical if the analyses are going to effect decisions and if solutions are going to be implemented as intended. We can perform the most complex analyses in the world; but if we want others to use the data, they must be able to understand the analyses, results, and uses.

One of the first considerations in reporting data analysis results is the audience—the people who need to understand and use these data. Staff are the most important recipients of schoolwide data analysis results. These data tell staff how they are doing and how they can improve what they are doing. We want staff to utilize the analyses to implement new ways of doing business, if needed.

We also want the community to understand the data analyses and resulting new approaches. What follows are ideas about communicating the data analysis results.

Communication Strategies

Many methods exist for reporting data results. It is important to match the method with the audience. For communication to a large audience, e.g., the public in general, you might want to use one or more of the following:

▼ *Article in the local newspaper by an education reporter.* A prepared fact sheet or press release can help keep the facts straight. An example press release is shown in Figure 9.1. The boxes in the press release are just guidelines.

▼ *Public meeting or news conference presented by the superintendent.* Make sure the superintendent has all of the facts as well as a thorough understanding of the data. Also, help the superintendent by thinking through typical questions that the public might ask. You might want to stage a practice news conference with staff to inform them and to rehearse for the real one.

▼ *Newsletters.* Schools often send newsletters home to parents. The results of the data analysis could be described in the newsletter with information about the changes implied by the results.

▼ *Special events.* If the data focus is on reading, for example, a special reading event might be set up for public participation. The results of the data could be reported that night in terms

Figure 9.1

Example Press Release

FOR IMMEDIATE RELEASE
Insert Date Here
Contact: Richard Long, Superintendent
Park School District
(500) 777-3715

Announce your Message and How the Community was Involved

PARK CITY, USA — Archer Elementary School announces the results of a recently completed analysis of the 2002-03 school year. "I am very pleased to announce that Archer Elementary School of the Park School District has taken a comprehensive look at how well they are serving their students and how they can do an even better job in the future," said Superintendent Richard Long. "The school analyzed parent, student, administrator, and teacher perceptions, demographic data, student achievement results, and school processes."

Background

As a part of their effort to continuously improve, Archer staff measured how well they are doing for children with their current approaches and determining what instructional strategies they need to change to get different results.

Data Analysis

The data show how the population and student achievement results of Archer have changed during the past five years. Archer's average Reading, Writing, and Math scores have not improved substantially," reported Principal Caroline Brown. "We studied our past scores to understand what skills need to be improved; we looked at our data to understand learning styles and perceptions of students and what attitudes need to be improved on the part of teachers, students, and the community; and, then we analyzed how to improve our instructional and assessment strategies to meet all of our students' needs."

Describe Plans for Improvement

Some tangible changes are being implemented in all subject areas. In the area of Reading, teachers will increase the minutes for daily K-3 reading instruction, and continue to encourage parents to read with their children for at least 15 minutes every night. In the area of math, teachers will increase the number of minutes each week that students are engaged in math. With respect to writing, teachers will ask students to write more often and in all subject areas, according to Brown.

Reference Attached Graphs

The attached graphs show the student achievement results for Archer, for the past five years.

End on a Positive

"I commend and am extremely proud of the Archer Elementary School staff for committing to this hard work of understanding where they can improve what they do for all students. Within two years, all of us are looking forward to seeing striking increases in student achievement. We need your help and continued support," said Superintendent Long.

that will help parents understand what they can do differently, and what teachers are going to do differently to improve reading at the school. Any handouts prepared for the audience could be sent home to those parents who were unable to attend.

▼ *A brief synopsis that can be shared at staff meetings.* For example, more than 50% of our fourth-grade students are at or above grade level for Reading.

▼ *School Portfolio.* A school portfolio is a wonderful container for housing the comprehensive data analysis of a school or district. In addition, a portfolio describes how the data are used to effect continuous improvement.

▼ *Web Sites.* Many schools have web sites that could be good communication vehicles for parents and community members with web access.

▼ *School Summary Report.* Short school summary reports can be set up to let the public know how the school is doing and what it learned from recent analyses. An example is shown for Archer Elementary School at the end of this chapter (Figure 9.13).

▼ *Other Methods.* Other ways to communicate findings might include telephone trees, speeches to service clubs, site council or leadership team briefings, and/or private meetings with business.

Each of these methods for disseminating information will require slightly different approaches to presenting the data visually and discussing it in the accompanying text. An article for the local newspaper will need to sound objective and professional, while a newsletter can sound warmer and more casual. The pages for the school portfolio will need to include all the details behind the analyses, for staff use, while a school summary report would generally summarize and highlight important results.

Communicating the Data Analysis Results

Whether communicating data analysis results to educators or non-educators, the communicator has an obligation to interpret all of the data, so pieces are not fragmented and so the data can be interpreted easily.

Graphs are powerful ways to communicate data analysis results. Data graphics display multiple measures in terms of points, lines, bars, symbols, and pictures. Graphs set the stage for discussion, convey a message, or reinforce a central point. Graphs are designed to be concise in conveying data and making the data readily digestible.

The power of graphs comes from their ability to convey data directly to the viewer. Viewers use their spatial intelligence to retrieve data from a graph—a source of intelligence different from the language-based intelligence of prose and verbal presentations. The audience sees graphs. For most people, the communication process becomes more direct and immediate through graphic displays. Data become more credible and more convincing when the audience has direct interaction with it.

Graphs allow us to move easily from the analytical to the descriptive and vice versa. They also raise the motivation of the audience to access and use the data.

Graphs break up the narrative in reports and encourage readers to engage in the material. They encourage the eye to compare different pieces of data and to reveal the data at several levels of detail—from a broad overview to the fine points. Graphs can show test score data, for instance, with confidence limits or in comparison to norms or standards.

Graphs must be meaningful, interesting, and well designed. They are meant to communicate information about relationships, especially where intensive inspection will deepen or induce understanding of the relationships. Readers should be able to make sense of a graph without reference to the text, and they should be enticed to think about substance rather than methodology.

The previous chapters show examples of graphs designed to provide overviews of a school's demographics, overviews of questionnaire results, summaries of student achievement results, example processes, and their intersections. In each of these examples, the graphs did not rely on the text for interpretation. The key to creating excellent graphs is to convey the greatest number of ideas with the least ink in the smallest space. This requires keeping graphs simple, clear, and easy to read and understand.

*A good graph is worth
a thousand words.*

Dennis Johnston

Different Types of Graphs

There are many ways to graph data. It is easy to choose a graph that can tell the comprehensive story of your data. It is just as easy to choose one that muddles the information. Appropriate graphs are simple—not complex—can stand alone, and are clear about the information they try to compare. The most common types of graphs used for displaying schoolwide data are pie, bar, and line graphs.

Pie Graphs

Use pie graphs to stress proportions or percentages of a population or category. Use no more than eight slices in any pie graph. When using color, do not use red and green together since 5% of the population cannot distinguish between red and green. Also, do not use patterns next to each other that result in optical illusions. Pie graphs are outstanding for displaying the proportion of a school's enrollment for one year, as in Figure 9.2.

Figure 9.2

Example Pie Graph

Make sure the title describes the information being displayed. ⟶

Add labels so everyone knows the information the data are relaying.

**Archer Elementary School
Student Enrollment by Percent Ethnicity
October 2003 (*N*=472)**

Order information in the legend from largest to smallest.

1.7%   1.7%   0.6%

46.2%

49.8%

■ Black
(*n*=235)
□ White
(*n*=218)
▨ Hispanic/Latino
(*n*=8)
■ Asian
(*n*=8)
□ American Indian
(*n*=3)

Bar Graphs

Bar graphs are the most highly recommended format for descriptive data. The bars can be shown horizontally or vertically. Bar graphs have an x-axis and y-axis, and they typically display means or frequencies for different categories. These graphs should be greater in width than height. Our eyes naturally look left to right and, therefore, horizontal graphs are more accessible to the eye. It is wise to stay away from three-dimensional and stacked bar graphs when it is difficult to comprehend the information being presented. Notice your personal preference as you look at Figure 9.3, converted into four different bar graphs, one set of flat graphs set up vertically and horizontally, and one set of three-dimensional graphs, set up vertically and horizontally.

Figure 9.3
Example Bar Graphs

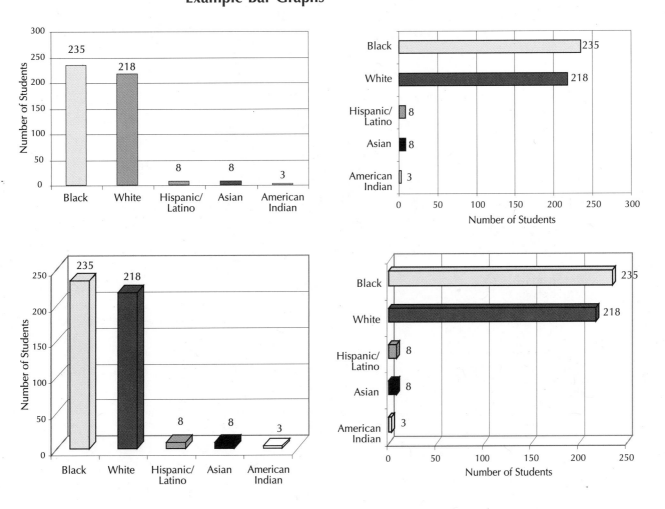

Figure 9.4, below, summarizes graph design considerations for bar graphs.

Figure 9.4

Design Considerations for Bar Graphs

Even if it leaves a large empty area in a graph, take care to make scales consistent when presenting a series of graphs, and use the correct scale to ensure accurate presentation of the data.

Keep the graph as clean as possible:
• reduce grid lines to the fewest needed for clarity
• label data within the graph wherever possible
• eliminate boxes around the legend and title
• use patterns sparingly
• you might want to move the legend to underneath the graph, if it is easier to read, or include a portion of the legend in the graph

Use data labels when it is hard to tell the number the bars represent.

Use a title that tells specifically what the graph represents.

Include "*n=*" in the legend.

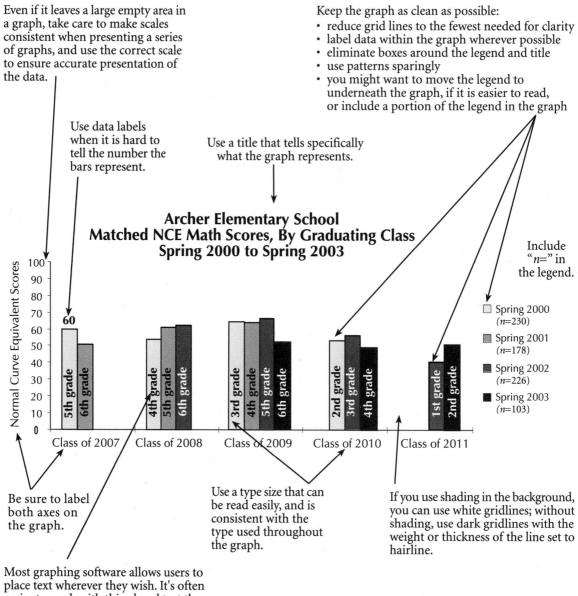

**Archer Elementary School
Matched NCE Math Scores, By Graduating Class
Spring 2000 to Spring 2003**

Be sure to label both axes on the graph.

Use a type size that can be read easily, and is consistent with the type used throughout the graph.

If you use shading in the background, you can use white gridlines; without shading, use dark gridlines with the weight or thickness of the line set to hairline.

Most graphing software allows users to place text wherever they wish. It's often easier to work with this placed text than with the automatically created labels generated by the software.

Make sure the colors contrast enough to show the data clearly, and use colors that will enable you to print or photocopy the graph in black and white.

Line Graphs

Line graphs give a lot of flexibility and are exceptionally good for showing a series of numbers over time. Line graphs can display complex data more effectively than bar graphs. For example, if a bar graph was used to display the data in Figure 9.5, six bars would be needed for each item.

Line graphs are outstanding for showing how different subgroups responded to items on a questionnaire. Line graphs enable a "big picture" look at the results of a questionnaire. For instance, Figure 9.5 shows a disaggregated line graph that is helpful in data analysis for continuous school improvement. One can see the overall response averages and individual subgroup averages at the same time. However, a graph such as Figure 9.5 would be best when following other less comprehensive graphs that have allowed readers to get to know the items in the graph. Readers would be able to pick out the varying subgroups very quickly. Figure 9.5 might only be used in-house for problem finding. There are too many lines for some audiences to read.

Design considerations for line graphs are found in Figure 9.5.

Figure 9.5

Design Considerations for Line Graphs

When graphing large numbers of subgroups (usually eight or more) with very similar responses, a graph may become difficult or even impossible to read. Be nice to your audience— if you think the chart is hard to read, it is! Consider breaking the analysis into two graphs, or even turning the graph. However, if a graph such as this one follows less congested graphs that allow readers to become familiar with the items in the graph, this graph would be great for spotting subgroup differences.

Be sure to include the number of people who make up each of the subgroups being graphed. (Subgroups fewer than 8 are generally considered to be too small to be considered in the graph.)

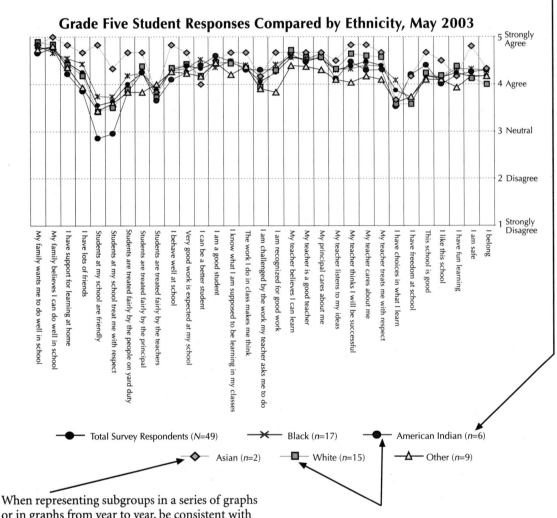

Grade Five Student Responses Compared by Ethnicity, May 2003

When representing subgroups in a series of graphs or in graphs from year to year, be consistent with color and with symbols. If Asian students in the school are lavender diamonds in one graph, make sure they are presented as lavender diamonds in subsequent graphs, so that comparisons can be made easily.

Use symbols that will show up either in color or when the graph is printed or copied in black and white. Each of the subgroups are represented here with different colors and different symbols.

Note: When disaggregating by subgroups, numbers do not always add up to the total number of respondents because some respondents do not identify themselves by the demographic, or they may have the option of indicating more than one subgroup in the demographic.

Explaining Questionnaire Results

It is just as important to describe questionnaire results as it is to describe student achievement test results. Be sure to—

- ▼ include the purpose for administering the questionnaire in your description
- ▼ explain that the results of the questionnaire are a snapshot in time that reflect where the school is right now
- ▼ start with a general overview of the data
- ▼ point out strengths and areas of concern
- ▼ show how you dug deeper and deeper into the data to find answers
- ▼ discuss how the school is going to use the data

The next three pages show graphs that are designed to help you find the information that can be considered for communication to your various audiences. Whether you decide to present it in more or less detail will depend upon what you learn from the graphs and how the results need to be presented to the audience in question.

Figure 9.6 shows the total responses for a group of students that responded to a questionnaire in 2003. The figure highlights various points of interest on the graph that should be considered when communicating the results of the questionnaire to an audience.

Figure 9.6

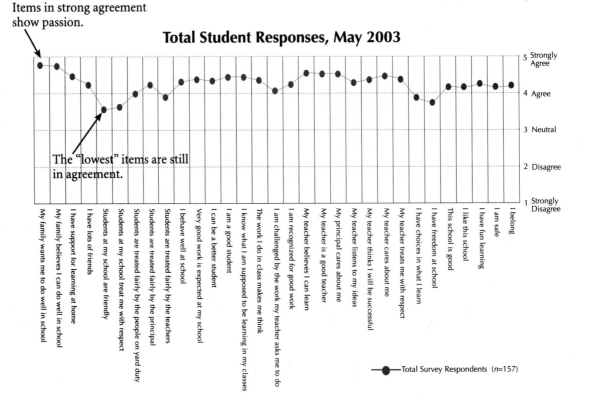

Total Student Responses, May 2003

Items in strong agreement show passion.

The "lowest" items are still in agreement.

Total Survey Respondents (*n*=157)

Things to look for:

- Overall responses being positive (agree), neutral, or negative (disagree).
- Highest averages and their relationship.
- Lowest averages and their relationship.

What we saw:

- Overall, these students are in strong agreement with the set of items (all but six items were higher than agree).
- Highest averages or items in which these students were in most agreement were related to their families wanting and believing that students can do well in school.
- A couple of items show passion in the responses, i.e., most students stated that they strongly agree with the two highest items.
- Lowest averages were about having choices in school and other students treating them with respect, possibly related.
- Disaggregation is needed to understand more about the averages.
- No item averages fell below the neutral point, or in disagreement.

The second graph (Figure 9.7) shows the same questionnaire responses broken down by grade level. Again, the figure highlights various points of interest to consider and some recommendations for further problem analysis.

Figure 9.7

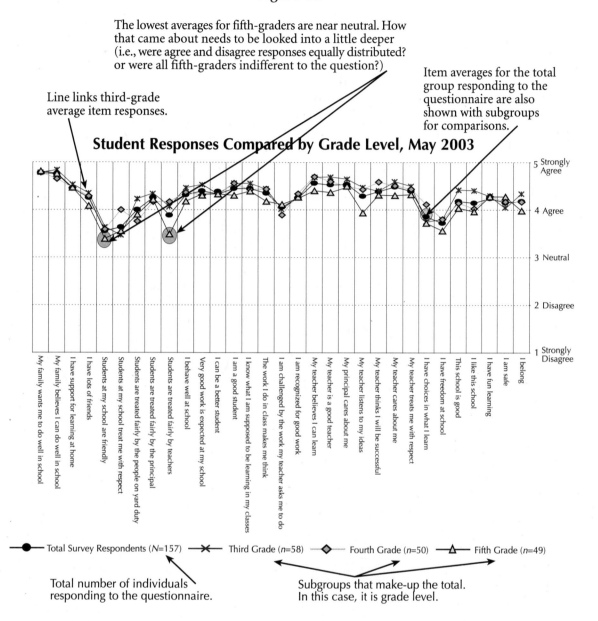

The lowest averages for fifth-graders are near neutral. How that came about needs to be looked into a little deeper (i.e., were agree and disagree responses equally distributed? or were all fifth-graders indifferent to the question?)

Item averages for the total group responding to the questionnaire are also shown with subgroups for comparisons.

Line links third-grade average item responses.

Total number of individuals responding to the questionnaire.

Subgroups that make-up the total. In this case, it is grade level.

Things to look for:

- Subgroups that "stick out" or look different from the others.
- Big gaps between one subgroup and the other subgroups.
- Differences in averages that result in opposite responses, such as agree-disagree.
- Subgroup trends that are unexpected.
- Size of subgroup that looks different from the other groups, although small numbers may still indicate issues that need to be addressed.
- Other analyses that would provide further understandings of the responses.

What we saw:

- There are few real differences between group averages.
- Third graders tend to be in strongest agreement with items on the questionnaire.
- Fifth graders tend to be in least agreement with questionnaire items.
- Fourth grade responses consistently fall in the middle of all the subgroups.
- Staff might want to understand how averages came about (i.e., look at the distribution of responses.)

The third graph (Figure 9.8) shows just the fifth-grade responses, disaggregated by ethnicity. The items to consider are the same as those presented in the previous figure. This graph shows what the reader learns from looking at the data. What we learn from this level of data is normally what would be discussed with staff and not necessarily presented to the public at large. In this particular case, there was a problem with students being friendly and treating each other with respect.

Figure 9.8

Looking at the responses by ethnicity, one can see that:

- American Indian students are in high disagreement that *Students at my school are friendly* and *Students at my school treat me with respect.*
- Black, Asian, White, and Other students are in low agreement with those statements.
- Asian students are in highest agreement with all items.

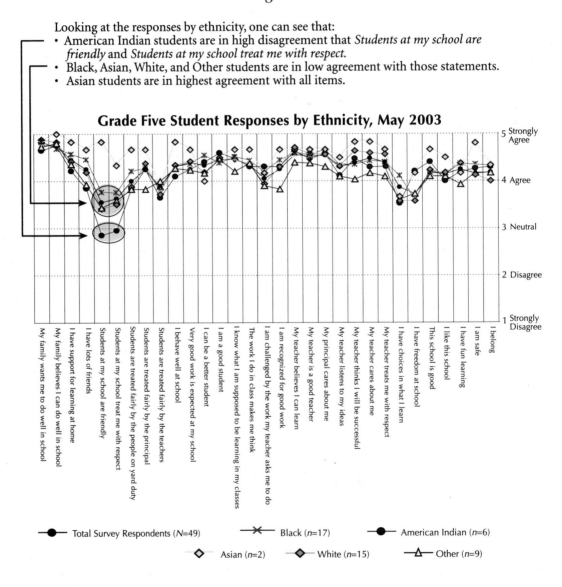

Grade Five Student Responses by Ethnicity, May 2003

Legend:
- Total Survey Respondents (*N*=49)
- Black (*n*=17)
- American Indian (*n*=6)
- Asian (*n*=2)
- White (*n*=15)
- Other (*n*=9)

Things to look for:

Issues that surface that need further investigation to understand the issues behind the responses. In this example, there are issues surfacing related to ethnicity and students treating each other with respect and in a friendly manner. Teachers might interview the fifth-grade class or disaggregate further to pinpoint an even more specific subgroup, such as American Indian males.

If the medium for communicating the results of the questionnaire is a school portfolio, you will want to describe questionnaire results in detail, i.e., you would display the whole graph and describe in detail what you found in that graph that you consider important. More often than not, the best way to present questionnaire results in their entirety is to use a line graph. With a line graph it is easy to get an overall picture of *agree* or *disagree* responses. It is easy to see where various subgroups fall, and you can get a great deal of information on one page.

Figure 9.9 provides an example narrative analysis for one questionnaire graph.

Figure 9.9

Interpreting Line Graphs—Sample Narrative Analysis

Students in grades three through five at Archer Elementary School responded to an *Education for the Future* questionnaire designed to measure how they feel about their learning environment in May 2003 (N=157). Students were asked to respond to items using a five-point scale: 1=strongly disagree; 2=disagree; 3=neutral; 4=agree; and, 5=strongly agree.

Average responses to each item on the questionnaire were graphed by the totals. The icons in the graph show the average responses to each item. The line joins the icons to help the reader know the distribution results. The line has no other meaning.

Students were most passionate in their responses, (scoring between 4.5 and 4.8 on the 5-point scale), to the following items, in descending order:

- ▼ My family wants me to do well in school
- ▼ My family believes I can do well in school

Total Student Responses, May 2003 (*N*=157)

5 Strongly Agree	4	3	2	Strongly 1 Disagree	
					I belong
					I am safe
					I have fun learning
					I like this school
					This school is good
					I have freedom at school
					I have choices in what I learn
					My teacher treats me with respect
					My teacher cares about me
					My teacher thinks I will be successful
					My teacher listens to my ideas
					My principal cares about me
					My teacher is a good teacher
					My teacher believes I can learn
					I am recognized for good work
					I am challenged by the work my teacher asks me to do
					The work I do in class makes me think
					I know what I am supposed to be learning in my classes
					I am a good student
					I can be a better student
					Very good work is expected at my school
					I behave well at school
					Students are treated fairly by the teachers
					Students are treated fairly by the principal
					Students are treated fairly by the people on yard duty
					Students at my school treat me with respect
					Students at my school are friendly
					I have lots of friends
					I have support for learning at home
					My family believes I can do well in school
					My family wants me to do well in school

▼ My teacher believes I can learn
▼ My principal cares about me
▼ My teacher is a good teacher

Students were in next strongest agreement (falling above 4.25 on the scale) with the following statements, in descending order:

▼ My teacher cares about me
▼ I know what I am supposed to be learning in my classes
▼ I am a good student
▼ I have support for learning at home
▼ My teacher treats me with respect
▼ Very good work is expected at my school
▼ My teacher thinks I will be successful
▼ The work I do in class makes me think
▼ I can be a better student
▼ I behave well at school
▼ My teacher listens to my ideas

The items which elicited a positive response that fell above 4.0 on the scale were, in descending order:

▼ I am recognized for good work
▼ Students are treated fairly by the principal
▼ I have lots of friends
▼ I have fun learning
▼ I belong
▼ This school is good
▼ I am safe
▼ I like this school
▼ I am challenged by the work my teacher asks me to do

Followed closely by, and continuing in agreement (above 3.5 on the scale), with the statements, in descending order:

▼ Students are treated fairly by the people on yard duty
▼ Students are treated fairly by teachers
▼ I have choices in what I learn
▼ I have freedom at school
▼ Students at my school treat me with respect
▼ Students at my school are friendly

If you are using a newsletter or a press release to communicate an important point that was revealed by the questionnaire, or you are discussing one particular item with the school board, you might want to show a portion of the graph and include a brief summary statement of what was learned. In that case, you can present that questionnaire item as a small bar graph included in the text, as shown in Figure 9.10.

Figure 9.10

Parents and the board may wish to be aware of the percentage of students at this school who do not feel their fellow students treat them with respect.

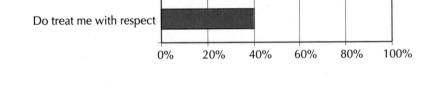

There are also times when you want to show questionnaire data over time in order to show positive change or to compare responses. Again, a line graph is an excellent choice to present data as a whole. Bar graphs can also be used to detail the number responding to each response option.

Figure 9.11 shows another way to communicate information. The line graph, sans the lines connecting icons, compares student responses to teacher predictions of student responses.

Figure 9.11

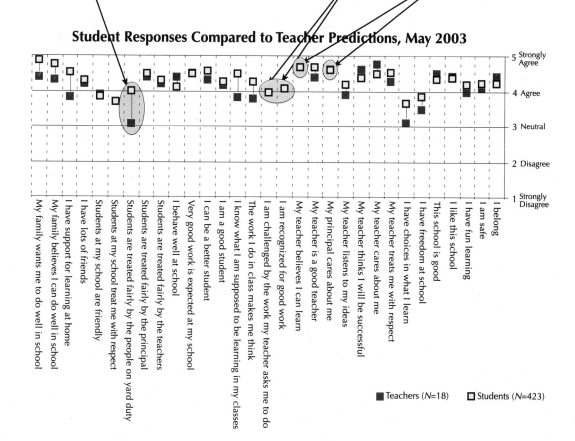

Look for greatest differences between groups. Real differences are those that have responses in two different response option categories (i.e., agree/disagree; agree/neutral).

Look for no differences between groups.

Student Responses Compared to Teacher Predictions, May 2003

5 Strongly Agree
4 Agree
3 Neutral
2 Disagree
1 Strongly Disagree

My family wants me to do well in school
My family believes I can do well in school
I have support for learning at home
I have lots of friends
Students at my school are friendly
Students at my school treat me with respect
Students are treated fairly by the people on yard duty
Students are treated fairly by the principal
Students are treated fairly by the teachers
I behave well at school
Very good work is expected at my school
I can be a better student
I am a good student
I know what I am supposed to be learning in my classes
The work I do in class makes me think
I am challenged by the work my teacher asks me to do
I am recognized for good work
My teacher believes I can learn
My teacher is a good teacher
My principal cares about me
My teacher listens to my ideas
My teacher thinks I will be successful
My teacher cares about me
My teacher treats me with respect
I have choices in what I learn
I have freedom at school
This school is good
I like this school
I have fun learning
I am safe
I belong

■ Teachers (*N*=18)   □ Students (*N*=423)

Things to look for:

- How well teachers predicted student responses, overall.
- Greatest differences.
- No differences.
- Relationships between (among) items with large (or no) differences.
- Further analyses required to understand the differences.

What we saw:

- Teachers were good predictors of what students said.
- More often than not, teachers' predictions were lower than students' actual responses.
- *Students are treated fairly by the people on yard duty* showed the greatest differences between student responses and teachers' predictions of what they thought the students would say.
- Teachers' predictions and student responses were essentially the same for twelve items.
- We would like to do this same comparison by grade level.

Figure 9.12 shows the distribution of responses in a bar graph form. The bar graphs tell you, by item, how the individuals making up the averages responded.

Figure 9.12

Bar graphs are a way to present numbers (or percentages) of individuals who chose each response option.

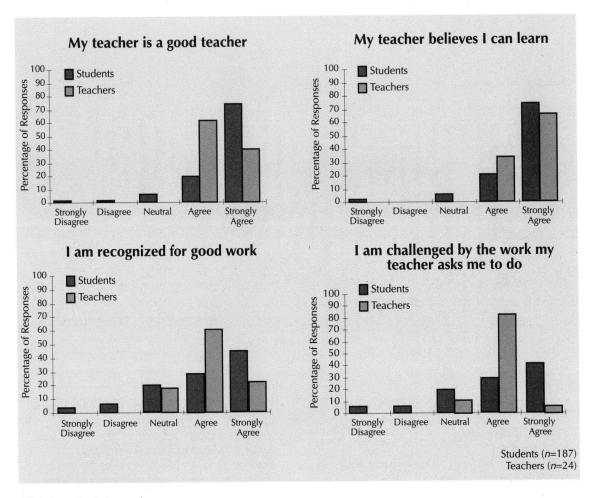

Things to look for:

- Where the averages came from—if an average came from a variety of responses, or if the majority of respondents marked the response option that equals the average.
- Items in which respondents are passionate (many responses *strongly agree* or *strongly disagree*).
- Discrepancies in responses by subgroups completing the questionnaire.
- The story told by comparing two subgroups or two years on the same graph, provided the items are consistent. (The comparison of two subgroups can show how "in tune" the predicting subgroup is to the predicted group. The comparison of two years can show how the attitudes changed or differences between two groups in different years.)

Interpreting Test Results

Many of us have been misquoted by reporters or have heard horror stories of misinterpretations related to reporting school measures, especially standardized test scores. Below are concepts to remember when communicating assessment results, especially to people without testing backgrounds.

▼ Make sure everyone writing about assessment results understands your purposes for conducting the assessments in the first place.

▼ If you use norms to describe your performance, define for the non-educator what the results mean, as well as other scores that have importance to you on a daily basis. Remember that 50% of the children in the country are below average, and 50% are above average on norm referenced tests. The norm is set at the 50th percentile, the point at which half of the scores are above and half of the scores are below.

▼ Do not compare scores across different measures or across different versions of the same test unless conversion tables are provided by the test publishers. There are some derived test scores (such as the normal curve equivalents) that can allow you to look at the same measures, which should be used over time. Percentile ranks, although they may look the same on different tests, are different because they have been specifically calculated for each test.

▼ Make sure that the reporting of standardized or norm-referenced tests—or any assessments of student learning—is reported within the context of many of the other variables that we know make a difference with standardized and norm referenced tests. These include demographics, perceptions, and processes used, among others.

▼ Use a simple graph to display the information you want everyone to see.

▼ Provide data results in context, with detail, so they can be interpreted appropriately. Try to stay away from statements that can be used as "sound bites" and put you at risk of being quoted out of context.

▼ Emphasize progress.

▼ Provide easy to understand information.

▼ Never lie about the results or attempt to keep them from the public. The result will be worse.

▼ Stay away from excuses and blame.

▼ Remember, there is no such thing as "off the record." Pull together a professional summary of what you want the public to know and stick to it.

▼ Never speculate.

Sometimes educators do all these things and still feel that the newspapers "do them in." We believe the best defense is a strong offense. Here are some ideas for the offense:

▼ As Americans, we have a right to publish almost anything we want in the editorial section of the local newspaper. Use that right to report what you want your community to know—if your education newspaper reporter does not do that for you.

▼ Hold a news conference.

▼ Create press releases that describe the context of the data and how you plan to use it.

▼ Publish annual reports in the format of a newspaper and distribute to the community. In some small town locations, your local newspaper will insert it with the newspaper. They will most likely distribute it free of charge.

▼ Keep your data analysis with your school improvement documentation, such as a school portfolio, that shows how you use data within the context of the school, and plan for improvement.

▼ Establish an action plan to discuss and make sure everyone understands the results and the actions to be taken based upon the results.

▼ Think through the questions you might get from the media or community and construct responses to—

  ◆ Why haven't all students been achieving?

  ◆ How many students are not achieving?

  ◆ What are you going to do about it?

  ◆ How do I know you are doing everything you can for my child?

  ◆ Why don't the neighboring school districts have the same problem?

  ◆ Do the neighboring school districts have the same problem?

- How are students taught to read?
- Can you tell me the names of the students not reading at grade level?
- Are these children all of one ethnicity or gender?
- How do you know your data are accurate?
- How do you know your standards are appropriate?

Chapter 6, *Student Learning,* contains a variety of examples of test results and student achievement data in graph form. More often than not, these data have been presented in bar graph form. You must first determine what you want to convey to the reader, then decide if a bar graph will be the best choice. Whether you choose to display those bars as horizontal or vertical depends upon the number of bars needed, and how much text you need to include to make the graph clear to the reader.

Chapter 6 covers the types of scores to use when communicating results in detail to an audience.

The most important thing to remember is clarity. Keep what you are saying clear. If you want to show the reader that a subgroup everyone was worried about last year is now doing better, include the information that shows that data. Don't bury the data in a graph that is more confusing than it needs to be.

Explaining Demographic Results

While educators feel that demographics are important factors in student achievement, they are often reluctant to talk about them to the public. They sometimes feel they will sound bigoted or biased, or that it is illegal to talk about student achievement by demographics in public. If the discussion is important enough to be taking place within the school walls, the discussion needs to surface outside of the school in order to make a difference.

There are ways to describe demographic data within the context of the other data analyses that will provide clarity and direction to both staff and community. Figure 9.13 is a classic example of a school population changing over time and reflects the growing diversity of many of our cities. Using a graph like this will help you show your Board of Education and the people who vote for school bonds that the numbers of children who come to our schools needing help in learning to speak and read English will continue to have an impact on staffing, budgeting, and student learning results. This type of graph will help your community predict how to meet the needs of these children and enhance the educational experience of all students at the school.

Here, again, the thing to remember is to communicate your point. If the growing Asian population is what you want to show your audience, make the Asian population bar stand out and make sure that the title clearly states what you want the audience to learn.

Figure 9.13

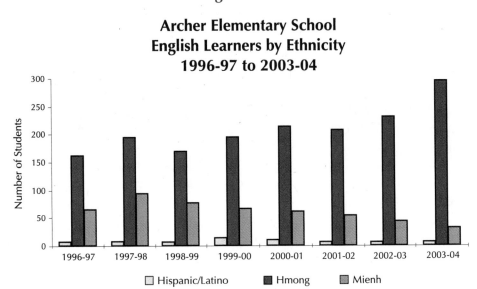

**Archer Elementary School
English Learners by Ethnicity
1996-97 to 2003-04**

Reporting the Big Picture

When we conduct comprehensive data analysis for continuous school improvement, we need to communicate the results as widely as possible, since we want everyone to understand the results. The ideal report is two-to-four pages long, or about 500 words, with high quality graphics that convey the story.

A summary of steps in presenting your school's data analysis report follows:

❶ Determine the message you want to convey about your data analysis results.

❷ Present the data as simply and clearly as possible to convey the message:

  ◆ Develop graphs with clear titles, legends, and numbers to convey the message.

  ◆ Only compare your data to the nation, state, or other schools and districts when appropriate.

  ◆ Never display or provide data that will allow individuals to be identified.

❸ Write a narrative interpretation of the graphs to prevent misinterpretations.

❹ State how parents and the community have helped and can continue to help.

❺ Always state what your school is doing, or plans to do, with the results.

Figure 9.14 shows a sample profile about Archer Elementary School, using the data gathered thus far, that everyone in the community can understand. (The press release shown earlier in this chapter in Figure 9.1 is another way to summarize the data.)

Figure 9.14

ARCHER ELEMENTARY SCHOOL PROFILE

Archer Elementary School
Caroline Brown, Principal

Park School District, Park City, USA
Profile of the 2003-04 School Year

INTRODUCTION

This school profile has been developed to provide our parents and community with information about our school, our successes, and the areas in which we have plans to improve.

Our focus is, and will be, to get all students proficient in all subject areas by 2013-14, as required by the *No Child Left Behind* (NCLB) legislation. This profile focuses on these efforts and offers suggestions about how you can assist. A review of the context of our school appears first.

We hope you enjoy this profile and find it to be a useful document. We would appreciate your comments and suggestions for improving both this report and our school.

Sincerely,
Caroline Brown, Principal
cbrown@parkcity.k12.us

MISSION

Our mission is to provide all students with a positive, secure, and supportive learning environment in which they can acquire the skills and attitudes that foster an enjoyment of learning; a respect for themselves and others; and the physical, emotional, and social competencies necessary to become responsible and productive citizens of the twenty-first century.

THE STUDENTS

Archer Elementary School, one of 18 elementary schools in Park School District, currently serves 472 students. Our population has decreased over the past five years, from around 581 in 1998-99 to the 472 students we have today. The graph below shows how the ethnic composition has changed during this time.

As you can see, we have fewer White students, more Black students, and approximately the same number of Hispanic/Latino, Asian, and American Indian students.

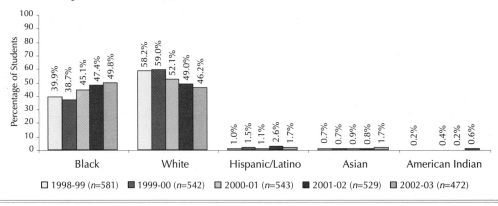

Page 1 of 4 pages

Figure 9.14 *(Continued)*

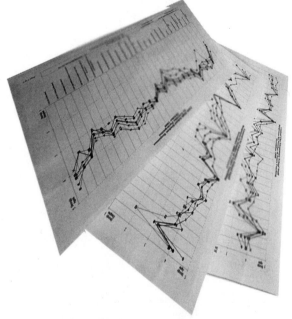

ARCHER ELEMENTARY SCHOOL PROFILE

Archer Elementary School   **Park School District, Park City, USA**
Caroline Brown, Principal   **Profile of the 2003-04 School Year**

THE STAFF AND CLASS SIZE

Twenty-six classroom teachers currently work at Archer. The average class size is 18 students—about what it has been for the past five years.

QUESTIONNAIRE ANALYSIS

To get a better understanding of the learning environment at Archer Elementary School and to measure change, staff administered student, staff, and parent questionnaires three years in a row. The purpose for administering the questionnaires was to understand from each constituency how they perceive the learning environment at Archer and to help staff learn how to improve everything they do.

Overall, the students, staff, and parents responded very positively to most of the items on the questionnaire. Our staff is happy with the students and their learning and appear to have gotten into teaching for the right reasons. They love to teach! The students are happy with their teachers and their learning, and were passionate about their families wanting them to do well in school. The parent responses echoed the same degree of satisfaction.

We want to continue to do better in all areas addressed by the questionnaire. We ask for your help with this. The students often commented in the open-ended responses about other students needing to be nicer and to behave better. The parent responses indicate parent concern for discipline and supervision. To this end, the staff have implemented a *Behavior Modification Program* as a solution to our school's biggest issue.

We need your involvement. Please read about this program in the brochure sent home with your child (also on our website: *http://parkcity.org*), and help us fully implement the concepts in the classroom and at home. We also encourage you to come to the school as often as you can. Read to your students, help them with their math. Show them, by your presence, that school is important.

Page 2 of 4 pages

Figure 9.14 *(Continued)*

ARCHER ELEMENTARY SCHOOL PROFILE

Archer Elementary School
Caroline Brown, Principal

Park School District, Park City, USA
Profile of the 2003-04 School Year

STUDENT ACHIEVEMENT RESULTS

Archer Elementary School and Park School District use the State Assessment Program (SAP) criterion-referenced test as our main basis for assessing student performance. Most of the test is given in grades three, four, eight, and ten. The SAP test results in the graphs below show the percentages of our students scoring at five reported levels of achievement—*Step 1, Progressing, Nearing Proficient, Proficient,* and *Advanced*—the way the data are reported to us, and compared to other schools of similar backgrounds. While the total numbers of students taking the test varied for the three years shown, the majority of Archer students fell into the *Nearing Proficient* and *Progressing* categories each year. Third-grade Science, 2001-02, was the exception. One can also see that in all subtests, except Science, the percentages of Archer students in the *Proficient* and *Advanced* categories, the two categories indicating proficiency, were lower than other schools with similar backgrounds:

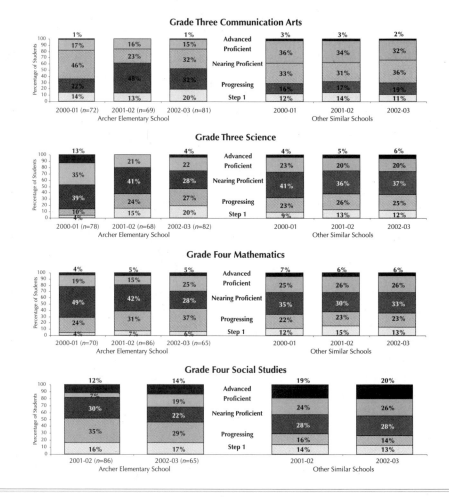

Page 3 of 4 pages

216

Figure 9.14 *(Continued)*

ARCHER ELEMENTARY SCHOOL PROFILE

Archer Elementary School
Caroline Brown, Principal

Park School District, Park City, USA
Profile of the 2003-04 School Year

2003-04 GOALS FOR IMPROVEMENT

Staff will continue to study current and past results to understand what we can do to ensure that all students meet or exceed the district standards. Staff know that if they want to change the results they have been getting, they must study and change the processes that produced the results. Our experienced teachers who are getting positive results will share teaching strategies with other teachers and help all teachers implement a continuum of learning that makes sense for *all* students in our school. Staff also recognize they need to continue to strengthen our partnership with parents.

WHAT PARENTS CAN DO TO HELP

We continue to encourage parents to:

- Read, in English, to or with your children—regardless of age—at least 15 minutes each night. Children love to read with their parents. Make reading an enjoyable experience—something to look forward to. Teachers have sent home a list of books in our library that are at an appropriate level for your child.
- Point out how math is used in everyday life (e.g., in recipes, with money, the gallons of gasoline that go into your car, distances).
- Engage your child in discussion as often as you can. Ask him or her what they did at school. Encourage your child to use new words as much as possible.
- Speak in English at home. Early English language fluency will make a difference in each student's achievement results in early grades, which will make all other learning easier.
- Let teachers know when there are things you feel are needed to assist your child's learning. Together we can make the difference.
- Make sure your child does not miss school, unless she or he is ill. It is very hard for your child to catch up with the others, and it is difficult for the class to move ahead together when children are absent.
- Please make sure there is a quiet, well-lit space, and a consistent time for your child to do homework. Homework is assigned to help with the daily concepts. When all students in a class have completed their homework, teachers can, more easily, move all students to that next level of achievement.
- Parents are invited and welcome to attend all professional development days at the school. Come learn along with us.
- Come volunteer to help in your child's classroom. This will give you an opportunity to see first-hand what teachers are trying to accomplish and for you to help make a difference in the learning of many children. Our teachers have a sign-up sheet posted next to their doors. We would love to have you with us.
- Stop by and read our School Portfolio. It describes the Archer vision, goals, and achievements. All data referred to in this profile are located in the portfolio.
- Attend our English classes for parents. The classes are free of charge and child care is provided.
- Look for announcements. We will soon be offering parenting and technology classes for parents.

Thank you for your continuing support.

Page 4 of 4 pages

Study Questions for Communicating the Results

The intent of the questions below is to help your school staff think through whom you want to inform of data analysis results, what messages you want to give, how the messages will get to them, and who will be responsible for getting the message out. An example appears in the first row for guidance.

Whom do you want to inform about your results?	What do you want them to know?	How will you get the message to them?	Who will be responsible for getting the message out?
Parents	▼ *How to help improve student reading skills* ▼ *Give some specific strategies*	▼ *Letter from each teacher sent home with students* ▼ *School profile* ▼ *Newspaper article*	▼ *Classroom teachers* ▼ *Principal* ▼ *District PIO (public information officer) to notify newspapers of what teachers are doing*

Summary

Gathering data and putting together comprehensive data analysis reports are difficult tasks for schools. Many schools have difficulty communicating data analysis results to the public largely because they do not have all of the pieces in one report. Once the data analyses are complete, a short, but comprehensive report can be very informative and useful for all stakeholders. This communication process must be planned and carefully written.

CONCLUSIONS AND RECOMMENDATIONS:
The Need for a Data Warehouse

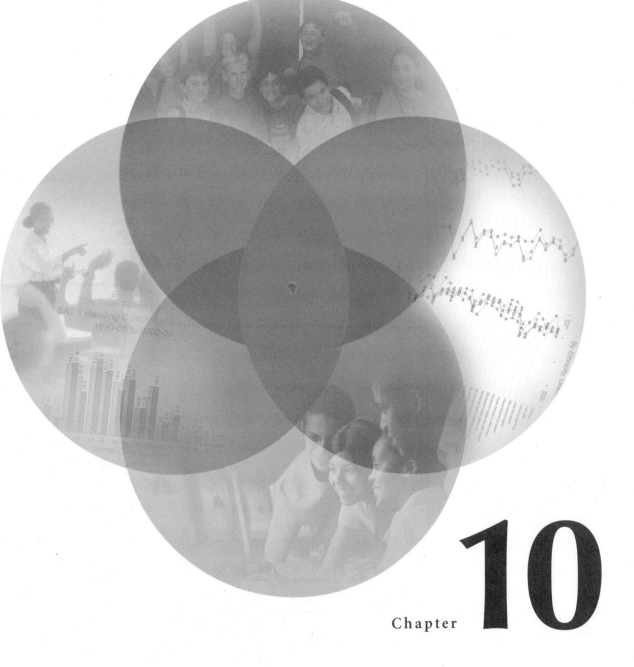

Chapter **10**

It is no longer an option for districts not to have databases and data analysis tools, or data warehouses, to help teachers and administratores use the data to understand what needs to change to get different results.

Throughout this book, the discussion has focused on why data are important, what data to collect and analyze, the importance of intersecting the data, and how to communicate the results. These activities are fairly straightforward, logical, and easy to perform – as long as you have access to the data and a tool for the data analysis work.

Many of the barriers mentioned in Chapter 1 which keep schools from doing this work are related to the mechanics behind the data collection and analysis—specifically, not having a useful database and/or data analysis tools. *It is no longer an option for districts not to have databases and data analysis tools, or data warehouses, to help teachers and administrators use the data to understand what needs to change to get different results.* Complex information needs to be reported, and districts themselves need to have the required information—and more—to make informed decisions for all students. Even though much of the required information is reported by subgroups, the ability to retrieve that data is dependent upon the data being linked to each individual student. A database, or preferably a data warehouse, is required.

This chapter reviews what a database or data warehouse is, how to select a data warehouse at the district level, recommendations for setting one up, and how to plan for a warehouse. Also included are a data warehouse needs analysis form and a discussion of who does the data analysis work.

Databases and Data Warehouses

A database is a system of organized and retrievable information that is easily accessible—preferably electronically. Telephone books, dictionaries, and encyclopedias are common databases that are organized alphabetically to make names, addresses, words, and subjects easy to find. Data warehouses are designed to allow the manipulation, updating, and control of multiple databases that are connected to one another via individual student identification numbers. Data warehouses allow school districts to analyze data across all four categories of data described throughout this book. Because we want to disaggregate and intersect the data in many ways, we need to be cautious about linking the data to individual students, as shown in Figure 10.1

Most schools maintain basic student information databases that house student demographic information, such as name, age, gender, ethnicity/race, language fluency, home language, special education disability, free/reduced lunch status, attendance, discipline records,

Figure 10.1

Multiple Measures / Data Elements

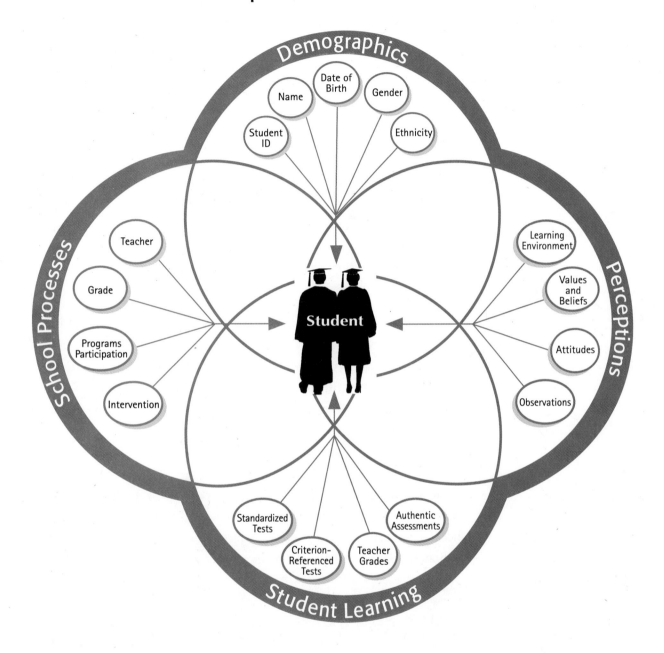

suspensions, expulsions, health, program participation, grades, courses, extra-curricular activities, home living situation, mobility (where students come from), retention, preschool attendance, and, sometimes, diagnostic assessments. These student information systems, more often than not, house the data, leaving the accessibility of the data somewhat limited. Many schools have never really used the information in these databases, because the need has never been there or the tools that come with the student information systems are cumbersome.

Some districts have more contemporary systems in place and are able to respond quickly and easily to requests for data at the school and individual student levels. More often, however, districts use different software systems, or offices in the same district, to maintain data on separate, sometimes incompatible, systems making the use of data to analyze student needs very difficult. For these districts, responding to school requests for data is often time-consuming and involves substantial programmer time.

Done well, data analysis is a massive activity requiring the technical support of knowledgeable people and a database or data warehouse. Districts are just now coming on board with acquiring data warehouses that will enable the storage of a large number of data elements and the analysis of data quickly, easily, accurately, and meaningfully.

Selecting a Data Warehouse

Districts must invest in a data warehouse to allow central office and school personnel to analyze and use the data that will help them and teachers close the achievement gap. Small districts can form consortiums and share the use of a data warehouse in order to bring down the costs per pupil.

Many vendors have confused district personnel about the issue of data warehouses—saying their products can do all that a district wants it to do.

If your school district does not have such a tool right now, there are at least eleven things you need to think about when acquiring a data warehouse, not necessarily in this order:

1. *Accessibility at different levels.* Most often, districts prefer all data stored at the district level, with accessibility at the school and classroom levels. You must decide how you will maintain security and whom you want to access the information. Also, having the data accessible at all levels does not mean that teachers and school administrators should be expected to perform all the analyses.

Most successful districts determine the most important analyses and provide them in report form to the schools and teachers, allowing school personnel the time to use the data and to dig deeper into the data. If teachers are trained to use the data warehouse and given time to use it, they will dig deeper into the data and get answers to questions they have never before been able to receive.

2. *Ability to build graphs automatically.* You want to be able to look over the data tables to check for accuracy; however, you want the data analysis tool to build graphs for you as well. If you want staffs to review the data, it is wise to put the data in picture form so everyone can see the resulting information in the same way.

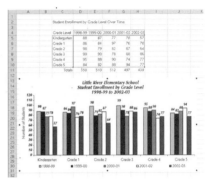

3. *Disaggregation and digging deeper on the fly.* When you perform an analysis that is starting to show interesting information or pose significant questions, you want to be able to analyze quickly and easily at the next deeper levels to understand how the results were obtained. You will also want to see if the results hold true for all subgroups.

4. *Point and click or drop and drag technology that is intuitive.* We want teachers and administrators to be able to use the database without having to refer to a manual for every analysis. The technology is available now to make complex data analysis work intuitive and easy. Related to this—I often hear people say they want a web-based or internet-based warehouse. I recommend rethinking this. Perhaps what these people are referring to are browser-based products that will allow access through a network. Your warehouse does not have to be on the Internet. In fact, think of the security issues that have to be considered. Also, when you go to browser-based or internet/web-based systems, and away from client-based software, networked to your intranet, you could lose the functionality you really want from a data analysis tool.

5. *The ability to create standard reports with a click of a button.* Some reports have to be created every year, such as *School Accountability Report Cards* or *Title 1* reports. If the same information is required each year, the product should allow you the flexibility to merely push a button the next year to recreate any report you want without spending a lot of time on it. When districts determine the information most important for schools to use, they should be able to create standard reports that can be

"batched" for all the schools. In other words, they could push a couple of buttons to create the same report for all the schools without creating each school report individually. Do not let vendors tell you that they have all the reporting capability thought out for you. You need the flexibility to create your own reports and to standardize and augment them. It is nice that they have most reports considered; however, they do not know what will appear as an issue for you in the future—nor do you.

6. *The ability to follow cohorts—the same groups of students—as they progress through their educational careers.* This is a complex analysis for data analysis tools. Most venders will tell you they can do this. You must learn to say these words when you speak with vendors—*Show Me!* By *cohorts,* we mean following the same groups of students over time—matched and unmatched.

7. *Longitudinal analyses.* This might sound like a "no brainer," but there are products on the market that can only perform analyses on data one year at a time. This is probably a good indication that you are dealing with flat database architecture and not a true complex data warehouse. Again, ask the vendors to show you a longitudinal analysis.

8. *Follow a student, or group of students, backwards.* In other words, if you want to understand how to predict and prevent some occurrences, such as high school drop-outs, you should be able to follow the dropouts from the past backward into your warehouse (as long as you have the data in the warehouse, regardless of the school they attended) to understand the students' common characteristics. That way you can also look for current students with those characteristics and do something different to prevent dropouts from occurring.

9. *You must like the people selling the product.* If you do not trust or like the people who sell the data warehouse, you probably will not like the engineering and customer service end of the company either. Companies hire people to carry out their mission and philosophy. Creating a data warehouse is a long-term, intensive, hands-on proposition. If the sales people promise to send you information and they never get back to you, you will probably feel as left alone when it comes to creating your warehouse. Additionally, data warehousing companies that really want your business will come to *you*—just ask. If they will not come to you, do not buy their product! There are companies that want to come to you to see your systems and to know what you need to make their product a success in your location. Now certainly a company can do some demonstrating using web tools; but at some point, the company should be willing to come to your location to meet you and to answer your specific questions. Companies that will not come to you because of your location should not have your business.

10. *True integration of disparate systems.* A true data warehouse can combine your student information system with your state testing data, on-going assessments, professional development information, and any other data you want included. A data warehouse is not a tool that takes your state testing data, disaggregates it by the demographics marked on the test, and gives you reports, as some vendors might lead you to believe.

11. *Talk with other school districts that purchased the product you are considering.* It would be great if you can find districts that are in varying stages of using the product. However, listen carefully to some of their complaints about the product. It might not be the product; it might be the district's own data. Many school districts state unhappiness with their data warehouses because they think it should be easier to set up than it is. They are also often hoping for more useable data. A data warehouse requires complex engineering—it is not a plug and play software program that will get you up and running in the same day. The next section will deal with these issues.

Be careful not to buy a data warehouse to solve only this year's problems. These are expensive systems that should be able to cross disparate data analysis systems to answer just about any data question you have in your schools or districts. You cannot, and should not, go through this buying process every year. Buy for the long haul.

Planning for a Data Warehouse for Your Needs

Designing a data warehouse, or thinking through all the issues in order to understand which database solution to commit to, is a time-consuming task, if done well, albeit very worthwhile. Beginning with the end in mind, the following procedure should be considered:

▼ define the scope of the project

▼ identify the needs of the potential users of the data warehouse

▼ articulate requirements of people who will be creating and maintaining the database

▼ determine hardware, financial, and human resource constraints that might affect the database design

The figures that follow (Figures 10.2 through 10.5) represent the steps required in thinking through a data warehouse solution for a district/school. The figures, followed by explanations, are organized by these topics found in the database needs analysis form in Figure 10.5:

▼ Determine the mission, goals, objective, uses, and users of the database

▼ Determine what data exist now (in a usable format)

▼ Determine the desired data

▼ Determine who is going to do the work

▼ Determine the levels of access, who will have access at each level, and how access will be obtained

Determine the Mission, Goals, Objectives, Uses, and Users of the Data Warehouse

Figure 10.2 shows the first steps in designing a database. These steps include determining the mission, getting buy-in, and creating a database system that serves many school and district needs and uses.

The mission is as important to the design, implementation, and maintenance of a data warehouse solution as it is for an organization. A mission provides a focus for a project and keeps everyone grounded. A mission needs to be identified by the committee established to design the data warehouse and revisited on an ongoing basis as the data warehouse is created. The mission will then need to be revisited when all members of the committee have met and uses and users of the data warehouse have been determined. Clear, quantifiable goals and objectives will help the mission become achievable. Goals and objectives will need to be revisited as uses are determined.

Identify who should be on the committee to assist with the design of the data warehouse. As district or school personnel think about selecting a data warehousing system for classroom, school, and district improvement, a committee has to be established that is comprised of people with diverse backgrounds and uses for data, including classroom teachers, database designers and programmers, school and district administrators, current data specialists for the district, clerical assistants for data entry, district, county, and/or regional education representatives, school board members, the general public, and other data users. It is important that people in all parts of the organization know that this selection work is going on, so anyone with special interests, abilities, or knowledge of existing or desired

Figure 10.2

**Determine the Mission, Goals, and Objectives,
Uses, and Users of the Data Warehouse**

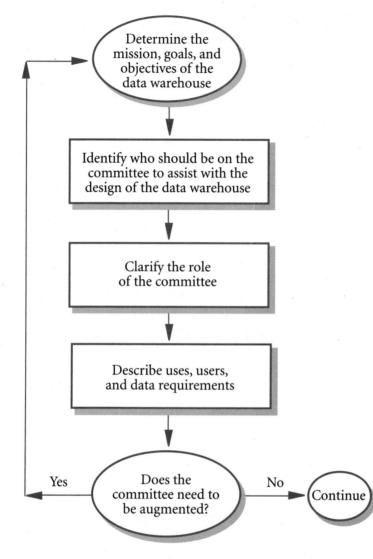

data can join the committee or provide input into the process. If all appropriate representatives cannot meet, a means of handling collaborative discussions has to be available. To not be all-inclusive, the district runs the risk of seemingly top-down decision-making, or worse, of not considering all district needs, uses, and purposes up front. The district also runs the risk of making critical errors because the perceptions and needs of all users were not taken into consideration. The needs of all those currently and potentially involved will be important to the future acceptance and success of the data warehouse project.

Clarify the role of the committee, including timelines. Committee members must clearly understand their common mission, role, and timeline for completing this design work. It is essential to document the role of the committee and each member's responsibility, so readers and potential users will understand the context of the final report. The following questions should be considered: *Is the committee's role to recommend to another group or to make an independent decision to purchase and implement a data warehouse system? When will the work be done?*

Describe purposes, uses, users, and data requirements. List the purposes for creating and using the data warehouse. Start with "real" needs. This list will grow as all that is possible is realized; then priorities will have to be assigned. For example: A purpose for a school district data warehouse is to provide the school district with information that will help administrators know how each school, grade level, and content area is performing with respect to school district standards, so that additional support may be provided where needed. Other purposes of this same data warehouse could be for schools in the district to access information about student achievement to ensure that all students are learning regardless of race, ethnicity, gender, language fluency, and economic background; and to provide teachers with historical student achievement data on all their students prior to the beginning of a new school year.

What are the desired uses of the data warehouse? Who must have access to the database in order to do their jobs? Who should have access to information to improve the way they are doing their jobs? How will security be maintained with multiple users? Will there be users with minimal software skills and experience? Will data warehouse managers be needed? If so, what will be their roles? How will potential users access the data warehouse (e.g., computer in classroom, access from home, via the Internet from any computer at any time).

Are there specific data elements required that are related to the desired uses? For example, if one use is to provide analyses to the State Department of Education for categorical programs, are there necessary data to identify, gather, and analyze? Another example would be a grade three teacher querying the data warehouse to examine his students' achievement scores on various measures over the past three years. These important considerations will probably uncover new information, or provide additional people to add to the data warehouse design committee.

Determine What Data Exists Now

Figure 10.3 shows steps in chronicling what data exists in the district and schools, and clarifying what usable data are already available.

Figure 10.3

Determine What Data Exist Now

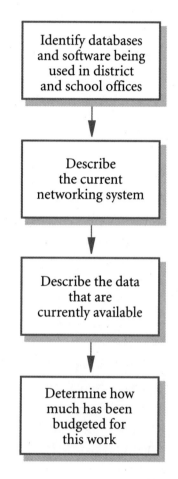

Identify the databases and software that are being used in the district and school offices. To understand how existing data can be imported into a data warehouse, currently used database programs and their capabilities must be analyzed. Find out what is being used, where, and for what purposes. This information will identify what is available and will clarify the level of compatibility between district, school office, and classroom software and hardware. We have seen districts purchase database programs or data warehouses that they expect schools to access, only to find that the schools do not have the hardware or software to connect to the main system. This analysis will also identify whether there is software being used that merely needs to be augmented, or hardware that needs updating. A district must do whatever is reasonably possible to ensure that schools can access and use the district data warehouse software. If the appropriate software and hardware are not available at the school level, their purchase must be included in the data warehouse budget or some other budget.

Describe the current networking system. A comprehensive data warehouse solution will require the use of your district and school network. Either your networking will be adequate or your district will need a new networking system. This is a major budgetary consideration, and a key issue in data access, design, and implementation.

Describe the data that are currently available. Consider the data that are currently available, their sources, and compatibility with different types of hardware and software. What does the district have and in what form? What data do the schools routinely gather? What does your county/regional office have? What can you get from the state database system? What can you get digitally from commercial test vendors or online data agencies? What do the schools share? You may find a wealth of data available that, for some reason or another, was unknown to all potential users. With existing data, a comprehensive data warehouse could be formed. It is important to include what some data warehouse engineers call a "data archaeologist" to make sure that existing data are cleaned up and made meaningful and usable. Some superintendents want to have data in the data warehouse for everything in the district. This is not always possible, cost-effective, or needed. We need to make sure that the data that are collected and stored for analysis are actually useful for attaining the school and district goals.

Determine how much has been budgeted for this work. How much is available for data warehouse development and maintenance, and how much is needed to do it right? If new hardware, software, and networking are required for the schools, make sure these are included in the budget. Database experts tell us that the costs for supporting multiple platforms is truly cost prohibitive for most schools. The cost of supporting two platforms is almost three times the cost of one $[1.75(x) + x]$. The cost of supporting three becomes exponential $x2$. It is extremely important to budget for all of the planning, design, implementation, training, maintenance work and time, and "hidden" costs that will appear.

Determine Desired Data

This piece of the database design requires reflective work about steps already covered:

▼ *What data are available and how does the district/school want to use the data?*

▼ *What other data are needed?*

Describe the data you want to include in the data warehouse. Occasionally, when a data warehouse system does not deliver the information needed by districts and schools, the fault may not be with the system. It might be an indication that additional data are needed rather than a new software program. However, it must also be a consideration that some data may not be appropriate for some data warehouse programs. For instance, districts and schools might earmark  questionnaire data as additional data desired. Unfortunately, if a questionnaire was not established with a data warehouse in mind, i.e., if the necessary identification was not included on the questionnaire initially, these data will not be linkable to all other records and, therefore, not appropriate for the type of database being used. Questionnaire data most often need to be gathered anonymously so respondents can feel that they can give candid responses. (Refer to the *Education for the Future Initiative* website, http://eff.csuchico.edu, for information about questionnaire database solutions.)

List all information—demographic, student achievement scores, teacher information, program participation, and so on, as discussed in the previous chapters—that needs to be included as part of the data.

Determine Who is Going To Do the Work

Figure 10.4 shows the different roles and responsibilities needed to get the data warehouse selected through it's maintenance. The discussion follows.

Determine who is going to perform the work required in selecting, implementing, and maintaining a data warehouse that will meet its mission. This will be a major budget issue.

Select the data warehouse design team. The design of a comprehensive data warehouse is an important task and one that requires database expertise. Determine a project manager and involve all the individual(s) who will be responsible for the design and implementation of this data warehouse system as early in the process as possible. It is highly recommended to have a knowledgeable data warehouse designer and systems programmer, with no commitments to a specific software product, as part of the design committee.

The data warehouse project manager should be knowledgeable about relational databases. She/he should know how to program desired reports and queries and how to work with a variety of school-based data. Data warehouse project managers should have a degree in computer science, coursework in statistics, and work experience in education. It is important that the project manager be able to listen to and understand users' needs and desired uses of data, and to be able to suggest ways to gather the appropriate data. Chances are you will need a systems programmer who will focus on the operating system and the hardware. Your situation may require an additional network person as well. Data will need some structural work to achieve a comprehensive flow between new and old data and new and old software. A data analyst, also called a data archaeologist, will need to be hired to clean up the data, verify the accuracy and consistency, and to make the data compatible and relatable. Cleansing the data includes: eyeballing the data for duplications and inconsistencies, understanding the data elements to know when an inappropriate number is a keyboard entry problem or some other error, and knowing how to "fix" it.

Identify who will input the data. Data sources will dictate who will import or input the data into the data warehouse and how the task will be accomplished. For example, if teachers and school administrators desire classroom specific information for use, the committee will need to recommend who will perform the data entry, and how it will be performed. Consistency, accuracy, security, and confidentiality are important considerations. This question requires reflecting on the

Figure 10.4

Determine Who is Going to do the Work

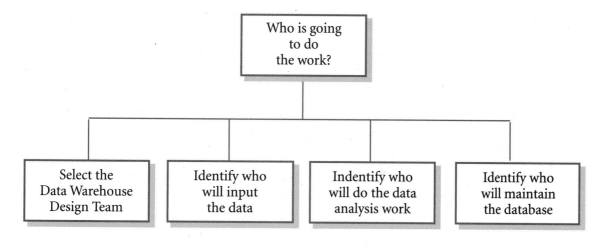

purposes and uses of the data warehouse, to the desired data, and the way they will be retrieved. If it is determined that classroom data will be input routinely, the data warehouse system will have to have a system and procedures for gathering and importing data into the system.

Identify who will produce the standard reports. Who will be responsible for producing standard reports? What do you want standard reports to look like? What about the production of additional reports? Some reports will depend on the human resources available at the district and school levels, with budget implications. A data distribution strategy is necessary.

Querying, the art of questioning the data warehouse to produce reports, was once the hardest part of the whole database equation. Now, data warehouse products have easy to use data analysis tools. Ad hoc querying without programming is available. Anyone setting up queries must intimately know what is in the data warehouse.

Identify who will maintain the data warehouse. Just like hardware and software, someone needs to be in charge of the maintenance and security of the data warehouse system. This individual needs to have database expertise and familiarity with the district's data, the schools' needs, and overall reporting needs. It is possible that routine maintenance may take place during off-school periods with data warehouse experts, or a data warehouse specialist may be employed full-time to continuously oversee and maintain the system.

Determine the Levels of Access, Who Will Have Access at Each Level, and How Access Will be Obtained

Once the data to include in the data warehouse and the standard reports have been determined, a plan of action for communicating information learned from the data will need to be established. Determine who will need the data warehouse information, and how they can get it. This is of major importance to the final selection of the data warehouse solution. Security is also a major consideration with access. The mission will drive this piece.

Needs Analysis Form

Figure 10.5 is a *Data Warehouse Needs Analysis* that can help school districts think through the uses, purposes, and requirements of a data warehouse so they can choose an appropriate data warehouse solution. Shown in what appears to be a linear process, the thinking through of data warehouse needs is really a cyclical process. The cyclical aspect comes into play when many issues become clearer in the ensuing steps and must be revisited more than once. Figure 10.5 is offered as a support in thinking through the issues.

Issues and Recommendations: Setting Up the Data Warehouse

As mentioned earlier in the chapter, many school districts are unhappy after they purchase their data warehouse because they think it should be easier than it is to set up. Sometimes, they are not able to get the information they want out of their warehouse in the format they want, and sometimes they are shocked by how little data they have in their warehouse.

Once you commit to buying a data warehouse, the hard work begins, unless you have started getting ready for it far in advance. Below are some of the issues that surface when school districts purchase their first data warehouse.

Issue #1: Most school districts are shocked by how long it takes to put a data warehouse together. Yes, the importing of your disparate data files will take time because of the sheer volume of the data and the complexity of the system. It could take 20 engineering hours—if it is done only once. Parts of most data warehouses end up being reinstalled more than once because of needed corrections. Additionally, testing the warehouse could take a couple of weeks. However, that is not what takes the longest time.

Figure 10.5

Data Warehouse Needs Analysis	
1. Determine the mission, goals, and objectives of the data warehouse.	
2. Identify who should be on the committee to assist with the design of the database.	
3. Clarify the role of the committee, including the timelines.	
4. Determine purposes, uses, users, and data requirements.	
5. Identify the databases and software that are being used in the district and school.	
6. Describe the current networking system.	
7. Describe what current software should do that is not now being done through current practices.	
8. Describe the data that are currently available.	
9. Determine how much has been budgeted for this work.	
10. Describe the data you want to include in the data warehouse.	
11. Select the data warehouse design team.	
12. Identify who will input the data.	
13. Identify who will produce the standard reports.	
14. Identify who will maintain the data warehouse.	
15. Determine the levels of access, who will have access at each level, and how access will be obtained.	

If you have not had to *clean* your data before, believe me, it is dirty! By dirty, we mean that there might not be consistent and unique identification numbers for students, and that student names might have been entered into each data file in different fashions, which could count the same student as multiple students (e.g., Victoria L. Bernhardt, Victoria Bernhardt, Vickie Bernhardt, Vickie L. Bernhardt, V. L. Bernhardt, V. Bernhardt could show up as six different students). These issues make the "cleaning up" of the data labor intensive and time consuming. If you are in a large school district, expect it to take a year to clean up your data—sometimes longer. There are programs that data warehousing companies can run to help you with the cleansing of your data; but, by and large, it comes down to someone checking the records in every file.

Issue #2: Many districts are disappointed at not being able to get the information they want out of their warehouse, in the format they want. This is usually a result of missing data. Sometimes districts think they sent to the warehousing company lots of good clean data in a usable format when, in reality, the data were incomplete and in hard-to-use formats. Corrupted backups and missing pieces of data are usually the culprits. Districts are also often disappointed to find that their student information systems may not permit the easy export of data, or that they made poor choices years ago in deciding how their data were to be organized.

Issue #3: Some districts are disappointed and shocked to learn they have been using a student information system for years that deletes the previous year's data when a new year is entered. There is nothing the data warehousing company can do for you on this one. Just make sure the necessary adjustments are made so it no longer happens this way.

Issue # 4: It is often hard to get data from some district departments— especially Human Resources. For many and varied reasons, some departments will want to hold on to their data. What can I say, but leadership cannot and should not allow this to happen.

Your district can cut the time it could take to put together a data warehouse, while getting you the data you want in useable form. Below are recommendations for getting started, and for working with a data warehouse company.

Recommendation # 1: Check now to see that you have one unique identification number for each student—regardless of how many times she/he enters or leaves the district. **Never recycle a student identification number. This is the only way to accurately match data over time. A lot of districts do not have a unified student information system, so a student's identification number will change when they go from school to school. In some cases a district will assign a student a new identification number when she/he withdraws and comes back; or even when she/he changes years. If you must assign new identification numbers, keep your old numbers in a field for reference.**

Recommendation # 2: Start cleansing your data now, and set procedures, districtwide, for how data will be entered into each data file. **Data warehousing companies have told me they have never experienced a school district submitting data that were 100% clean. Get all departments on board with the warehouse and the cleansing of data. Set districtwide processes and procedures for entering data, and monitor their use.**

Recommendation # 3: Review all the data you would like to have in your data warehouse—even list the numbers that should appear. This will serve three important functions:

1. It will help you see what you have, what you don't have, and how accurate your data systems are.

2. It is extremely helpful to any data warehousing company with which you would contract. They will see what you want, and how the data ought to appear. It will help them spot errors much more quickly that they could correct without involving you and your time.

3. It will help you correctly identify all the fields you will want included—now and/or for the future.

Recommendation #4: Do not expect your first data warehouse to be perfect. **The first warehouse build is often best at pointing out problems. A good data warehousing company will work with you on correcting the problems, and give you multiple builds.**

Recommendation #5: Know your student information system. Make sure you know what data are in it, where it is kept, and how to get the data out. When buying a Student Information System, make sure it has easy export and import functionality. Also, make sure a new year's data will not overwrite historical data. You will never be able to retrieve these data.

Recommendation #6: Before exporting your data, talk with the data warehousing company about what format would be the best and what is needed in the data. This relates back to the earlier issue of making sure you contract with a company that wants to work with you.

Recommendation #7: Assign a champion to work with the data warehousing company and to "own" the district data and data issues. Districts that have a data leader, who can get the company what it needs in the format it needs to be in, decrease the overall time it takes to pull a data warehouse together.

Recommendation #8: Follow, methodically, all directions and instructions given to you by the data warehousing company. A data warehouse is a big investment, requiring much of your time and that of busy engineers. Everyone involved should work to be sure that time is well spent.

Recommendation #9: When sending data to the data warehousing company, identify and document the information being sent. It is better to document too much rather than too little. Data warehousing companies tell me all the time that districts send data files without column headers. In other words, the engineers have no idea what they are working with. Worse yet, these same districts do not return the engineer's calls for weeks.

Recommendation #10: Talk with the engineers who are loading your data to make sure you are going to get what you want. In other words, communicate, communicate, communicate. And stay in touch.

Overall, consider the far-reaching consequences of your decisions; make sure a decision isn't going to cause issues a few years down the road.

Who Does the Data Analysis Work?

For the types of data analyses discussed in this book and described as comprehensive data analyses, it would be ideal if someone at the district level did the major analyses. With a good strong data analyzer tool and data warehouse, the district person can do the analyses for all the schools, at all grade levels, and all subtests in one query. A clerk can then copy and paste the individual results into graphing templates. (Graphing templates are provided on CD-Roms for all K-12 educational levels in the *Using Data to Improve Student Learning* series.)

Our passion with data analysis is getting the results into the hands of teachers and giving them the time to study the results of the analyses, instead of having them use their time performing the analyses. In our ideal world, at minimum, teachers would start the school year with historical data on each student in their class(es). They would know what the students know and what they need to know. Also in our ideal world, teachers would be using ongoing measurements in their classrooms to make sure all students are progressing and mastering the content.

Let's say your district does not have a data warehouse and provides only the state assessment results on paper; you can still use these data in meaningful ways. At minimum, schools can graph average scores over time—if there have been positive improvements in the school, you should see increases in scores. If the school is making a positive impact on students, student cohort scores should increase over time—they should never go backward. Don't forget the powerful demographic data gathered through your student information system.

Who does all this at the school level, if there is no district support for the analysis, depends on your school make-up. Often instructional coaches, assistant principals, teachers on special assignment, and/or the Leadership Teams do this work.

Summary

What makes the difference in schools successfully closing student achievement gaps and schools that do not succeed in closing the achievement gaps is the effective use of data. Many times the reason schools do not use data to this end is that the data just are not easily accessible to them; and, when they are, the data may not be in a form that will help them achieve the analyses for which they are planning.

If you take your schoolwide data and follow some of the examples within this book, you will get a good look at where your school is as a system. If you want to change the results you are getting, you must improve the processes that create the results. To know what to improve, you have to know where you are right now, with data.

If all teachers in your school knew what the students know when they start their course or grade level, focused their effective instructional strategies on teaching to the standards, assessed in an ongoing fashion to know if the students are improving, student learning results would increase in a very short period of time.

Data warehouses can link student information together to create analyses that allow the understanding of the impact of different programs and processes on achieving school success, and the identification of differences that may occur related to subgroupings (e.g., gender, ethnicity, poverty, language proficiency).

School districts should start by studying what already exists at the district or school levels, carefully think about what specific data are needed, and clarify the types of reports that would be helpful in finding answers to their questions. If at all possible, a data warehouse will make comprehensive data analysis doable, easy to accomplish, and replicable over time.

APPENDIX A
Sample Questionnaires

On the pages that follow are six of *Education for the Future's* most popular student, teacher, and parent questionnaires. Schools working with *Education for the Future* have used these questionnaires since 1991, and we offer them here as examples of questionnaires that work. Before you administer any of these questionnaires, please consider administering them online. (See *http://eff.csuchico.edu.*)

Please note that these questionnaires cannot be copied and scanned as they appear in this book. One would need to set them up to be scanned, or to be administered online. Chapter 5 includes details of questionnaire administration and analysis.

The questionnaire examples that follow include:

▼ Student (Kindergarten to Grade 3) Questionnaire

▼ Student (Grades 1 to 12) Questionnaire

▼ Student (Middle/High School) Questionnaire

▼ Teaching Staff Questionnaire

▼ Parent (K-12) Questionnaire

▼ Parent (High School) Questionnaire

Education for the Future

Students

Please complete this form using a No. 2 pencil. Be sure to completely fill in the circle that describes best what you think or how you feel. Thank you!

PLEASE USE NO. 2 PENCIL

RIGHT	WRONG

I am in:
- ○ Kindergarten
- ○ First Grade
- ○ Second Grade
- ○ Third Grade

I am:
(fill in all that apply)
- ○ Black
- ○ American Indian/ Alaskan Native
- ○ Asian
- ○ White
- ○ Hispanic/Latino
- ○ Other

I am:
- ○ Boy
- ○ Girl

When I am at school, I feel:

	☹ ①	😐 ②	☺ ③
I belong	①	②	③
I am safe	①	②	③
I have fun learning	①	②	③
I like this school	①	②	③
This school is good	①	②	③
My teacher cares about me	①	②	③
My principal cares about me	①	②	③
My teacher is a good teacher	①	②	③
My teacher believes I can learn	①	②	③
The work I do in class makes me think	①	②	③
I know what I am supposed to be learning in my classes	①	②	③
I am a good student	①	②	③
I can be a better student	①	②	③
I behave well at school	①	②	③
Students at my school are friendly	①	②	③
I have lots of friends	①	②	③
My family believes I can do well in school	①	②	③
My family wants me to do well in school	①	②	③

Page 1 of 2

244

Education for the Future

What do you like about this school?

What do you wish was different at this school?

Education for the Future

Students

Please complete this form using a No. 2 pencil. Be sure to completely fill in the circle that describes best what you think or how you feel. Thank you!

PLEASE USE NO. 2 PENCIL

RIGHT	WRONG

I am in:
- ○ 1st Grade
- ○ 2nd Grade
- ○ 3rd Grade
- ○ 4th Grade
- ○ 5th Grade
- ○ 6th Grade
- ○ 7th Grade
- ○ 8th Grade
- ○ 9th Grade
- ○ 10th Grade
- ○ 11th Grade
- ○ 12th Grade

I am:
(fill in all that apply)
- ○ Black (African-American)
- ○ American Indian/ Alaskan Native
- ○ Asian
- ○ White (Caucasian)
- ○ Hispanic/Latino
- ○ Other

I am:
- ○ Boy
- ○ Girl

When I am at school, I feel:

	Strongly Disagree	Disagree	Neutral	Agree	Strongly Agree
I belong	①	②	③	④	⑤
I am safe	①	②	③	④	⑤
I have fun learning	①	②	③	④	⑤
I like this school	①	②	③	④	⑤
This school is good	①	②	③	④	⑤
I have freedom at school	①	②	③	④	⑤
I have choices in the way I learn	①	②	③	④	⑤
My teacher treats me with respect	①	②	③	④	⑤
My teacher cares about me	①	②	③	④	⑤
My teacher thinks I will be successful	①	②	③	④	⑤
My teacher listens to my ideas	①	②	③	④	⑤
My principal cares about me	①	②	③	④	⑤
My teacher is a good teacher	①	②	③	④	⑤
My teacher believes I can learn	①	②	③	④	⑤
I am recognized for good work	①	②	③	④	⑤
I am challenged by the work my teacher asks me to do	①	②	③	④	⑤
The work I do in class makes me think	①	②	③	④	⑤
I know what I am supposed to be learning in my classes	①	②	③	④	⑤
I am a good student	①	②	③	④	⑤
I can be a better student	①	②	③	④	⑤
Working hard will make me do well in school	①	②	③	④	⑤
Very good work is expected at my school	①	②	③	④	⑤
I behave well at school	①	②	③	④	⑤
Students are treated fairly by teachers	①	②	③	④	⑤
Students are treated fairly by the principal	①	②	③	④	⑤
Students are treated fairly by campus supervisors	①	②	③	④	⑤
Students at my school treat me with respect	①	②	③	④	⑤
I am safe from bullies	①	②	③	④	⑤
Students at my school are friendly	①	②	③	④	⑤
I have lots of friends	①	②	③	④	⑤
I have support for learning at home	①	②	③	④	⑤
My family believes I can do well in school	①	②	③	④	⑤
My family wants me to do well in school	①	②	③	④	⑤

Page 1 of 2

Education for the Future

What do you like about this school?

What do you wish was different at this school?

Education for the Future

Middle/High School Students

Please complete this form using a No. 2 pencil.
Be sure to completely fill in the circle that
describes best what you think or how you feel.
Thank you!

| PLEASE USE NO. 2 PENCIL |
| RIGHT | WRONG |

	Strongly Disagree	Disagree	Neutral	Agree	Strongly Agree
I feel safe at this school	①	②	③	④	⑤
I feel like I belong at this school	①	②	③	④	⑤
I feel challenged at this school	①	②	③	④	⑤
I have opportunities to choose my own projects	①	②	③	④	⑤
I feel that I am in charge of what I learn	①	②	③	④	⑤
Teachers encourage me to assess the quality of my own work	①	②	③	④	⑤
This school is preparing me well for what I want to do after high school	①	②	③	④	⑤
My teachers treat me fairly	①	②	③	④	⑤
My school administrators treat me fairly	①	②	③	④	⑤
My campus supervisors treat me fairly	①	②	③	④	⑤
The office staff treat me fairly	①	②	③	④	⑤
Other students at this school treat me fairly	①	②	③	④	⑤
The work at this school is challenging	①	②	③	④	⑤
I find what I learn in school to be relevant to real life	①	②	③	④	⑤
I feel successful at school	①	②	③	④	⑤
This school is fun	①	②	③	④	⑤
I like this school	①	②	③	④	⑤
This is a good school	①	②	③	④	⑤
I like the students at this school	①	②	③	④	⑤
Students at this school like me	①	②	③	④	⑤
I like to learn	①	②	③	④	⑤
Doing well in school makes me feel good about myself	①	②	③	④	⑤
Working hard will make me do well in school	①	②	③	④	⑤
I am doing my best in school	①	②	③	④	⑤
Participating in extracurricular activities is important to me	①	②	③	④	⑤

Page 1 of 3

Education for the Future

Middle/High School Students

	Strongly Disagree	Disagree	Neutral	Agree	Strongly Agree

My teachers:

	Strongly Disagree	Disagree	Neutral	Agree	Strongly Agree
expect students to do their best	①	②	③	④	⑤
expect me to do my best	①	②	③	④	⑤
are understanding when students have personal problems	①	②	③	④	⑤
set high standards for learning in their classes	①	②	③	④	⑤
help me gain confidence in my ability to learn	①	②	③	④	⑤
know me well	①	②	③	④	⑤
care about me	①	②	③	④	⑤
make learning fun	①	②	③	④	⑤
are excited about the subjects they teach	①	②	③	④	⑤
give me individual attention when I need it	①	②	③	④	⑤

In my classes, time is spent:

listening to the teacher talk	①	②	③	④	⑤
in whole class discussions	①	②	③	④	⑤
working in small groups	①	②	③	④	⑤
answering questions from a book or worksheet	①	②	③	④	⑤
working on projects or research	①	②	③	④	⑤
doing work that I find meaningful	①	②	③	④	⑤
using computers	①	②	③	④	⑤

I learn well when:

I am working on projects or research	①	②	③	④	⑤
the teacher is leading a discussion with the whole class	①	②	③	④	⑤
I am working in a small group	①	②	③	④	⑤
I am working by myself	①	②	③	④	⑤

I feel ready for the real world, with reference to:

my ability to write	①	②	③	④	⑤
my ability to read	①	②	③	④	⑤
my ability with mathematics	①	②	③	④	⑤
my ability to process information	①	②	③	④	⑤
my presentation skills	①	②	③	④	⑤
my technology skills	①	②	③	④	⑤
my ability to learn on my own outside of a classroom	①	②	③	④	⑤

Page 2 of 2

Education for the Future

Middle/High School Students

What do you like about this school?

What do you wish was different at this school?

Student Demographic Data

I am: (fill in all that apply)
- ○ Black (African-American)
- ○ American Indian/Alaskan Native
- ○ Asian
- ○ White (Caucasian)
- ○ Filipino
- ○ Hispanic/Latino
- ○ Middle Eastern
- ○ Pacific Islander
- ○ Other _____

I am in the:
- ○ 6th Grade
- ○ 7th Grade
- ○ 8th Grade
- ○ 9th Grade
- ○ 10th Grade
- ○ 11th Grade
- ○ 12th Grade

I am:
- ○ Female
- ○ Male

I participate in: (fill in all that apply)
- ○ Athletics (includes Cheerleading/Flag Team)
- ○ School Clubs
- ○ Instrumental Music
- ○ Vocal Music
- ○ Drama
- ○ Speech/Debate
- ○ Not connected to any school club or regular extracurricular activity

I came to this school as a:
- ○ 6th Grader
- ○ 7th Grader
- ○ 8th Grader
- ○ Freshman
- ○ Sophomore
- ○ Junior
- ○ Senior

Immediately after graduation, I plan to: (fill in all that apply)
- ○ Go to a 2-year community college
- ○ Go to a 4-year college
- ○ Enter a training or apprenticeship program
- ○ Get a full-time job
- ○ Join the military
- ○ Get married
- ○ Other _____

Education for the Future

Teaching Staff

Please fill in the circle that best describes your beliefs or feelings, using the scale to the right. Please use a No. 2 pencil. Thank you!

	Strongly Disagree	Disagree	Neutral	Agree	Strongly Agree

(1) I feel:

	SD	D	N	A	SA
like I belong at this school	①	②	③	④	⑤
that the staff cares about me	①	②	③	④	⑤
that learning can be fun	①	②	③	④	⑤
that learning is fun at this school	①	②	③	④	⑤
recognized for good work	①	②	③	④	⑤
intrinsically rewarded for doing my job well	①	②	③	④	⑤
clear about what my job is at this school	①	②	③	④	⑤
that others are clear about what my job is at this school	①	②	③	④	⑤

(2) I work with people who:

	SD	D	N	A	SA
treat me with respect	①	②	③	④	⑤
respect each other	①	②	③	④	⑤
collaborate with each other to make student learning consistent across grade levels	①	②	③	④	⑤
are committed to continuous improvement	①	②	③	④	⑤
provide one another feedback on their teaching	①	②	③	④	⑤

(3) My administrators:

	SD	D	N	A	SA
treat me with respect	①	②	③	④	⑤
are effective instructional leaders	①	②	③	④	⑤
facilitate communication effectively	①	②	③	④	⑤
support me in my work with students	①	②	③	④	⑤
support shared decision making	①	②	③	④	⑤
allow me to be an effective instructional leader	①	②	③	④	⑤
are effective in helping us reach our vision	①	②	③	④	⑤
actively encourage staff to collaborate	①	②	③	④	⑤

(4) I believe student achievement can increase through:

	SD	D	N	A	SA
differentiating instruction	①	②	③	④	⑤
effective professional development related to our vision	①	②	③	④	⑤
teaching to the state standards	①	②	③	④	⑤
the use of computers	①	②	③	④	⑤
providing a threat-free environment	①	②	③	④	⑤
close personal relationships between students and teachers	①	②	③	④	⑤
addressing student learning styles	①	②	③	④	⑤
effective parent involvement	①	②	③	④	⑤
using ongoing student assessments related to state standards	①	②	③	④	⑤
student self-assessments	①	②	③	④	⑤
teacher use of student achievement data	①	②	③	④	⑤

(5) I love:

	SD	D	N	A	SA
working at this school	①	②	③	④	⑤
seeing the results of my work with students	①	②	③	④	⑤
to teach	①	②	③	④	⑤

Education for the Future

Teaching Staff

	Strongly Disagree	Disagree	Neutral	Agree	Strongly Agree

(6) I believe:

every student can learn	①	②	③	④	⑤
the instructional program at this school is challenging	①	②	③	④	⑤
this school provides an atmosphere where every student can succeed	①	②	③	④	⑤
quality work is expected of all students at this school	①	②	③	④	⑤
quality work is expected of me	①	②	③	④	⑤
quality work is expected of all the adults working at this school	①	②	③	④	⑤
the vision for this school is clear	①	②	③	④	⑤
the vision for this school is shared	①	②	③	④	⑤
we have an action plan in place which will get us to our vision	①	②	③	④	⑤
this school has a good public image	①	②	③	④	⑤
it is important to communicate often with parents	①	②	③	④	⑤
I communicate with parents often about their child's progress	①	②	③	④	⑤
student outcomes for my class(es) are clear to me	①	②	③	④	⑤
student outcomes for my class(es) are clear to my students	①	②	③	④	⑤
learning is fun in my classroom	①	②	③	④	⑤

(7) I work effectively with:

students with learning disabilities	①	②	③	④	⑤
English learners	①	②	③	④	⑤
ethnically/racially diverse students	①	②	③	④	⑤
students who live in poverty	①	②	③	④	⑤
low-achieving students	①	②	③	④	⑤

(8) Morale is high on the part of:

teachers	①	②	③	④	⑤
students	①	②	③	④	⑤
support staff	①	②	③	④	⑤
our school administrators	①	②	③	④	⑤

Education for the Future

Standards Assessment for
Elementary School Teachers only *(Middle/High Teachers skip to question #16)*

*The analysis of the following questions will inform staff of where your school is in the process of implementing state standards, and what support structures are needed to make the effective implementation of standards possible. Only **group** results will be used. Individuals will not be identified. It is okay if you do not know a set of standards now. This assessment will show your school's progress over time. Please answer the questions to the best of your ability, with the first answers that come to mind. Use N/A when the question is not applicable to your situation. Completely fill in the circle, using the scale to the right. Thank you!*

(9) How well do you know the state standards at your grade level(s) for the following content areas?

	Just know they exist	Have skimmed	Have read at least once	Have read in-depth	Am very knowledgeable
English/Language Arts	①	②	③	④	⑤
Mathematics	①	②	③	④	⑤
Science	①	②	③	④	⑤
Social Studies	①	②	③	④	⑤
Technology	①	②	③	④	⑤

(10) How well do you know the state standards just below your grade level(s) for the following content areas?

English/Language Arts	①	②	③	④	⑤
Mathematics	①	②	③	④	⑤
Science	①	②	③	④	⑤
Social Studies	①	②	③	④	⑤
Technology	①	②	③	④	⑤

(11) How well do you know the state standards just above your grade level(s) for the following content areas?

English/Language Arts	①	②	③	④	⑤
Mathematics	①	②	③	④	⑤
Science	①	②	③	④	⑤
Social Studies	①	②	③	④	⑤
Technology	①	②	③	④	⑤

(12) How well would you say you know what it would look like, sound like, and feel like if you were teaching to the standards 100% of the time?

	Not at All	Little Bit	Getting There	Well	Extremely Well
English/Language Arts	①	②	③	④	⑤
Mathematics	①	②	③	④	⑤
Science	①	②	③	④	⑤
Social Studies	①	②	③	④	⑤
Technology	①	②	③	④	⑤

(13) How much of the time are you implementing the standards in your classroom for the following content areas?

	0%	25%	50%	75%	100%
English/Language Arts	①	②	③	④	⑤
Mathematics	①	②	③	④	⑤
Science	①	②	③	④	⑤
Social Studies	①	②	③	④	⑤
Technology	①	②	③	④	⑤

Education for the Future

Standards Assessment for *Middle and High* School Teachers only

*The analysis of the following questions will inform staff of where your school is in the process of implementing state standards, and what support structures are needed to make the effective implementation of standards possible. Only **group** results will be used. Individuals will not be identified. It is okay if you do not know a set of standards now. This assessment will show your school's progress over time. Please answer the questions to the best of your ability, with the first answers that come to mind. Use N/A when the question is not applicable to your situation. Completely fill in the circle, using the scale to the right. Thank you!*

	Just know they exist	Have skimmed	Have read at least once	Have read in-depth	Am very knowledgeable
(14) How well do you know the state standards for your grade level(s) and content areas?	①	②	③	④	⑤
(15) How well do you know the state standards for your content area(s) that precede your grade level(s)?	①	②	③	④	⑤
(16) How well do you know the state standards for your content area(s) that follow your grade level(s)?	①	②	③	④	⑤
(17) For those of you who teach upper grades, how well do you know content expectations students will encounter in higher education?	①	②	③	④	⑤
	Not at All	Little Bit	Getting There	Well	Extremely Well
(18) How well would you say you know what it would look like, sound like, and feel like if you were teaching to the standards 100% of the time?	①	②	③	④	⑤

Standards Assessment for ALL Teachers

(19) How much would each of the following help you to better know the standards for your grade level(s)?	Not at All	Probably Not	Not Sure	A Lot	A Great Deal
Grade-level meetings about standards	①	②	③	④	⑤
Cross-grade-level meetings about standards	①	②	③	④	⑤
Schoolwide meetings about standards	①	②	③	④	⑤
Professional development on how to teach to the standards	①	②	③	④	⑤
Feedback from classroom observations	①	②	③	④	⑤
Demonstration lessons	①	②	③	④	⑤
Peer coaching	①	②	③	④	⑤
Other _____	①	②	③	④	⑤

(20) Which of the following statements describes how you use standards to design instruction?
(Select one statement that best applies.)

I teach the curriculum and instructional strategies our school/district has adopted	○
I follow the textbooks, and I believe they are aligned to the state standards	○
I am pretty sure my instructional strategies are already aligned to the state standards	○
I take my existing instructional plans and indicate where the standards are being taught	○
I study the standards and create instruction to take students from where they are to where the standards say they should be by the end of the year	○
I study the standards, determine outcomes related to the standards, frequently assess where students are with respect to the standards, and adapt my lesson plans to create instruction to take students to where they need to be by the end of the year	○
I teach the standards through ongoing assessments	○

Education for the Future

Teaching Staff

Standards Assessment for ALL Teachers

(21) What percentage of your students do you think will meet the standards by the end of the school year?
(Select the option that best applies.)

○ 0%	○ 11–20%	○ 31–40%	○ 51–60%	○ 71–80%	○ 91–100%
○ 1–10%	○ 21–30%	○ 41–50%	○ 61–70%	○ 81–90%	

(22) What do you do when your students do not learn the standards?
(Select *all* the boxes that apply and add other strategies, as appropriate.)

I reteach the content	○
I reteach the content, in different ways	○
I adapt my instructional strategies to the learning styles of individual students	○
After reteaching, I assess the students in different ways	○
I get help from others in the school, such as colleagues and/or specialists	○
I move on to make sure the curriculum gets covered	○
I cannot make a student learn	○
_____ Other	○

(23) How much support do you receive from your school administrators to ensure that:

	No Support	Hardly Any	There is a system for support	Good Support	Continuous Support
you are teaching to the standards	①	②	③	④	⑤
your students are learning the standards	①	②	③	④	⑤
all teachers at your grade level/content area are teaching to the *same* standards	①	②	③	④	⑤
teachers across grade levels are teaching to standards	①	②	③	④	⑤
teachers across grade levels are using the standards to build a continuum of learning that makes sense for all students	①	②	③	④	⑤
teachers are using formative assessments to verify student mastery of standards	①	②	③	④	⑤

(24) How much support do you receive from your colleagues to ensure that:

	No Support	Hardly Any	There is a system for support	Good Support	Continuous Support
you are teaching to the standards	①	②	③	④	⑤
your students are learning the standards	①	②	③	④	⑤
all teachers at your grade level are teaching to the *same* standards	①	②	③	④	⑤
teachers across grade levels are teaching to standards	①	②	③	④	⑤
teachers across grade levels are using the standards to build a continuum of learning that makes sense for all students	①	②	③	④	⑤
teachers are using formative assessments to verify student mastery of standards	①	②	③	④	⑤

	Not at All	Little Bit	Getting There	Believe	Strongly Believe
(25) To what extent do you believe teachers and instructional staff can make the necessary changes to improve student learning?	①	②	③	④	⑤
(26) To what extent do you believe school leadership can facilitate the necessary changes to improve student learning?	①	②	③	④	⑤

	Not at All	Little Bit	Getting There	Committed	Strongly Committed
(27) How committed are you to making necessary changes to improve student learning?	①	②	③	④	⑤

Education for the Future

Teaching Staff

What would it take to improve student learning in this school?

Demographic Data

For each item, please select the description that applies to you. These demographic data are used for summary analyses; some descriptions will not be reported if groups are so small that individuals can be identified.

What grade level(s) do you teach?
(Mark all that apply.)

○ Pre K   ○ Grade 6
○ Kindergarten   ○ Grade 7
○ Grade 1   ○ Grade 8
○ Grade 2   ○ Grade 9
○ Grade 3   ○ Grade 10
○ Grade 4   ○ Grade 11
○ Grade 5   ○ Grade 12

I am a(n):

○ Classroom Teacher
○ Instructional Assistant
○ Certificated Staff
  (other than a classroom teacher)
○ Classified Staff
  (other than an instructional assistant)

How long have you been a teacher?

○ 1st Year
○ 2–3 Years
○ 4–6 Years
○ 7–10 Years
○ 11–14 Years
○ 15–20 Years
○ 21–25 Years
○ 26+ Years

What content do you teach?
(Mark all that apply.)

○ Elementary   ○ The Arts
○ English/Language Arts   ○ Physical Education/Health
○ Mathematics   ○ Special Education
○ Science   ○ Vocational Education
○ Social Studies   ○ Industrial Education
○ Technology   ○ Other_____
○ Foreign Language

What are your teaching qualifications?
(Mark all that apply.)

○ Emergency Credential
○ Elementary Credential
○ Middle Credential
○ Secondary Credential
○ Special Education
○ Intervention Specialist
○ Literacy Specialist/Coach
○ Math Specialist/Coach
○ Classroom Instructional Assistant
○ Other_____

Thank you!

Education for the Future

Parents

Please complete this form using a No. 2 pencil. Be sure to completely fill in the circle that describes best what you think or how you feel. Thank you!

PLEASE USE NO. 2 PENCIL

	RIGHT			WRONG		

	Strongly Disagree	Disagree	Neutral	Agree	Strongly Agree
I feel welcome at my child's school	①	②	③	④	⑤
I am informed about my child's progress	①	②	③	④	⑤
I know what my child's teacher expects of my child	①	②	③	④	⑤
My child is safe at school	①	②	③	④	⑤
My child is safe going to and from school	①	②	③	④	⑤
There is adequate supervision during school	①	②	③	④	⑤
There is adequate supervision before and after school	①	②	③	④	⑤
Teachers show respect for the students	①	②	③	④	⑤
Students show respect for other students	①	②	③	④	⑤
The school meets the social needs of the students	①	②	③	④	⑤
The school meets the academic needs of the students	①	②	③	④	⑤
The school expects quality work of its students	①	②	③	④	⑤
The school has an excellent learning environment	①	②	③	④	⑤
I know how well my child is progressing in school	①	②	③	④	⑤
I like the school's report cards/progress report	①	②	③	④	⑤
I respect the school's teachers	①	②	③	④	⑤
I respect the school's principal	①	②	③	④	⑤
Overall, the school performs well academically	①	②	③	④	⑤
The school succeeds at preparing children for future work	①	②	③	④	⑤
The school has a good public image	①	②	③	④	⑤
The school's assessment practices are fair	①	②	③	④	⑤
My child's teacher helps me to help my child learn at home	①	②	③	④	⑤
I support my child's learning at home	①	②	③	④	⑤
I feel good about myself as a parent	①	②	③	④	⑤

Children's grades:
- ○ Kindergarten
- ○ First Grade
- ○ Second Grade
- ○ Third Grade
- ○ Fourth Grade
- ○ Fifth Grade
- ○ Sixth Grade
- ○ Seventh Grade
- ○ Eighth Grade
- ○ Ninth Grade
- ○ Tenth Grade
- ○ Eleventh Grade
- ○ Twelfth Grade

Number of children in this school:
① ② ③ ④ ⑤ ⑥ ⑦ ⑧ ⑨

My native language is:
- ○ Chinese
- ○ English
- ○ Japanese
- ○ Korean
- ○ Spanish
- ○ Vietnamese
- ○ Other _____

Number of children in the household:
① ② ③ ④ ⑤ ⑥ ⑦ ⑧ ⑨

Ethnic background:
(fill in all that apply)
- ○ Black
- ○ American Indian/Alaskan Native
- ○ Asian
- ○ White
- ○ Hispanic/Latino
- ○ Other _____

Responding:
- ○ Mother
- ○ Father
- ◉ Guardian
- ○ Other

Education for the Future

What are the strengths of this school?

What needs to be improved?

Education for the Future

High School Parents

Please complete this form using a No. 2 pencil. Be sure to completely fill in the circle that describes best what you think or how you feel. Thank you!

| PLEASE USE NO. 2 PENCIL |
| RIGHT | WRONG |

	Strongly Disagree	Disagree	Neutral	Agree	Strongly Agree
I feel welcome at my child's school	①	②	③	④	⑤
My child is safe at school	①	②	③	④	⑤
My child is safe going to and from school	①	②	③	④	⑤
There is adequate supervision during school	①	②	③	④	⑤
There is adequate supervision before and after school	①	②	③	④	⑤
I am informed about my child's progress at school	①	②	③	④	⑤
My calls to the school are returned in a timely manner	①	②	③	④	⑤
I know what my child's teachers expect of my child	①	②	③	④	⑤
My child knows what his/her teachers expect of him/her	①	②	③	④	⑤
New students receive adequate orientation to the school and the programs offered	①	②	③	④	⑤
The school provides adequate information to students about attending college after graduation	①	②	③	④	⑤
The school provides adequate information about non-college options after graduation	①	②	③	④	⑤
The school provides an adequate calendar of school activities	①	②	③	④	⑤
The school clearly communicates how parent volunteers can help	①	②	③	④	⑤
Parent volunteers are made to feel appreciated	①	②	③	④	⑤
Parent volunteers are vital to the school community	①	②	③	④	⑤
I respect the school's teachers	①	②	③	④	⑤
I respect the school's principal	①	②	③	④	⑤
Students are treated fairly by the teachers	①	②	③	④	⑤
Students are treated fairly by administration	①	②	③	④	⑤
Students are treated fairly by other students	①	②	③	④	⑤
The school meets the social needs of the students	①	②	③	④	⑤
The school meets the academic needs of the students	①	②	③	④	⑤
The school expects quality work of its students	①	②	③	④	⑤
The school's assessment practices are fair	①	②	③	④	⑤
Overall, the school performs well academically	①	②	③	④	⑤
There is adequate recognition of student successes	①	②	③	④	⑤
The school succeeds at preparing its students for future work	①	②	③	④	⑤
Teachers help me know how to support my child's learning at home	①	②	③	④	⑤
I support my child's learning at home	①	②	③	④	⑤
Overall, the school has a good public image	①	②	③	④	⑤
I would recommend this school to other families	①	②	③	④	⑤

Education for the Future

High School Parents

What are the strengths of this school?

What needs to be improved?

Demographics

Number of children in this school:
① ② ③ ④ ⑤ ⑥ ⑦ ⑧ ⑨

Number of children in the household:
① ② ③ ④ ⑤ ⑥ ⑦ ⑧ ⑨

Children's grades:
O Kindergarten
O First Grade
O Second Grade
O Third Grade
O Fourth Grade
O Fifth Grade
O Sixth Grade
O Seventh Grade
O Eighth Grade
O Ninth Grade
O Tenth Grade
O Eleventh Grade
O Twelfth Grade

My native language is:
O Chinese
O English
O Japanese
O Korean
O Spanish
O Vietnamese
O Other _____

Ethnic background:
(fill in all that apply)
O Black (African-American)
O American Indian/Alaskan Native
O Asian
O White (Caucasian)
O Hispanic/Latino
O Other _____

I am a graduate of this high school:
O Yes
O No

Responding:
O Mother
O Father
O Guardian
O Other

APPENDIX B
Continuous Improvement Continuums for Schools

These *Education for the Future Continuous Improvement Continuums,* adapted from the *Malcolm Baldrige Award Program for Quality Business Management,* provide an authentic means for measuring schoolwide improvement and growth. Districts and schools use these Continuums as a vehicle for ongoing self-assessment. They use the results of the assessment to acknowledge their accomplishments, to set goals for improvement, and to keep school districts and partners apprised of the progress they have made in their school improvement efforts.

Understanding the Continuums

These Continuums, extending from *one* to *five* horizontally, represent a continuum of expectations related to school improvement with respect to an *Approach* to the Continuum, *Implementation* of the approach, and the *Outcome* that results from the implementation. A *one* rating, located at the left of each Continuum, represents a school that has not yet begun to improve. *Five,* located at the right of each Continuum, represents a school that is one step removed from "world class quality." The elements between *one* and *five* describe how that Continuum is hypothesized to evolve in a continuously improving school. Each Continuum moves from a reactive mode to a proactive mode—from fire fighting to prevention. The *five* in *Outcome* in each Continuum is the target.

Vertically, the *Approach, Implementation,* and *Outcome* statements, for any number *one* through *five,* are hypotheses. In other words, the *implementation* statement describes how the *approach* might look when implemented, and the *outcome* is the "pay-off" for implementing the approach. If the hypotheses are accurate, the outcome will not be realized until the approach is actually implemented.

Using the Continuums

Use the *Continuous Improvement Continuums* (CICs) to understand where your school is with respect to continuous improvement. The results will hopefully provide that sense of urgency needed to spark enthusiasm for your school improvement efforts.

Start the assessment by stating or creating the ground rules, setting the tone for a safe and confidential assessment, and explaining why you are doing this. Provide a brief overview of the seven sections, taking each section one or two at a time, and having each staff member read the related Continuum and make independent assessments of where she/he believes the school is with respect to *Approach, Implementation,* and *Outcome.* We recommend using individual 8 1/2 x 11 copies of the Continuums for individual assessments. Then, have each staff member note where she/he believes the school is with a colorful sticker or marker on a large poster of the Continuum. The markers allow all staff to see how much they are in agreement with one another. If only one color is used for the first assessment, another color can be used for the next assessment, and so forth, to help gauge growth over time, or you can plan to use two different charts for gauging progress over time such as in the photos below.

When all dots or marks have been placed on the enlarged Continuum, look at the agreement or disagreement of the ratings. Starting with *Approach*, have staff discuss why they believe the school is where they rated it. Keep discussing until the larger group comes to consensus on one number that reflects where the school is right now. You might need to make a quick check on where staff is with respect to coming to consensus, using a thumbs up, thumbs down "vote." Keep discussing the facts until consensus is reached. Do not average the results—it does not produce a sense of urgency for improvement. We cannot emphasize this enough! Keep discussing until agreement can be reached by everyone on a number that represents where "we" are right now. When that consensus is reached, record the number and move to *Implementation* and then *Outcome*. Determine *Next Steps*. Proceed in the same way through the next six categories.

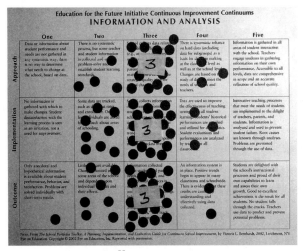

Fall Assessment

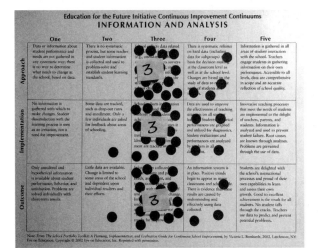

Spring Assessment

During the assessments, make sure someone records the discussions of the Continuum assessments. Schools might want to exchange facilitators with a neighboring school to have someone external to the school facilitate the assessments. This will enable everyone in the school to participate and provide an unbiased and competent person to lead the consensus-building piece. Assessing over time will help staff see that they are making progress. The decision of how often to assess on the *Continuous Improvement Continuums* is certainly up to the school. We recommend twice a year—about mid-fall and mid-spring—when there is time (or has been time) to implement next steps. Over time, once a year might be sufficient.

Using these Continuums will enable you and your school to stay motivated, to shape and maintain your shared vision, and will assist with the continuous improvement of all elements. Take pictures of the resulting charts. Even if your consensus number does not increase, the dots will most probably come together over time showing shifts in whole staff thinking.

Remember that where your school is at any time is just where it is. The important thing is what you do with this information. Continuous improvement is a never-ending process which, when used effectively, will ultimately lead your school toward providing a quality program for *all* children.

School Continuous Improvement Continuums
INFORMATION AND ANALYSIS

	One	Two	Three	Four	Five
Approach	Data or information about student performance and needs are not gathered in any systematic way; there is no way to determine what needs to change at the school, based on data.	There is no systematic process, but some teacher and student information is collected and used to problem solve and establish student learning standards.	School collects data related to student performance (e.g., attendance, achievement) and conducts surveys on student, teacher, and parent needs. The information is used to drive the strategic quality plan for school change.	There is systematic reliance on hard data (including data for subgroups) as a basis for decision making at the classroom level as well as at the school level. Changes are based on the study of data to meet the needs of students and teachers.	Information is gathered in all areas of student interaction with the school. Teachers engage students in gathering information on their own performance. Accessible to all levels, data are comprehensive in scope and an accurate reflection of school quality.
Implementation	No information is gathered with which to make changes. Student dissatisfaction with the learning process is seen as an irritation, not a need for improvement.	Some data are tracked, such as drop-out rates and enrollment. Only a few individuals are asked for feedback about areas of schooling.	School collects information on current and former students (e.g., student achievement and perceptions), analyzes and uses it in conjunction with future trends for planning. Identified areas for improvement are tracked over time.	Data are used to improve the effectiveness of teaching strategies on all student learning. Students' historical performances are graphed and utilized for diagnostics. Student evaluations and performances are analyzed by teachers in all classrooms.	Innovative teaching processes that meet the needs of students are implemented to the delight of teachers, parents, and students. Information is analyzed and used to prevent student failure. Root causes are known through analyses. Problems are prevented through the use of data.
Outcome	Only anecdotal and hypothetical information is available about student performance, behavior, and satisfaction. Problems are solved individually with short-term results.	Little data are available. Change is limited to some areas of the school and dependent upon individual teachers and their efforts.	Information collected about student and parent needs, assessment, and instructional practices is shared with the school staff and used to plan for change. Information helps staff understand pressing issues, analyze information for "root causes," and track results for improvement.	An information system is in place. Positive trends begin to appear in many classrooms and schoolwide. There is evidence that these results are caused by understanding and effectively using data collected.	Students are delighted with the school's instructional processes and proud of their own capabilities to learn and assess their own growth. Good to excellent achievement is the result for all students. No student falls through the cracks. Teachers use data to predict and prevent potential problems.

School Continuous Improvement Continuums
STUDENT ACHIEVEMENT

	One	Two	Three	Four	Five
Approach	Instructional and organizational processes critical to student success are not identified. Little distinction of student learning differences is made. Some teachers believe that not all students can achieve.	Some data are collected on student background and performance trends. Learning gaps are noted to direct improvement of instruction. It is known that student learning standards must be identified.	Student learning standards are identified, and a continuum of learning is created throughout the school. Student performance data are collected and compared to the standards in order to analyze how to improve learning for all students.	Data on student achievement are used throughout the school to pursue the improvement of student learning. Teachers collaborate to implement appropriate instruction and assessment strategies for meeting student learning standards articulated across grade levels. All teachers believe that all students can learn.	School makes an effort to exceed student achievement expectations. Innovative instructional changes are made to anticipate learning needs and improve student achievement. Teachers are able to predict characteristics impacting student achievement and to know how to perform from a small set of internal quality measures.
Implementation	All students are taught the same way. There is no communication with students about their academic needs or learning styles. There are no analyses of how to improve instruction.	Some effort is made to track and analyze student achievement trends on a school-wide basis. Teachers begin to understand the needs and learning gaps of students.	Teachers study effective instruction and assessment strategies to implement standards and to increase their students' learning. Student feedback and analysis of achievement data are used in conjunction with implementation support strategies.	There is a systematic focus on implementing student learning standards and on the improvement of student learning schoolwide. Effective instruction and assessment strategies are implemented in each classroom. Teachers support one another with peer coaching and/or action research focused on implementing strategies that lead to increased achievement and the attainment of the shared vision.	All teachers correlate critical instructional and assessment strategies with objective indicators of quality student achievement. A comparative analysis of actual individual student performance to student learning standards is utilized to adjust teaching strategies to ensure a progression of learning for all students.
Outcome	There is wide variation in student attitudes and achievement with undesirable results. There is high dissatisfaction among students with learning. Student background is used as an excuse for low student achievement.	There is some evidence that student achieve-ment trends are available to teachers and are being used. There is much effort, but minimal observable results in improving student achievement.	There is an increase in communication between students and teachers regarding student learning. Teachers learn about effective instructional strategies that will implement the shared vision, including student learning standards, and meet the needs of their students. They make some gains.	Increased student achievement is evident schoolwide. Student morale, attendance, and behavior are good. Teachers converse often with each other about preventing student failure. Areas for further attention are clear.	Students and teachers conduct self-assessments to continuously improve performance. Improvements in student achievement are evident and clearly caused by teachers' and students' understandings of individual student learning standards, linked to appropriate and effective instructional and assessment strategies. A continuum of learning results. No students fall through the cracks.

School Continuous Improvement Continuums
QUALITY PLANNING

	One	Two	Three	Four	Five
Approach	No quality plan or process exists. Data are neither used nor considered important in planning.	The staff realize the importance of a mission, vision, and one comprehensive action plan. Teams develop goals and timelines, and dollars are allocated to begin the process.	A comprehensive school plan to achieve the vision is developed. Plan includes evaluation and continuous improvement.	One focused and integrated schoolwide plan for implementing a continuous improvement process is put into action. All school efforts are focused on the implementation of this plan that represents the achievement of the vision.	A plan for the continuous improvement of the school, with a focus on students, is put into place. There is excellent articulation and integration of all elements in the school due to quality planning. Leadership team ensures all elements are implemented by all appropriate parties.
Implementation	There is no knowledge of or direction for quality planning. Budget is allocated on an as-needed basis. Many plans exist.	School community begins continuous improvement planning efforts by laying out major steps to a shared vision, by identifying values and beliefs, the purpose of the school, a mission, vision, and student learning standards.	Implementation goals, responsibilities, due dates, and timelines are spelled out. Support structures for implementing the plan are set in place.	The quality management plan is implemented through effective procedures in all areas of the school. Everyone commits to implementing the plan aligned to the vision, mission, and values and beliefs. All share responsibility for accomplishing school goals.	Schoolwide goals, mission, vision, and student learning standards are shared and articulated throughout the school and with feeder schools. The attainment of identified student learning standards is linked to planning and implementation of effective instruction that meets students' needs. Leaders at all levels are developing expertise because planning is the norm.
Outcome	There is no evidence of comprehensive planning. Staff work is carried out in isolation. A continuum of learning for students is absent.	The school community understands the benefits of working together to implement a comprehensive continuous improvement plan.	There is evidence that the school plan is being implemented in some areas of the school. Improvements are neither systematic nor integrated schoolwide.	A schoolwide plan is known to all. Results from working toward the quality improvement goals are evident throughout the school. Planning is ongoing and inclusive of all stakeholders.	Evidence of effective teaching and learning results in significant improvement of student achievement attributed to quality planning at all levels of the school organization. Teachers and administrators understand and share the school mission and vision. Quality planning is seamless and all demonstrate evidence of accountability.

School Continuous Improvement Continuums
PROFESSIONAL LEARNING

	One	Two	Three	Four	Five
Approach	There is no professional development. Teachers, principals, and staff are seen as interchangeable parts that can be replaced. Professional development is external and usually equated to attending a conference alone. Hierarchy determines "haves" and "have-nots."	The "cafeteria" approach to professional development is used, whereby individual teachers choose what they want to take, without regard to an overall school plan.	The shared vision, school plan, and student needs are used to target focused professional development for all employees. Staff is inserviced on relevant instructional and leadership strategies.	Professional development and data-gathering methods are used by all teachers and are directed toward the goals of the shared vision and the continuous improvement of the school. Teachers have ongoing conversations about student achievement data. Other staff members receive training in their content areas. Systems thinking is considered in all decisions.	Leadership and staff continuously improve all aspects of the learning organization through an innovative, data-driven, and comprehensive continuous improvement process that prevents student failures. Effective job-embedded professional development is ongoing for implementing the vision for student success. Traditional teacher evaluations are replaced by collegial coaching and action research focused on student learning standards. Policies set professional development as a priority budget line-item. Professional development is planned, aligned, and lead to the achievement of student learning standards.
Implementation	Teacher, principal, and staff performance is controlled and inspected. Performance evaluations are used to detect mistakes.	Teacher professional development is sporadic and unfocused, lacking an approach for implementing new procedures and processes. Some leadership training begins to take place.	Teachers are involved in year-round quality professional development. The school community is trained in shared decision making, team building concepts, effective communication strategies, and data analysis at the classroom level.	Teachers, in teams, continuously set and implement student achievement goals. Leadership considers these goals and provides necessary support structures for collaboration. Teachers utilize effective support approaches as they implement new instruction and assessment strategies. Coaching and feedback structures are in place. Use of new knowledge and skills is evident.	Teams passionately support each other in the pursuit of quality improvement at all levels. Teachers make bold changes in instruction and assessment strategies focused on student learning standards and student learning styles. A teacher as action researcher model is implemented. Staffwide conversations focus on systemic reflection and improvement. Teachers are strong leaders.
Outcome	No professional growth and no staff or student performance improvement. There exists a high turnover rate of employees, especially administrators. Attitudes and approaches filter down to students.	The effectiveness of professional development is not known or analyzed. Teachers feel helpless about making schoolwide changes.	Teachers, working in teams, feel supported and begin to feel they can make changes. Evidence shows that shared decision making works.	A collegial school is evident. Effective classroom strategies are practiced, articulated schoolwide, are reflective of professional development aimed at ensuring student achievement, and the implementation of the shared vision, that includes student learning standards.	True systemic change and improved student achievement result because teachers are knowledgeable of and implement effective, differentiated teaching strategies for individual student learning gains. Teachers' repertoire of skills are enhanced, and students are achieving. Professional development is driving learning at all levels.

School Continuous Improvement Continuums
LEADERSHIP

	One	Two	Three	Four	Five
Approach	Principal as decision maker. Decisions are reactive to state, district, and federal mandates. There is no knowledge of continuous improvement.	A shared decision-making structure is put into place and discussions begin on how to achieve a school vision. Most decisions are focused on solving problems and are reactive.	Leadership team is committed to continuous improvement. Leadership seeks inclusion of all school sectors and supports study teams by making time provisions for their work.	Leadership team represents a true shared decision-making structure. Study teams are reconstructed for the implementation of a comprehensive continuous improvement plan.	A strong continuous improvement structure is set into place that allows for input from all sectors of the school, district, and community, ensuring strong communication, flexibility, and refinement of approach and beliefs. The school vision is student focused, based on data, and appropriate for school/community values, and meeting student needs.
Implementation	Principal makes all decisions, with little or no input from teachers, the community, or students. Leadership inspects for mistakes.	School values and beliefs are identified; the purpose of school is defined; a school mission and student learning standards are developed with representative input. A structure for studying approaches to achieving student learning standards is established.	Leadership team is active on study teams and integrates recommendations from the teams' research and analyses to form a comprehensive plan for continuous improvement within the context of the school mission. Everyone is kept informed.	Decisions about budget and implementation of the vision are made within teams, by the principal, by the leadership team, and by the full staff as appropriate. All decisions are communicated to the leadership team and to the full staff.	The vision is implemented and articulated across all grade levels and into feeder schools. Quality standards are reinforced throughout the school. All members of the school community understand and apply the quality standards. Leadership team has systematic interactions and involvement with district administrators, teachers, parents, community, and students about the school's direction. Necessary resources are available to implement and measure staff learning related to student learning standards.
Outcome	Decisions lack focus and consistency. There is no evidence of staff commitment to a shared vision. Students and parents do not feel they are being heard. Decision-making process is clear and known.	The mission provides a focus for all school improvement and guides the action to the vision. The school community is committed to continuous improvement. Quality leadership techniques are used sporadically.	Leadership team is seen as committed to planning and quality improvement. Critical areas for improvement are identified. Faculty feel included in shared decision making.	There is evidence that the leadership team listens to all levels of the organization. Implementation of the continuous improvement plan is linked to student learning standards and the guiding principles of the school. Leadership capacities for implementing the vision among teachers are evident.	Site-based management and shared decision making truly exists. Teachers understand and display an intimate knowledge of how the school operates. Teachers support and communicate with each other in the implementation of quality strategies. Teachers implement the vision in their classrooms and can determine how their new approach meets student needs and leads to the attainment of student learning standards. Leaders are standards-driven at all levels.

School Continuous Improvement Continuums
PARTNERSHIP DEVELOPMENT

	One	Two	Three	Four	Five
Approach	There is no system for input from parents, business, or community. Status quo is desired for managing the school.	Partnerships are sought, but mostly for money and things.	School has knowledge of why partnerships are important and seeks to include businesses and parents in a strategic fashion related to student learning standards for increased student achievement.	School seeks effective win-win business and community partnerships and parent involvement to implement the vision. Desired outcomes are clearly identified. A solid plan for partnership development exists.	Community, parent, and business partnerships become integrated across all student groupings. The benefits of outside involvement are known by all. Parent and business involvement in student learning is refined. Student learning *regularly* takes place beyond the school walls.
Implementation	Barriers are erected to close out involvement of outsiders. Outsiders are managed for least impact on status quo.	A team is assigned to get partners and to receive input from parents, the community, and business in the school.	Involvement of business, community, and parents begins to take place in some classrooms and after school hours related to the vision. Partners begin to realize how they can support each other in achieving school goals. School staff understand what partners need from the partnership.	There is a systematic utilization of parents, community, and businesses schoolwide. Areas in which the active use of these partnerships benefit student learning are clear.	Partnership development is articulated across all student groupings. Parents, community, business, and educators work together in an innovative fashion to increase student learning and to prepare students for the 21st Century. Partnerships are evaluated for continuous improvement.
Outcome	There is little or no involvement of parents, business, or community at-large. School is a closed, isolated system.	Much effort is given to establishing partner-ships. Some spotty trends emerge, such as receiving donated equipment.	Some substantial gains are achieved in implementing partnerships. Some student achievement increases can be attributed to this involvement.	Gains in student satisfaction with learning and school are clearly related to partnerships. All partners benefit.	Previously non-achieving students enjoy learning with excellent achievement. Community, business, and home become common places for student learning, while school becomes a place where parents come for further education. Partnerships enhance what the school does for students.

School Continuous Improvement Continuums

CONTINUOUS IMPROVEMENT AND EVALUATION

	One	Two	Three	Four	Five
Approach	Neither goals nor strategies exist for the evaluation and continuous improvement of the school organization or for elements of the school organization.	The approach to continuous improvement and evaluation is problem solving. If there are no problems, or if solutions can be made quickly, there is no need for improvement or analyses. Changes in parts of the system are not coordinated with all other parts.	Some elements of the school organization are evaluated for effectiveness. Some elements are improved on the basis of the evaluation findings.	All elements of the school's operations are evaluated for improvement and to ensure congruence of the elements with respect to the continuum of learning students experience.	All aspects of the school organization are rigorously evaluated and improved on a continuous basis. Students, and the maintenance of a comprehensive learning continuum for students, become the focus of all aspects of the school improvement process.
Implementation	With no overall plan for evaluation and continuous improvement, strategies are changed by individual teachers and administrators only when something sparks the need to improve. Reactive decisions and activities are a daily mode of operation.	Isolated changes are made in some areas of the school organization in response to problem incidents. Changes are not preceded by comprehensive analyses, such as an understanding of the root causes of problems. The effectiveness of the elements of the school organization, or changes made to the elements, is not known.	Elements of the school organization are improved on the basis of comprehensive analyses of root causes of problems, client perceptions, and operational effectiveness of processes.	Continuous improvement analyses of student achievement and instructional strategies are rigorously reinforced within each classroom and across learning levels to develop a comprehensive learning continuum for students and to prevent student failure.	Comprehensive continuous improvement becomes the way of doing business at the school. Teachers continuously improve the appropriateness and effectiveness of instructional strategies based on student feedback and performance. All aspects of the school organization are improved to support teachers' efforts.
Outcome	Individuals struggle with system failure. Finger pointing and blaming others for failure occurs. The effectiveness of strategies is not known. Mistakes are repeated.	Problems are solved only temporarily and few positive changes result. Additionally, unintended and undesirable consequences often appear in other parts of the system. Many aspects of the school are incongruent, keeping the school from reaching its vision.	Evidence of effective improvement strategies is observable. Positive changes are made and maintained due to comprehensive analyses and evaluation.	Teachers become astute at assessing and in predicting the impact of their instructional strategies on individual student achievement. Sustainable improvements in student achievement are evident at all grade levels, due to continuous improvement.	The school becomes a congruent and effective learning organization. Only instruction and assessment strategies that produce quality student achievement are used. A true continuum of learning results for all students and staff. The impact of improvements is increasingly measurable.

APPENDIX C
Continuous Improvement Continuums for Districts

These *Education for the Future Continuous Improvement Continuums,* adapted from the *Malcolm Baldrige Award Program for Quality Business Management,* provide an authentic means for measuring schoolwide improvement and growth. Districts and schools use these Continuums as a vehicle for ongoing self-assessment. They use the results of the assessment to acknowledge their accomplishments, to set goals for improvement, and to keep school districts and partners apprised of the progress they have made in their district improvement efforts.

Understanding the Continuums

These Continuums, extending from *one* to *five* horizontally, represent a continuum of expectations related to district improvement with respect to an *Approach* to the Continuum, *Implementation* of the approach, and the *Outcome* that results from the implementation. A *one* rating, located at the left of each Continuum, represents a district that has not yet begun to improve. *Five,* located at the right of each Continuum, represents a district that is one step removed from "world class quality." The elements between *one* and *five* describe how that Continuum is hypothesized to evolve in a continuously improving district. Each Continuum moves from a reactive mode to a proactive mode—from fire fighting to prevention. The *five* in *Outcome* in each Continuum is the target.

Vertically, the *Approach, Implementation,* and *Outcome* statements, for any number *one* through *five,* are hypotheses. In other words, the *implementation* statement describes how the *approach* might look when implemented, and the *outcome* is the "pay-off" for implementing the approach. If the hypotheses are accurate, the outcome will not be realized until the approach is actually implemented.

Using the Continuums

Use the *Continuous Improvement Continuums* (CICs) to understand where your district is with respect to continuous improvement. The results will hopefully provide that sense of urgency needed to spark enthusiasm for your district improvement efforts.

Start the assessment by stating or creating the ground rules, setting the tone for a safe and confidential assessment, and explaining why you are doing this. Provide a brief overview of the seven sections, taking each section one or two at a time, and having each staff member read the related Continuum and make independent assessments of where she/he believes the district is with respect to *Approach, Implementation,* and *Outcome.* We recommend using individual 8 1/2 x 11 copies of the Continuums for individual assessments. Then, have each staff member note where she/he believes the district is with a colorful sticker or marker on a large poster of the

Continuum. The markers allow all staff to see how much they are in agreement with one another. If only one color is used for the first assessment, another color can be used for the next assessment, and so forth, to help gauge growth over time, or you can plan to use two different charts for gauging progress over time such as in the photos below.

When all dots or marks have been placed on the enlarged Continuum, look at the agreement or disagreement of the ratings. Starting with *Approach,* have staff discuss why they believe the district is where they rated it. Keep discussing until the larger group comes to consensus on one number that reflects where the district is right now. You might need to make a quick check on where staff is with respect to coming to consensus, using a thumbs up, thumbs down "vote." Keep discussing the facts until consensus is reached. Do not average the results—it does not produce a sense of urgency for improvement. We cannot emphasize this enough! Keep discussing until agreement can be reached by everyone on a number that represents where "we" are right now. When that consensus is reached, record the number and move to *Implementation* and then *Outcome.* Determine *Next Steps.* Proceed in the same way through the next six categories.

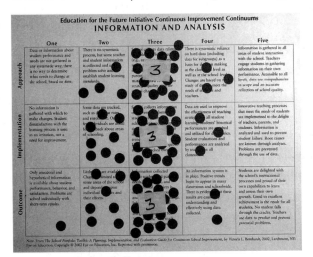

Fall Assessment

During the assessments, make sure someone records the discussions of the Continuum assessments. Districts might want to exchange facilitators with a neighboring district to have someone external to the district facilitate the assessments. This will enable everyone in the district to participate and provide an unbiased and competent person to lead the consensus-building piece. Assessing over time will help staff see that

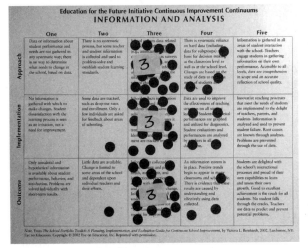

Spring Assessment

they are making progress. The decision of how often to assess on the *Continuous Improvement Continuums* is certainly up to the district. We recommend twice a year—about mid-fall and mid-spring—when there is time (or has been time) to implement next steps. Over time, once a year might be sufficient.

Using these Continuums will enable you and your district to stay motivated, to shape and maintain your shared vision, and will assist with the continuous improvement of all elements. Take pictures of the resulting charts. Even if your consensus number does not increase, the dots will most probably come together over time showing shifts in whole staff thinking.

Remember that where your district is at any time is just where it is. The important thing is what you do with this information. Continuous improvement is a never-ending process which, when used effectively, will ultimately lead your district toward providing a quality program for *all* children.

District Continuous Improvement Continuums
INFORMATION AND ANALYSIS

	One	Two	Three	Four	Five
Approach	Data or information about school student performance and needs are not gathered in any systematic way. The district does not provide assistance in helping schools understand what needs to change at the school and classroom levels, based on data.	There is no systematic process for data analysis across the district. Some school, teacher, and student information are collected and used to problem solve and establish student-learning standards across the district.	School district collects data related to school and student performance (e.g., attendance, enrollment, achievement), and surveys students, staff, and parents. The information is used to drive the strategic quality plan for district and school improvement.	There is systematic reliance on hard data (including data for subgroups) as a basis for decision making at the district, school, and classroom levels. Changes are based on the study of data to meet the educational needs of students and teachers.	Information is gathered in all areas of student interaction with the school. The district engages administrators and teachers in gathering information on their own performance. Accessible to all schools, data are comprehensive in scope and an accurate reflection of school and district quality.
Implementation	No information is gathered with which to make district or school changes. Student dissatisfaction with the learning process is seen as an irritation, not a need for improvement.	Some data are tracked, such as attendance, enrollment, and drop-out rates. Only a few individuals are asked for feedback about areas of schooling and district operations.	The district collects information on current and former students (e.g., student achievement and perceptions), analyzes and uses it in conjunction with future trends for planning. Identified areas for improvement are tracked over time.	Data are used to provide feedback to improve the effectiveness of teaching strategies on all student learning. Schools' historical performances are graphed and utilized for diagnosis by the district.	Innovative teaching processes that meet the needs of students are implemented across the district. Information is analyzed and used to prevent student failure. Root causes are known through analyses. Problems are prevented through the use of data.
Outcome	Only anecdotal and hypothetical information are available about student performance, behavior, and satisfaction. Problems are solved individually with short-term results.	Little data are available. Change is limited to some areas of the district and dependent upon individual administrators and their efforts.	Information collected about school needs, effective assessment, and instructional practices are shared with all school and district staff and used to plan for school and district improvement. Information helps staff understand pressing issues, analyze information for "root causes," and track results for improvement.	An information system is in place. Positive trends begin to appear in many schools and districtwide. There is evidence that these results are caused by understanding and effectively using the data collected.	Schools are delighted with their instructional processes and proud of their own capabilities to learn and assess their own growth. Good to excellent achievement is the result for all schools. Schools use data to predict and prevent potential problems. No student falls through the cracks.

District Continuous Improvement Continuums
STUDENT ACHIEVEMENT

	One	Two	Three	Four	Five
Approach	Instructional and organizational processes critical to student success are not identified. Little distinction of student learning differences is made. Some schools believe that not all students can achieve.	Some data are collected on student background and performance trends. Learning gaps are noted to direct improvement of instruction. It is known that student learning standards must be identified.	Student learning standards are identified, and a continuum of learning is created across the district. Student performance data are collected and compared to the standards in order to analyze how to improve learning for all students.	Data on student achievement are used throughout the district to pursue the improvement of student learning. The district ensures that teachers collaborate to implement appropriate instruction and assessment strategies for meeting student learning standards articulated across grade levels. All teachers believe that all students can learn.	The district makes an effort to exceed student achievement expectations. Innovative instructional changes are made to anticipate learning needs and improve student achievement. District makes sure that teachers are able to predict characteristics impacting student achievement and to know how to perform from a small set of internal quality measures.
Implementation	All students are taught the same way. There is no communication between the district and schools about students' academic needs or learning styles. There are no analyses of how to improve instruction.	Some effort is made to track and analyze student achievement trends on a districtwide basis. District begins to understand the needs and learning gaps within the schools.	Teachers across the district study effective instruction and assessment strategies to implement standards and to increase students' learning. Student feedback and analysis of achievement data are used in conjunction with implementation support strategies.	There is a systematic focus on implementing student learning standards and on the improvement of student learning districtwide. Effective instruction and assessment strategies are implemented in each school. District supports teachers supporting one another with peer coaching and/or action research focused on implementing strategies that lead to increased achievement.	All teachers correlate critical instructional and assessment strategies with objective indicators of quality student achievement. A comparative analysis of actual individual student performance to student learning standards is utilized to adjust teaching strategies to ensure a progression of learning for all students.
Outcome	There is wide variation in student attitudes and achievement with undesirable results. There is high dissatisfaction among students with learning. Student background is used as an excuse for low student achievement.	There is some evidence that student achievement trends are available to schools and are being used. There is much effort, but minimal observable results in improving student achievement.	There is an increase in communication among district and schools, students, and teachers regarding student learning. Teachers learn about effective instructional strategies that will implement the shared vision, student learning standards, and how to meet the needs of students. The schools make some gains.	Increased student achievement is evident districtwide. Student morale, attendance, and behavior are good. Teachers converse often with each other about preventing student failure. Areas for further attention are clear.	Schools and teachers conduct self-assessments to continuously improve performance. Improvements in student achievement are evident and clearly caused by teachers' and students' understandings of individual student learning standards, linked to appropriate and effective instructional and assessment strategies. A continuum of learning results. No students fall through the cracks.

District Continuous Improvement Continuums
QUALITY PLANNING

	One	Two	Three	Four	Five
Approach	No quality plan or process exists. Data are neither used nor considered important in planning.	The district realizes the importance of a mission, vision, and one comprehensive action plan. Teams develop goals and timelines, and dollars are allocated to begin the process.	A comprehensive plan to achieve the district vision is developed. Plan includes evaluation and continuous improvement.	One focused and integrated districtwide plan for implementing a continuous improvement process is put into action. All district efforts are focused on the implementation of this plan that represents the achievement of the vision.	A plan for the continuous improvement of the district, with a focus on students, is put into place. There is excellent articulation and integration of all elements in the district due to quality planning. Leadership team ensures all elements are implemented by all appropriate parties.
Implementation	There is no knowledge of or direction for quality planning. Budget is allocated on an as-needed basis. Many plans exist.	School district community begins continuous improvement planning efforts by laying out major steps to a shared vision, by identifying values and beliefs, the purpose of the district, a mission, vision, and student learning standards.	Implementation goals, responsibilities, due dates, and timelines are spelled out. Support structures for implementing the plan are set in place.	The quality management plan is implemented through effective procedures in all areas of the district. Everyone commits to implementing the plan aligned to the vision, mission, and values and beliefs. All share responsibility for accomplishing district goals.	Districtwide goals, mission, vision, and student learning standards are shared and articulated throughout the district and with feeder schools. The attainment of identified student learning standards is linked to planning and implementation of effective instruction that meets students' needs. Leaders at all levels are developing expertise because planning is the norm.
Outcome	There is no evidence of comprehensive planning. Staff work is carried out in isolation. A continuum of learning for students is absent.	The school district community understands the benefits of working together to implement a comprehensive continuous improvement plan.	There is evidence that the district plan is being implemented in some areas of the district. Improvements are neither systematic nor integrated districtwide.	A districtwide plan is known to all. Results from working toward the quality improvement goals are evident throughout the district. Planning is ongoing and inclusive of all stakeholders.	Evidence of effective teaching and learning results in significant improvement of student achievement attributed to quality planning at all levels of the district organization. Teachers and administrators understand and share the district mission and vision. Quality planning is seamless and all demonstrate evidence of accountability.

District Continuous Improvement Continuums
PROFESSIONAL LEARNING

	One	Two	Three	Four	Five
Approach	There is no professional development. Teachers, principals, and staff are seen as interchangeable parts that can be replaced. Professional development is external and usually equated to attending a conference alone. Hierarchy determines "haves" and "have-nots."	The "cafeteria" approach to professional development is used, whereby individual teachers and administrators choose what they want to take, without regard to an overall district plan.	The shared vision, district plan and student needs are used to target focused professional development for all employees. Staff is inserviced on relevant instructional and leadership strategies.	Professional development and data-gathering methods are used by all teachers and administrators, and are directed toward the goals of the shared vision and the continuous improvement of the district and schools. Teachers have ongoing conversations about student achievement data. All staff members receive training in their content areas. Systems thinking is considered in all decisions.	Leadership and staff continuously improve all aspects of the learning organization through an innovative, data-driven, and comprehensive continuous improvement process that prevents student failures. Effective job-embedded professional development is ongoing for implementing the vision for student success. Traditional teacher evaluations are replaced by collegial coaching and action research focused on student learning standards. Policies set professional development as a priority budget line-item. Professional development is planned, aligned, and leads to the achievement of student learning standards.
Implementation	District staff, principals, teachers, and school staff performance is controlled and inspected. Performance evaluations are used to detect mistakes.	Teacher professional development is sporadic and unfocused, lacking an approach for implementing new procedures and processes. Some leadership training begins to take place.	The district ensures that teachers are involved in year-round quality professional development. The school community is trained in shared decision making, team building concepts, effective communication strategies, and data analysis.	Teachers, in teams, continuously set and implement student achievement goals. Leadership considers these goals and provides necessary support structures for collaboration. Teachers utilize effective support approaches as they implement new instruction and assessment strategies. Coaching and feedback structures are in place. Use of new knowledge and skills is evident.	Teams passionately support each other in the pursuit of quality improvement at all levels. Teachers make bold changes in instruction and assessment strategies focused on student learning standards and student learning styles. A *teacher as action researcher* model is implemented. Staffwide conversations focus on systemic reflection and improvement. Teachers are strong leaders.
Outcome	No professional growth and no staff or student performance improvement. There exists a high turnover rate of employees, especially administrators. Attitudes and approaches filter down to students.	The effectiveness of professional development is not known or analyzed. Teachers feel helpless and unsupported in making schoolwide changes.	Teachers, working in teams, feel supported by the district and begin to feel they can make changes. Evidence shows that shared decision making works.	A collegial school district is evident. Effective classroom strategies are practiced, articulated schoolwide. These strategies, focused on student learning standards, are reflective of professional development aimed at ensuring student learning and the implementation of the shared vision.	True systemic change and improved student achievement result because teachers are knowledgeable of and implement effective, differentiated teaching strategies for individual student learning gains. Teachers' repertoire of skills is enhanced and students are achieving. Professional development is driving learning at all levels.

District Continuous Improvement Continuums
LEADERSHIP

	One	Two	Three	Four	Five
Approach	The School Board is decision maker. Decisions are reactive to state, district, and federal mandates. There is no knowledge of continuous improvement.	A shared decision-making structure is put into place and discussions begin on how to achieve a district vision. Most decisions are focused on solving problems and are reactive.	District leadership team is committed to continuous improvement. Leadership seeks inclusion of all school sectors and supports study teams by making time provisions for their work.	District leadership team represents a true shared decision-making structure. Study teams are reconstructed for the implementation of a comprehensive continuous improvement plan.	A strong continuous improvement structure is set into place that allows for input from all sectors of the district, school, and community; ensuring strong communication, flexibility, and refinement of approach and beliefs. The district vision is student focused, based on data and appropriate for district/school/community values, and meeting student needs.
Implementation	The School Board makes all decisions, with little or no input from administrators, teachers, the community, or students. Leadership inspects for mistakes.	District values and beliefs are identified; the purpose of district is defined; a district mission and student learning standards are developed with representative input. A structure for studying approaches to achieving student learning standards is established.	The district leadership team is active on study teams and integrates recommendations from the teams' research and analyses to form a comprehensive plan for continuous improvement within the context of the district mission. Everyone is kept informed.	Decisions about budget and implementation of the vision are made within teams, by the school board, by the leadership team, by the individual schools, and by the full staff, as appropriate. All decisions are communicated to the leadership team and to the full staff.	The vision is implemented and articulated across all grade levels and into feeder schools. Quality standards are reinforced throughout the district. All members of the district community understand and apply the quality standards. Leadership team has systematic interactions and involvement with district administrators, teachers, parents, community, and students about the district's direction. Necessary resources are available to implement and measure staff learning related to student learning standards.
Outcome	Although the decision-making process is clearly known, decisions are reactive and lack focus and consistency. There is no evidence of staff commitment to a shared vision. Students and parents do not feel they are being heard.	The mission provides a focus for all district and school improvement and guides the action to the vision. The school community is committed to continuous improvement. Quality leadership techniques are used sporadically.	The district leadership team is seen as committed to planning and quality improvement. Critical areas for improvement are identified. Faculty feel included in shared decision making.	There is evidence that the district leadership team listens to all levels of the organization. Implementation of the continuous improvement plan is linked to student learning standards and the guiding principles of the school. Leadership capacity for implementing the vision throughout the district is evident.	Site-based management and shared decision making truly exists. Teachers understand and display an intimate knowledge of how the school and district operate. Schools support and communicate with each other in the implementation of quality strategies. Teachers implement the vision in their classrooms and can determine how their new approaches meet student needs and lead to the attainment of student learning standards. Leaders are standards-driven at all levels.

Copyright © 1991–2009 Education for the Future Initiative, Chico, CA.

District Continuous Improvement Continuums
PARTNERSHIP DEVELOPMENT

	One	Two	Three	Four	Five
Approach	There is no system for input from parents, business, or community. Status quo is desired for managing the school district.	Partnerships are sought, but mostly for money and things.	School district has knowledge of why partnerships are important and seeks to include businesses and parents in a strategic fashion related to student learning standards for increased student achievement.	School district seeks effective win-win business and community partnerships and parent involvement to implement the vision. Desired outcomes are clearly identified. A solid plan for partnership development exists.	Community, parent, and business partnerships become integrated across all student groupings. The benefits of outside involvement are known by all. Parent and business involvement in student learning is refined. Student learning regularly takes place beyond the school and district walls.
Implementation	Barriers are erected to close out involvement of outsiders. Outsiders are managed for least impact on status quo.	A team is assigned to get partners and to receive input from parents, the community, and business in the school district.	Involvement of business, community, and parents begins to take place in some schools and after school hours related to the vision. Partners begin to realize how they can support each other in achieving district goals. District staff understand what partners need from the partnership.	There is systematic utilization of parents, community, and businesses districtwide. Areas in which the active use of these partnerships benefit student learning are clear.	Partnership development is articulated across all district groupings. Parents, community, business, and educators work together in an innovative fashion to increase student learning and to prepare students for the Twenty-first Century. Partnerships are evaluated for continuous improvement.
Outcome	There is little or no involvement of parents, business, or community at-large. The district is a closed, isolated system.	Much effort is given to establishing partnerships. Some spotty trends emerge, such as receiving donated equipment.	Some substantial gains are achieved in implementing partnerships. Some student achievement increases can be attributed to this involvement.	Gains in student satisfaction with learning and school are clearly related to partnerships. All partners benefit.	Previously non-achieving students enjoy learning with excellent achievement. Community, business, and home become common places for student learning, while school becomes a place where parents come for further education. Partnerships enhance what the school district does for students.

District Continuous Improvement Continuums

CONTINUOUS IMPROVEMENT AND EVALUATION

	One	Two	Three	Four	Five
Approach	Neither goals nor strategies exist for the evaluation and continuous improvement of the district organization or for elements of the organization.	The approach to continuous improvement and evaluation is problem-solving. If there are no problems, or if solutions can be made quickly, there is no need for improvement or analyses. Changes in parts of the system are not coordinated with all other parts.	Some elements of the district organization are evaluated for effectiveness. Some elements are improved on the basis of the evaluation findings.	All elements of the district's operations are evaluated for improvement. Efforts are consistently made to ensure congruence of the elements with respect to the continuum of learning that students experience.	All aspects of the district organization are rigorously evaluated and improved on a continuous basis. Students, and the maintenance of a comprehensive learning continuum for students, become the focus of all aspects of the school district improvement process.
Implementation	With no overall plan for evaluation and continuous improvement, strategies are changed by individual schools, teachers, and/or administrators only when something sparks the need to improve. Reactive decisions and activities are a daily mode of operation.	Isolated changes are made in some areas of the district organization in response to problem incidents. Changes are not preceded by comprehensive analyses, such as an understanding of the root causes of problems. The effectiveness of the elements of the district organization is not known.	Elements of the district organization are improved on the basis of comprehensive analyses of root causes of problems, client perceptions, and operational effectiveness of processes.	Continuous improvement analyses of student achievement and instructional strategies are rigorously reinforced within each classroom and across learning levels to develop a comprehensive learning continuum for students and to prevent student failure.	Comprehensive continuous improvement becomes the way of doing business throughout the district. Teachers continuously improve the appropriateness and effectiveness of instructional strategies based on student feedback and performance. All aspects of the district organization are improved to support teachers' efforts.
Outcome	Individuals struggle with system failure. Finger pointing and blaming others for failure occur. The effectiveness of strategies is not known. Mistakes are repeated.	Problems are solved only temporarily and few positive changes result. Additionally, unintended and undesirable consequences often appear in other parts of the system. Many aspects of the school district are incongruent, keeping the district from reaching its vision.	Evidence of effective improvement strategies is observable. Positive changes are made and maintained due to comprehensive analyses and evaluation.	Teachers become astute at assessing and in predicting the impact of their instructional strategies on individual student achievement. Sustainable improvements in student achievement are evident at all grade levels due to continuous improvement supported by the district.	The district becomes a congruent and effective learning organization. Only instruction and assessment strategies that produce quality student achievement are used. A true continuum of learning results for all students and staff. The impact of improvements is increasingly measurable.

GLOSSARY OF TERMS

The Glossary provides brief definitions of data analysis and testing terms used throughout *Data Analysis for Continuous School Improvement,* Second Edition.

▼ **Achievement**

The demonstration of student performance measured against learning goals, learning objectives, or standards.

▼ **Achievement Gap**

The difference between how well low-income and minority children perform on standardized tests, as compared with their peers. For many years, low-income and minority children have been falling behind their white peers in terms of academic achievement.

▼ **Accountability**

The act of being responsible to somebody else or to others. It also means capable of being explained.

▼ **Action**

Specific steps, tasks, or activity used to implement a strategy.

▼ **Action Plan**

The part of continuous school improvement planning that describes the tasks that must be performed, when they will be performed, who is responsible, and how much they will cost to implement.

▼ **Action Research**

Teachers and/or administrators raise questions about the best way to improve teaching and learning, systematically study the literature to answer the questions, implement the best approach(es), and analyze the results.

▼ **Adequate Yearly Progress (AYP)**

An individual state's measure of yearly progress toward achieving state academic standards. *Adequate Yearly Progress* is the minimum level of improvement that states, school districts, and schools must achieve each year.

▼ **Affinity Diagram**

A visual picture or chart of reflective thinking. The result is that more participants are likely to deal with problems that emerge.

▼ **Aggregate**

Combining the results of all groups that make up the sample or population.

▼ **Alignment**

An arrangement of groups or forces in relation to one another. In continuous school improvement planning, we align all parts of the system to the vision. With curriculum, we align instruction and materials to student learning standards.

▼ **Analysis**

The examination of facts and data to provide a basis for effective decisions.

▼ **Analysis of Variance (ANOVA)**

ANOVA is an inferential procedure to determine if there is a significant difference among sample means.

▼ **Anticipated Achievement Scores**

An estimate of the average score for students of similar ages, grade levels, and academic aptitude. It is an estimate of what we would expect an individual student to score on an achievement test.

▼ **Articulation**

The varied process of integrating the school/district aligned curriculum across disciplines and between grade levels and connecting it to real-life situations; also presenting it to all stakeholders and implementing it district/school wide.

▼ **Assessment**

Gathering and interpretation of student performance, primarily for the purpose of enhancing learning. Also used for the improvement of a program and/or strategies.

▼ **Authentic Assessment**

Refers to a variety of ways to assess a student's demonstration of knowledge and skills. Authentic assessments may include performances, projects, exhibitions, and portfolios.

▼ **Bar Graph**

A pictorial representation that uses bars to display data, usually frequencies, percentages, and averages.

▼ **Baseline Data**

Information collected to comprise a reference set for comparison of a second set of data collected at a later time; used to interpret changes over time, usually after some condition has been changed for research purposes that sets the standard for any research that follows in the same project.

▼ **Benchmark**

A standard against which something can be measured or assessed.

▼ **Brainstorming**

The act of listing ideas without judgment. Brainstorming generates creative ideas spontaneously.

▼ **Cadres or Action Teams**

Groups or teams of educators who agree to accept responsibility to study new approaches, plan for the implementation of new strategies or programs, and get work done without every staff member's involvement.

▼ **Case Studies**

Reviewing student's work, and/or another teacher's example lessons, which can lead to quality discussions and improved practices.

▼ **Cause and Effect**

The relationship and complexities between a problem or effect and the possible causes.

▼ **Coaching**

Teachers form teams of two or three to observe each other, plan together, and talk and encourage each other in meaningful ways while reflecting on continuously improving instructional practices.

▼ **Cognitive Abilities or Skills Index**

An age-dependent, normalized standard score based on a student's performance on a cognitive skills test with a mean of 100 and standard deviation of 16. The score indicates a student's overall cognitive ability or academic aptitude relative to students of similar age, without regard to grade level.

▼ **Cohort**

A group of individuals sharing a particular statistical or demographic characteristic, such as the year they were in a specific school grade level. Following cohorts over time helps teachers understand the effects particular circumstances may have on results. Matched cohort studies follow the same individuals over time, and unmatched cohort studies follow the same group over time.

▼ **Cohort Analysis**

The reorganization of grade level data to look at the groups of students progressing through the grades together over time.

▼ **Collaboration**

Evidence of two of more concerned groups (i.e., teachers, aides, itinerant and resource teachers, parents, community representatives, etc.), working together to improve the school program.

▼ **Collaborative**

Working jointly with others, especially in an intellectual endeavor.

▼ **Comprehensive Action Plan**

Defining the specific actions needed to implement the vision, setting forth when the actions will take place, designating who is responsible for accomplishing the action, how much it will cost, and where to get the funds.

▼ **Confidence Interval**

Used in inferential statistics, a range of values that a researcher can estimate, with a certain level of confidence, where the population parameter is located.

▼ **Congruent**

Corresponding to, or consistent with, each other or something else.

▼ **Consensus**

Decision making where a group finds a proposal acceptable enough that all members can support it; no member actively opposes it.

▼ **Content Standard**

Description of the knowledge or skills that educators want students to learn.

▼ **Continuous**

In the context of continuous school improvement, continuous means the ongoing review of the data, the implementation of the plan, and the progress being made.

▼ **Continuous Improvement**

Keeping the process of planning, implementing, evaluating, and improving alive over time.

▼ **Continuous Improvement and Evaluation**

The section of the school portfolio that assists schools to further understand where they are and what they need to do to move forward in the big picture of continuous school improvement.

▼ **Continuous Improvement Continuums (CICs)**

As developed by *Education for the Future Initiative,* CICs are seven rubrics that represent the theoretical flow of systemic school improvement. The *Continuous Improvement Continuums* take the theory and spirit of continuous school improvement, interweave educational research, and offer practical meaning to the components that must change simultaneously and systematically.

▼ **Continuous School Improvement**

By *continuous school improvement,* we mean measuring and evaluating processes on an ongoing basis to identify and implement improvement.

▼ **Continuous School Improvement Plan**

A plan for improvement, based on data, that will help create and manage change. The process of answering the following questions: *Who are we? How do we do business? What are our strengths and areas for improvement? Why do we exist? Where do we want to be? What are the gaps? What are the root causes of the gaps? How can we get to where we want to be? How will we implement? How will we evaluate our efforts?*

▼ **Control Groups**

Control groups serve as a baseline in making comparisons with treatment groups and are necessary when general effectiveness of the treatment is unknown. During an experiment, the control group is studied the same as the experimental groups, except that it does not receive the treatment of interest.

▼ **Convenience Sampling**

Convenience sampling is done when one wants to survey people who are ready and available, and not hassle with trying to get everyone in the population ready and willing to complete the questionnaire.

▼ **Correlation**

A statistical analysis that helps one see the relationship of scores in one distribution to scores in another distribution. Correlation coefficients have a range of −1.0 to +1.0. A correlation of around zero indicates no relationship. Correlations of .8 and higher indicate strong relationships.

▼ **Criteria**

Characteristics or dimensions of student performance.

▼ **Criterion-referenced Tests**

Tests that judge how well a test taker does on an explicit objective, learning goal, or criteria relative to a pre-determined performance level. There is no comparison to any other test takers.

▼ **Culture**

Attitudes, values, beliefs, goals, norms of behavior, and practices that characterize a group.

▼ **Curriculum Alignment**

A curriculum in which what is taught, how it is taught, and how it is assessed is intentionally based on, but not limited to, the state *Core Curriculum Content Standards and Assessment*—the sequence of learning in an aligned curriculum is articulated and constantly discussed, monitored, and revised.

▼ **Curriculum Development and Implementation**

The way content is designed and delivered. Teachers must think deeply about the content, student-learning standards, and how it must be managed and delivered, or put into practice.

▼ **Curriculum Implementation**

Putting the curriculum into practice.

▼ **Curriculum Mapping and Webbing**

Approaches that require teachers to align the curriculum and student learning standards by grade levels, and then across grade levels to ensure a continuum of learning that makes sense for all students.

▼ **Data Cleansing**

The process of ensuring that all values in a database are consistent and correctly recorded.

▼ **Data-driven Decision Making**

Making decisions based on demographic, student learning, perceptions, and school process data. True data-driven decision making has at the center of every decision the guiding principles of the learning organization.

▼ **Data Mining**

Techniques for finding patterns and trends in large data sets. The process of automatically extracting valid, useful, previously unknown, and ultimately comprehensible information from large databases. Just doing common data analysis is not data mining.

▼ **Data Table**

The source of data for tables and graphs. In building graphs with a software program, one would need to create a data table from which to create the graphs or tables.

▼ **Data Warehouse**

A single, large database that has collected relevant information from several other sources into a single, accessible format designed to be used for decision making. The data warehouse is created to house data imported from many other data sources that are not designed to work together or to share information.

▼ **Database**

A storage mechanism for data that eliminates redundancy and conflict among multiple data files. Data is entered once and is then available to all programs that need it.

▼ **Deciles**

The values of a variable that divide the frequency distribution into ten equal frequency groups. The ninth decile shows the number (or percentage) of the norming group that scored between 80 and 89 NCE, for example.

▼ **Demographics**

Statistical characteristics of a population, such as average age, number of students in a school, percentages of ethnicities, etc. Disaggregation with demographic data allows us to isolate variations among different subgroups.

▼ **Derived Score**

A score that is attained by performing some kind of mathematical operation on a raw score for comparison within a particular grade (e.g., T-scores, NCE, etc.).

▼ **Descriptive Statistics**

Direct measurement (i.e. mean, median, percent correct) of each member of a group or population. Descriptive statistics can include graphing.

▼ **Diagnostic**

Assessment/evaluation carried out prior to instruction that is designed to determine a student's attitude, skill, or knowledge in order to identify specific student needs.

▼ **Diagnostic Tests**

Usually standardized and normed, diagnostic tests are given before instruction begins to help the instructor(s) understand student learning needs. Many different score types are used with diagnostic tests.

▼ **Different Ways of Knowing (DWOK)**

A standards-based, interdisciplinary, arts-infused curriculum that promotes collaborative learning and higher–order thinking.

▼ **Disaggregate**

Separating the results of different groups that make up the sample or population.

▼ **Disaggregated Data**

To *disaggregate* means to separate a whole into its parts. In education, this term means that test results are sorted into groups of students by gender, those who are economically disadvantaged, by racial and ethnic minority groups, disabilities, or by English fluency. This practice allows administrators and teachers to see more than just the average score for the school. Instead, administrators and teachers can see how each student group is performing.

▼ **Diverse/Diversity**

The inclusion of differences based on gender, race, disability, age, national origin, color, economic status, religion, geographic regions, and other characteristics. Achieving diversity requires respect of differences; valuing differences; supporting, encouraging, and promoting differences; and affirmation initiatives, such as recruitment, placement, and retention.

▼ **Educationally Significant**

Gains in student achievement, school, or program results can be considered educationally significant, even though they are not statistically significant.

▼ **Evaluation**

Making judgments about the quality of overall student performance for the purpose of communicating student achievement. Evaluation also is the study of the impact of a program or process.

▼ **Examining Student Data**

Conversations around individual student data results and the processes that created the results. This approach can be a significant form of professional development when skilled team members facilitate the discussions.

▼ **Examining Student Work**

Ensures that what students learn is aligned to the learning standards. It also shows teachers the impact of their actions.

▼ **Exemplars**

Models or examples of excellent work that meet stated criteria or levels of performance.

▼ **Experimental Design**

The detailed planning of an experiment, made beforehand, to insure the data collected is appropriate and obtained in a way that will lead to an objective analysis, with valid inferences. Preferably, the design will maximize the amount of information that can be gained, given the amount of effort expended.

▼ **Fluency**

The capacity to read text accurately and quickly.

▼ **Flow Chart**

A flowchart illustrates the steps in a process. By visualizing the process, a flow chart can quickly help identify bottlenecks or inefficiencies where a process can be streamlined or improved.

▼ **Focus Group**

A group convened to gather information about processes or practices that need to be examined.

▼ **Formative**

Assessments at regular intervals of a student's progress, with accompanying feedback in order to help the student's performance and to provide direction for improvement of a program for individual students or for a whole class.

▼ **Frequency**

The number of times a given score occurs in a distribution.

▼ **Frequency Distribution**

Describes how often observations fall within designated categories. It can be expressed as numbers, percents, and deciles, to name just a few possibilities.

▼ **Gain Score**

The difference between two administrations of the same test. Gain scores are calculated by subtracting the previous score from the most recent score. One can have negative gains, which are actually losses.

▼ **Gaps**

The difference between where the school is now and where the school wants to be in the future. It is this gap that gets translated into goals, objectives, strategies, and actions in the action plan.

▼ **Goals**

Achievements or end results. Goal statements describe the intended outcome of the vision and are stated in terms that are broad, general, abstract, and non-measurable. Schools should have only two or three goals.

▼ **Grade-level Analysis**

Looking at the same grade level over time.

▼ **Grade-level Equivalent**

The grade and month of the school year for which a given score is the actual or estimated average. Based on a 10-month school year, scores would be noted as 3.1 for grade three, first month, 5.10 for grade five, tenth month, etc.

▼ **Grades**

Subjective scores given by teachers to students for performance.

▼ **Guiding Principles**

The vision of the school, or district, that is based on the purpose and mission of the organization, created from the values and beliefs of the individuals to make up the organization. Everything that is done in the organization ought to be aligned to its guiding principles.

▼ **Holistic**

Emphasizing the organic or functional relation between parts and the whole.

▼ **Horizontal Articulation or Coordination**

Indicates that the curriculum is carefully planned within grade levels. In effect, this would mean that every primary grade throughout the school/district will teach the same curriculum—also every grade six social studies class; every grade ten health class; every grade twelve physics class, and so on.

▼ **Inferential Statistics**

Statistical analysis concerned with the measurement of only a sample from a population and then making estimates, or inferences, about the population from which the sample was taken; inferential statistics help generalize the results of data analyses.

▼ **Information and Analysis**

Establishes systematic and rigorous reliance on data for decision making in all parts of the organization. This section of the school portfolio sets the context of the learning organization.

▼ **Intersections**

Analyzing the overlapping of measures (demographics, perceptions, school processes, student learning) enables schools to predict what they must do to meet the needs of all the students they have, or will have in the future.

▼ **Interval Scale**

Intervals are meaningful with a relative zero point. Can calculate mode, median, mean, range, standard deviation, etc.

▼ **Item Analysis**

Reviewing each item on a test or assessment to determine how many students missed the particular item. A general term for procedures designed to access the usefulness of a test item.

▼ **Latent Trait Scale**

A scaled score obtained through one of several mathematical approaches collectively known as Latent-trait procedures or Item Response Theory. The particular numerical values used in the scale are arbitrary, but higher scores indicate more knowledgeable test takers or more difficult items.

▼ **Leadership**

Providing needed assistance to schools to think through and plan for their vision, shared decision making, and other structures that will work with their specific population.

▼ **Learner-Centered**

An environment created by educators focusing on the needs and learning styles of all students.

▼ **Learning**

A process of acquiring knowledge, skills, understanding, and/or new behaviors.

▼ **Learning Environment**

Any setting or location, inside or outside the school, used to enhance the instruction of students.

▼ **Learning Goal**

A target for learning: a desired skill, knowledge, or behavior.

▼ **Line Graph**

Line graphs give a lot of flexibility and are exceptionally good for showing a series of numbers over time. Line graphs can display complex data more effectively than bar graphs.

▼ **Matched Cohorts**

Looking at the same students (individual, not groups) progressing through the grades over time.

▼ **Maximum**

The highest actual score or the highest possible score on a test.

▼ **Mean**

Average score in a set of scores; calculated by summing all the scores and dividing by the total number of scores.

▼ **Means**

Methods, strategies, actions, and processes by which a school plans to improve student achievement.

▼ **Measures**

A way of evaluating something; how we know we have achieved the objective.

▼ **Median**

The score that splits a distribution in half: 50 percent of the scores lie above and 50 percent of the scores lie below the median. If the number of scores is odd, the median is the middle score. If the number of scores is even, one must add the two middle scores and divide by two to calculate the median.

▼ **Minimum**

The lowest score or the lowest possible score on a test.

▼ **Mission**

A brief, clear, and compelling statement that serves to unify an organization's efforts. A mission has a finish line for its achievement and is proactive. A mission should walk the boundary between the possible and impossible.

▼ **Mobility**

The reference to the movement of students in and out of a school or district.

▼ **Mode**

The score that occurs most frequently in a scoring distribution.

▼ **Multiple Measures**

Using more than one method of assessment, gathered from varying points of view, in order to understand the multifaceted world of school from the perspective of everyone involved.

▼ **N**

The number of students in the group being described, such as the number taking a test or completing a questionnaire.

▼ **Needs Assessment**

Questions that help staff understand their professional development needs. At the same time, if done well, this assessment can lead to quality staff conversations and sharing of knowledge.

▼ **No Child Left Behind**

The No Child Left Behind Act of 2001 reauthorized the 1965 Elementary and Secondary Education Act. NCLB calls for increased accountability for states, school districts, and schools; choices for parents and students; greater flexibility for states, school districts, and schools regarding Federal education funds; establishing a Reading First initiative to ensure every child can read by end of grade three; and improving the quality of teachers.

▼ **Nominal Scale**

Qualitative, categorical information. Numbers represent categories, e.g., 1=male, 2=female.

▼ **Normal Curve**

The bell-shaped curve of the normal distribution.

▼ **Normal Curve Equivalent (NCE)**

Equivalent scores are standard scores with a mean of 50, a standard deviation of 21.06, and a range of 1 to 99.

▼ **Normal Distribution**

A distribution of scores or other measures that in graphic form has a distinctive bell-shaped appearance. In a normal distribution, the measures are distributed symmetrically about the mean. Cases are concentrated near the mean and decrease in frequency, according to a precise mathematical equation, the farther one departs from the mean. Also known as a normal curve.

▼ **Normalized Standard Score**

A transformation procedure used to make scores from different tests more directly comparable. Not only are the mean and the standard deviation of the raw score distribution changed, as with a linear standard score transformation, but the shape of the distribution is converted to a normal curve. The transformation to a normalized z-score involves two steps: 1) compute the exact percentile rank of the raw score; and 2) determine the corresponding z-score for that exact percentile rank from a table of areas under the normal curve.

▼ **Norming Group**

A representative group of students whose results on a norm-referenced test help create the scoring scales with which others compare their performance. The norming group's results are professed to look like the normal curve.

▼ **Norm-referenced Test**

Any test in which the score acquires additional meaning by comparing it to the scores of people in an identified norming group. A test can be both norm- and criterion-referenced. Most standardized achievement tests are referred to as norm-referenced.

▼ **Norms**

The distribution of test scores and their corresponding percentile ranks, standard scores, or other derived scores of some specified group called the norming group. For example, this may be a national sample of all fourth graders, a national sample of all fourth-grade males, or perhaps all fourth graders in some local district.

▼ **Norms versus Standards**

Norms are not standards. Norms are indicators of what students of similar characteristics did when confronted with the same test items as those taken by students in the norming group. Standards, on the other hand, are arbitrary judgments of what students should be able to do, given a set of test items.

▼ **Objectives**

Goals that are redrafted in terms that are clearly tangible. Objective statements are narrow, specific, concrete, and measurable. When writing objectives, it is important to describe the intended results, rather than the process or means to accomplish them, and state the time frame.

▼ **Observation**

Teacher and observer agree on what is being observed, the type of information to be recorded, when the observation will take place, and how the information will be analyzed. The observee is someone implementing strategies and actions that others want to know. Observer might be a colleague, a supervisor, or a visitor from another location.

▼ **Open-ended Response Items**

Questions that require students to combine content knowledge and application of process skills in order to communicate an answer.

▼ **Ordinal**

Ordinal provides information about size or direction; numbers ordered along underlying dimension, but no information about distance between points.

▼ **Outcome**

Successful demonstration of learning that occurs at the culmination point of a set learning experiences.

▼ **Over Time**

No less than three years.

▼ **Parameter**

A parameter is a population measurement that characterizes one of its features. An example of a parameter is the mode. The mode is the value in the population that occurs most frequently. Other examples of parameters are a population's mean (or average) and its variance.

▼ **Partnerships**

Teachers developing relationships with parents, businesses in the community, scientists, and/or university personnel to help students achieve student learning standards, and to bring about real world applications for student learning and deeper understandings of content.

▼ **Pearson Correlation Coefficient**

The most widely-used correlation coefficient determines the extent to which two variables are proportional to each other; measures the strength and direction of a linear relationship between the x and y variables.

▼ **Percent Correct**

A calculated score implying the percentage of students meeting and exceeding some number, usually a cut score, or a standard. Percent passing equals the number passing the test divided by the number taking the test.

▼ **Percent Proficient**

Percent Proficient, Percent Mastery, or Percent Passing are terms that represent the percentage of students who pass a particular test at a level above a cut score, as defined by the test creators or the test interpreters.

▼ **Percentile**

A point on the normal distribution below which a certain percentage of the scores fall. For example, if 70 percent of the scores fall below a raw score of 56, then the score of 56 is at the 70th percentile. The term *local percentile* indicates that the norm group is obtained locally. The term *national percentile* indicates that the norm group represents a national group.

▼ **Percentile Rank (PR)**

Percentage of students in a norm group (e.g., national or local) whose scores fall below a given score. Range is from 1 to 99. A 50th percentile ranking would mean that 50 percent of the scores in the norming group fall below a specific score.

▼ **Perceptions Data**

Information that reflects opinions and views of questionnaire respondents.

▼ **Performance Assessment**

Refers to assessments that measure skills, knowledge, and ability directly—such as through performance. In other words, if you want students to learn to write, you assess their ability on a writing activity.

▼ **Performance Standard**

Identification of the desired level of proficiency at which educators want a content standard to be mastered.

▼ **Pie Chart or Pie Graph**

A graph in a circular format, used to display percentages of something, such as the percentage of a school or district population, by ethnicity.

▼ **Population**

Statisticians define a population as the entire collection of items that is the focus of concern. Descriptive Statistics describe the characteristics of a given population by measuring each of its items and then summarizing the set of measures in various ways. Inferential Statistics make educated inferences about the characteristics of a population by drawing a random sample and appropriately analyzing the information it provides.

▼ **Press Release**

Article written by school public information official or an education reporter for a local newspaper.

▼ **Process Mapping**

School processes are instruction, curriculum, and assessment strategies used to ensure the learning of all students. Mapping or flow charting school processes can help staff objectively look at how students are being taught.

▼ **Processes**

Measures that describe what is being done to get results, such as programs, strategies, and practices.

▼ **Professional Development**

Planned activities that help staff members, teachers, and administrators change the manner in which they work, i.e., how they make decisions; gather, analyze, and use data; plan, teach, and monitor achievement; evaluate personnel; and assess the impact of new approaches to instruction and assessment on students.

▼ **Program Evaluation**

The examination of a program to understand its quality and impact.

▼ **Purpose**

The aim of the organization; the reason for existence.

▼ **Quality Planning**

Developing the elements of a strategic plan including a vision, mission, goals, action plan, outcome measures, and strategies for continuous improvement and evaluation. Quality planning is a section of the school portfolio.

▼ **Quality**

A standard for excellence.

▼ **Quartiles**

Three quartiles—Q1, Q2, Q3—divide a distribution into four equal groups (Q1=25th percentile; Q2=50th percentile; Q3=75th percentile).

▼ **Query**

A request one makes to a database that is returned to the desktop. Understanding and knowing how to set up queries or to ask questions of the database is very important to the information discovery process.

▼ **Quota Sampling**

Divides the population being studied into subgroups such as male and female, or young, middle, and old, to ensure that you set a quota of responses.

▼ **Range**

A measure of the spread between the lowest and the highest scores in a distribution, calculated by subtracting the lowest score from the highest score.

▼ **Ratio**

A proportional relationship between two different numbers or quantities.

▼ **Raw Scores**

A person's observed score on a test or subtest. The number of questions answered correctly on a test or subtest. A raw score is simply calculated by adding the number of questions answered correctly.

▼ **Regression**

An analysis that results in an equation that describes the nature of the relationship among variables. Simple regressions predict an object's value on a criterion variable when given its value on one predictor variable. Multiple regressions predict an object's value on a criterion variable when given its value on each of several predictor variables.

▼ **Relational Database**

A type of database that allows the connection of several databases to each other. The data and relations between them are stored in table form. Relational databases are powerful because they require few assumptions about how data are related and how they will be extracted from the database.

▼ **Relationships**

Looking at two or more sets of analyses to understand how they are associated or what they mean to each other.

▼ **Reliability**

The consistency with which an assessment measures what it intends to measure.

▼ **Research**

The act of methodically collecting information about a particular subject to discover facts or to develop a plan of action based on the facts discovered.

▼ **RIT Scale Scores**

Named for George Rasch, who developed the theory of this type of measurement, RIT scores are scaled scores that come from a series of tests created by the Northwest Evaluation Association (NWEA). The tests that draw from an item bank are created to align with local curriculum and state standards.

▼ **Root Cause**

As used in the continuous school improvement plan, refers to the deep underlying reason for a specific situation. While a symptom may be made evident from a needs assessment or gap analysis—the symptom (low student scores) is not the cause. To find a root cause or causes one often has to ask Why? at least five levels down to uncover the root reasons for the symptom.

▼ **Rubric**

A scoring tool that rates performance according to clearly stated levels of criteria. The scales can be numeric or descriptive.

▼ **Sample**

In statistical terms, a random sample is a set of items that have been drawn from a population in such a way that each time an item is selected, every item in the population has an equal opportunity to appear in the sample. In practical terms, it is not so easy to draw a random sample.

▼ **Scaled Scores**

A mathematical transformation of a raw score. It takes the differences in the difficulty of test forms into consideration and is useful for teaching changes over time.

▼ **School Improvement Planning**

Planning to implement the vision requires studying the research, determining strategies that will work with the students, and determining what the vision would look like, sound like, and feel like when the vision is implemented, and how to get all staff members implementing the vision.

▼ **School Portfolio**

A professional development tool that gathers evidence about the way work is done in the school and a self-assessment tool to ensure the alignment of all parts of the learning organization to the vision. A school portfolio can also serve as a principal portfolio.

▼ **School Processes**

Instruction, curriculum, and assessment strategies used to ensure the learning of all students.

▼ **School Profile**

A two to four page summary that presents a picture of a school. Usually includes demographic and achievement information, as well as analysis of other available data.

▼ **Scientifically-based Research**

The revised *Elementary and Secondary Education Act,* recently approved by Congress and also known as the *No Child Left Behind Act of 2001,* mandates that educators base school programs and teaching practices on Scientifically Based Research. This includes everything from teaching approaches to drug abuse prevention. Scientifically Based Research means research that involves the application of rigorous, systematic, and objective procedures to obtain reliable and valid knowledge relevant to education activities and programs.

▼ **Self-assessment**

Assessment by the individual performing the activity.

▼ **Shared Decision Making**

A process whereby all stakeholders within a school are engaged and meaningfully involved in the planning and decision-making process of that school.

▼ **Simple Sample**

A smaller version of the larger population that can be considered representative of the population. One classroom of students can be a simple sample, or one school in the district. This is typically used when administering a very large questionnaire.

▼ **Skewed Distribution**

Most of the scores are found near one end of the distribution. When most of the scores are grouped at the lower end, it is positively skewed. When most of the scores are grouped at the upper end, it is negatively skewed.

▼ **Snowball Sampling**

Relies on members of one group completing the questionnaire to identify other members of the population to complete the questionnaire.

▼ **Socioeconomic Status (SES)**

An indication of the level of poverty in which a student lives. Most school districts use whether or not a student qualifies for free/reduced lunch as an indicator. Other school districts use more complex equations that include mother's level of education and the like.

▼ **Standard**

A guideline or description that is used as a basis for judgment—exemplary performance; an objective ideal; a worthy and tangible goal.

▼ **Standard Deviation**

Measure of variability in a set of scores. The standard deviation is the square root of the variance. Unlike the variance, the standard deviation is stated in the original units of the variable. Approximately 68 percent of the scores in a normal distribution lie between plus one and minus one standard deviation. The more scores cluster around the mean, the smaller the variance.

▼ **Standard Scores**

A group of scores having a desired mean and standard deviation. A z-score is a basic standard score. Other standard scores are computed by first converting a raw score to a z-score (sometimes normalized), multiplying the transformation by the desired standard deviation, and then adding the desired mean to the product. The raw scores are transformed this way for reasons of convenience, comparability, and ease of interpretation.

▼ **Standardized Tests**

Tests that are uniform in content, administration, and scoring. Standardized tests can be used for comparing results across classrooms, schools, school districts, and states.

▼ **Standards**

Consistent expectations of all learners.

▼ **Standards-based Assessments**

A collection of items that indicate how much students know and/or are able to do with respect to specific standards.

▼ **Stanines**

A nine-point normalized standard score scale. It divides the normal curve distribution of scores into nine equal points: 1 to 9. The mean of a stanine distribution is 5, and the standard deviation is approximately 2.

▼ **Statistically Significant**

Statistical significance of a result is the probability that the observed relationship in a sample occurred by pure chance; indicates that there is at least a 95% probability of the result that did not happen by chance.

▼ **Strategies**

Procedures, methods, or techniques to accomplish an objective.

▼ **Stratified Random Sample**

One which divides the population into subgroups, and then a random sample is selected from each of the groups. This approach would be used when you want to make sure that you hear from all the groups of people you want to study.

▼ **Student Achievement Data**

Information that reflects a level of knowledge, skill, or accomplishment, usually in something that has been explicitly taught.

▼ **Study Groups**

Teams or groups of educators meet to learn new strategies or programs, to review new publications, or to review student work together.

▼ **Summative**

Assessment or evaluation designed to provide information; used in making judgments about a student's achievement at the end of a period of instruction.

▼ **Symptom**

A symptom is the outward (most visible) indicator of a deeper root cause.

▼ **System**

School districts are systems. A system is the sum of the interactions between and among its component parts.

▼ **Systemic**

Affecting or relating to a system as a whole.

▼ **Systematic**

Refers to approaches that are repeatable and that use data and information so that improvement and learning are possible.

▼ **Systems Perspective**

Viewing the school as a whole or perceiving the combination of related structures/components of the school and community (i.e., indicators and standards for school improvement), organized into a complex whole.

▼ **Systems Thinking**

Systems thinking would have continuous improvement teams focusing on improving how the parts of the system interact and support one another towards achievement of common goals.

▼ **T-Chart**

Used to compare and contrast information or to show relationships. It is used to help people see the opposite dimension of an issue.

▼ **T-Scores**

A calculated standard score with a mean of 50 and a standard deviation of 10. T-scores are obtained by the following formula: $T=10z+50$. T-scores are sometimes normalized.

▼ **Table**

A data structure comprised of rows and columns, like a spreadsheet.

▼ **Teacher Portfolios**

The process and product of documenting a teacher as learner; includes reflections, observations, and evidence. Portfolios can be used for many things, such as, self-assessment, employment, supervision to replace traditional teacher evaluation, and for peer collaboration.

▼ **Tests of Significance**

Procedures that use samples to test claims about population parameters. Significance tests can estimate a population parameter, with a certain amount of confidence, from a sample.

▼ **Trends**

Direction that is given from a learning organization's data. Usually need three years of data to see a trend.

▼ **Triangulation**

The term used for combining three or more student achievement measures to get a more complete picture of student achievement.

▼ **Validity**

The degree to which an assessment strategy measures what it is intended to measure.

▼ **Values and Beliefs**

The core of who we are, what we do, and how we think and feel. Values and beliefs reflect what is important to us; they describe what we think about work and how we think it should operate. Core values and beliefs are the first step in reaching a shared vision.

▼ **Variance**

A measure of the dispersion, or variability, of scores about their mean. The population variance is calculated by taking the average of the squared deviations from the mean—a deviation being defined as an individual score minus the mean.

▼ **Variation**

All systems and processes vary. It is essential to understand what type of variation is present before trying to correct or improve the system. Two types of variation are *common cause* and *special cause*. Special cause variation must be eliminated before a system can be improved.

▼ **Vertical Articulation or Alignment**

Indicates that the curriculum is carefully planned and sequenced from beginning learning and skills to more advanced learning and skills. Vertical articulation speaks to what is taught from pre-school through upper grades and is sometimes noted simply as "K-12 Curriculum."

▼ **Vision**

A specific description of what the learning organization will be like when the mission is achieved. A vision is a mental image. It must be written in practical, concrete terms that everyone can understand and see in the same way.

▼ **z-Scores**

A standard score with a mean of zero and a standard deviation of one. A z-score is obtained by the following formula: z = raw score (x) minus the mean, divided by the standard deviation (sd). A z-score is sometimes normalized.

REFERENCES AND RESOURCES

The references used in this book, along with other resources that will assist busy school administrators and teachers in conducting quality data analyses, appear below.

Airasian, P. W. (1994). *Classroom assessment.* New York, NY: McGraw-Hill, Inc.

Ammerman, M. (1998). *The root cause analysis handbook: A simplified approach to identifying, correcting, and reporting workplace errors.* New York, NY: Quality Resources.

Ardovino, J., Hollingsworth, J., & Ybarra, S. (2000). *Multiple measures: Accurate ways to assess student achievement.* Thousand Oaks, CA: Corwin Press, Inc.

Armstrong, J., & Anthes, K. (2001). How data can help: Putting information to work to raise student achievement. In *American School Board Journal,* 38-41.

Arter, J. (1999). *Teaching about performance assessment.* Portland, OR: Northwest Regional Educational Laboratory.

Arter, J., & The Classroom Assessment Team, Laboratory Network Program. (1998). *Improving classroom assessment: A toolkit for professional developers: Alternative Assessment.* Aurora, CO: MCREL.

Arter, J., & Busick, K. (2001). *Practice with student-involved classroom assessment.* Portland, OR: Assessment Training Institute, Inc.

Arter, J., & McTighe, J. (2001). *Scoring rubrics in the classroom: Using performance criteria for assessing and improving student performance.* In Guskey, T.R., & Marzano, R.J. (Series Eds.). *Experts in Assessment.* Thousand Oaks, CA: Corwin Press, Inc.

Aschbacher, P. R., & Herman, J. L. (1991). *Guidelines for effective score reporting.* (CSE Technical Report No. 326). Los Angeles, CA: University of California, Center for Research on Evaluation, Standards and Student Testing (CRESST).

Baldrige National Quality Program. (2002). *Education criteria for performance excellence.* Gaithersburg, MD: National Institute of Standards and Technology. Available: www.quality.nist.gov

Barth, P., Haycock, K., Jackson, H., Mora, K., Ruiz, P., Robinson, S., & Wilkins, A. (Eds.). (1999). *Dispelling the myth: High poverty schools exceeding expectations.* Washington, DC: Education Trust in Cooperation with the Council of Chief State School Officers and partially funded by the U.S. Department of Education.

Bernhardt, V. L. (1998). *Data analysis for comprehensive schoolwide improvement.* Larchmont, NY: Eye on Education, Inc.

Bernhardt, V. L. (1999). *The school portfolio: A comprehensive framework for school improvement* (2nd ed.). Larchmont, NY: Eye on Education, Inc.

Bernhardt, V.L. (1999, June). *Databases can help teachers with standards implementation.* Monograph No. 5. California Association for Supervision and Curriculum Development (CASCD).

Bernhardt, V. L. (2000). *Designing and using databases for school improvement.* Larchmont, NY: Eye on Education, Inc.

Bernhardt, V. L. (2000). Intersections: New routes open when one type of data crosses another. *Journal of Staff Development,* 21(1), 33-36.

Bernhardt, V. L. (2002). *The school portfolio toolkit: A planning, implementation, and evaluation guide for continuous school improvement.* Larchmont, NY: Eye on Education, Inc.

Bernhardt, V. L. (2003). *Using Data to Improve Student Learning in Elementary Schools.* Larchmont, NY: Eye on Education, Inc.

Bernhardt, V. L. (2003). No Schools Left Behind. *Educational Leadership,* 60(5), 26-30.

Bernhardt, V. L., von Blanckensee, L., Lauck, M., Rebello, F., Bonilla, G., & Tribbey, M. (2000). *The example school portfolio, A companion to the school portfolio: A comprehensive framework for school improvement.* Larchmont, NY: Eye on Education, Inc.

Bobko, P. (2001). *Correlation and regression: Applications for industrial/organizational psychology and management.* (2nd ed.). Thousand Oaks, CA: Sage Publications, Inc.

Blythe, T., & Associates. (1998). *The teaching for understanding guide.* San Francisco, CA: Jossey-Bass, Inc.

Carr, N. (2001). Making data count: Transforming schooling through data-driven decision making. *American School Board Journal,* 34-37.

Cawelti, G. (Ed.). (1999). *Handbook of research on improving student achievement* (2nd ed.). Arlington, VA: Educational Testing Service.

Chenoweth, T., & Everhart, R.B. (1993). *The restructured school: How do you know if something is happening* (Report No. ISSN-0032-0684). East Lansing, MI: National Center for Research on Teacher Learning. (ERIC Document Reproduction Service No. EJ462413)

Clarke, D. (1997). *Constructive assessment in mathematics: Practical steps for classroom teachers.* Berkeley, CA: Key Curriculum Press.

Clune, B., & Webb, N. (2001-02). WCER Highlights. Madison, WS: University of Wisconsin-Madison, Wisconsin Center for Education Research.

Commission on Instructionally Supportive Assessment. (2001). *Building tests to support instruction and accountability.* Available: http://www.aasa.org.

Conzemius, A., & O'Neill, J. (2001). *Building shared responsibility for student learning.* Alexandria, VA: Association for Supervision and Curriculum Development.

Corda. (2003). Available: http://www.corda.com.

Creighton, T. B. (2001). *Schools and data: The educator's guide for using data to improve decision-making.* Thousand Oaks, CA: Corwin Press, Inc.

Creswell, J. W. (2003). *Research design: Qualitative, quantitative, and mixed methods approaches.* Thousand Oaks, CA: SAGE publications.

Dann, R. (2002). *Promoting assessment as learning.* New York, NY: RoutledgeFalmer.

Darling-Hammond, L., Berry, B., & Toreson, A. (2001). Does Teacher Certification Matter? Evaluating the Evidence. *Educational Evaluation and Policy Analysis,* 23(1), 57-77.

Deming, W. E. (1986). *Out of the crisis.* Cambridge, MA: MIT Press.

DuFour, R., & Eaker, R. (1998). *Professional learning communities at work: Best practices for enhancing student achievement.* Alexandria, VA: Association for Supervision and Curriculum Development.

Educators in Connecticut's Pomperaug Regional School District 15. (1996). *A teacher's guide to performance-based learning and assessment.* Alexandria, VA: Association for Supervision and Curriculum Development.

Elmore, R. F. (2000). *Building a new structure for school leadership.* Washington, DC: The Albert Shanker Institute.

English, F. W. (2000). *Deciding what to teach and test: Developing, aligning, and auditing the curriculum.* Thousand Oaks, CA: Corwin Press, Inc.

Falk, B. (2000). *The heart of the matter: Using standards and assessment to learn.* Portsmouth, NH: Heinemann.

Fullan, M. (2001). *Leading a culture of change.* New York, NY: Jossey-Bass/Pfeiffer.

Fullan, M. (2002). *Changing forces with a vengeance.* New York, NY: RoutledgeFalmer.

Garmston, R.J., & Wellman, B.M. (1997). *The adaptive school: A sourcebook for developing collaborative groups.* Norwood, MA: Christopher-Gordon Publishers, Inc.

Glatthorn, A. A. (1999). *Performance standards & authentic learning.* Larchmont, NY: Eye on Education, Inc.

Glatthorn, A. A., & Fontana, J. (Eds.). (2000). *Coping with standards, tests, and accountability: Voices from the classroom.* Washington, DC: National Education Association.

Gredler, M. (1999). *Classroom assessment and learning.* Needham Heights, MA: Allyn & Bacon.

Gupta, K. (1999). *A practical guide to needs assessment.* San Francisco, CA: Jossey-Bass, Inc.

Guskey, T. (2000). *Evaluating professional development.* Thousand Oaks, CA: Corwin Press, Inc.

Guskey, T. R., & Bailey, J. M. (2001). Developing grading and reporting systems for student learning. In Guskey, T.R. & Marzano, R.J. (Series Eds.). *Experts in assessment.* Thousand Oaks, CA: Corwin Press, Inc.

Haladyna, T. M., Nolan, S. B., & Haas, N. S. (1991). Raising standardized achievement test scores and the origins of test score pollutions. *Educational Researcher,* 20(5), 2-7.

Haycock, K. (1999). *Results: Good teaching matters.* Oxford, OH: National Staff Development Council.

Henry, G. (1997). *Creating effective graphs: Solutions for a variety of evaluation data.* Editor-in-chief. New Directions for Evaluation, a publication of the American Evaluation Association..

Henry, T. (2001, June 11). Lawmakers move to improve literacy, the 'new civil right.' *USA Today,* pp. A1-2.

Herman, J. L., & Golan, S. (1991). *Effects of standardized testing on teachers and learning—another look.* (CSE Technical Report No. 334). Los Angeles, CA: University of California, Center for Research on Evaluation, Standards and Student Testing (CRESST).

Holcomb, E. L. (1999). *Getting excited about data.* Thousand Oaks, CA: Corwin Press, Inc.

Holly, P.J. (2003). *Conceptualizing a new path: Data-driven school improvement series.* Princeton, NJ: Educational Testing Service.

Isaac, S., & William, B. M. (1997). *Handbook in research and evaluation for education and the behavioral sciences* (3rd ed.). San Diego, CA: Educational and Industrial Testing Services.

Johnson, D. W., & Johnson, R. T. (2002). *Introduction: Cooperative learning and assessment.* Needham Heights, MA: Allyn & Bacon.

Johnson, R. S. (2002). *Using data to close the achievement gap: How to measure equity in our schools.* Thousand Oaks, CA: Corwin Press, Inc.

Joint Commission Resources. (2002). *Root cause analysis in healthcare: Tools and techniques.* Indianapolis, IN: Joint Commission Resources.

Kachigan, S. K. (1991). *Multivariate statistical analysis: A conceptual introduction* (2nd ed.). New York, NY: Radius Press.

Kain, D. L. (1996). *Looking beneath the surface: Teacher collaboration through the lens of grading practices.* Teachers College Record, Summer, 569-587.

Kifer, E. (2000). *Large-scale assessment: Dimensions, dilemmas, and policy.* Thousand Oaks, CA: Corwin Press, Inc.

Killion, J. (2002). *Assessing impact: Evaluating staff development.* Oxford, OH: National Staff Development Council.

Koretz, D., Stecher, B., Klein, S., & McCaffrey, D. (1994). The Vermont portfolio assessment program: Finding and implications. *Educational Measurement: Issues and Practice, 13*(3), 5-16.

Kosslyn, S. (1994). *Elements of graph design.* New York, NY: W. H. Freeman and Company.

Kouzes, J. M., & Posner, B. Z. (2002). *The leadership challenge: How to keep getting extraordinary things done in organizations.* (2nd Ed.). San Francisco, CA: Jossey-Bass Publishers.

Krueger, R. A. (2000). *Focus groups: A practical guide for applied research.* (3rd ed.). Thousand Oaks, CA: Sage Publications, Inc.

Kubiszyn, T., & Borich, G. (1996). *Educational testing and measurement: Classroom application and practice.* (5th ed.) New York, NY: HarperCollins.

Lambert, L. (2003). *Leadership capacity for lasting school improvement.* Alexandria, VA: Association for Supervision and Curriculum Development.

Lambert, L. (1998). *Building leadership capacity in schools.* Alexandria, VA: Association for Supervision and Curriculum Development.

Lazear, D. (1998). *The rubrics way: Using MI to assess understanding.* Tucson, AZ: Zephyr Press.

Linn, R. L., Baker, E. L., & Dunbar, S. B. (1991). *Complex, performance-based assessment: Expectations and validation guide.* (CSE Technical Report No. 331). Los Angeles, CA: University of California, Center for Research on Evaluation, Standards and Student Testing (CRESST).

Lissitz, R. W., & Schafer, W. D. (2002). (Eds.). *Assessment in educational reform: Both means and ends.* Needham Heights, MA: Allyn & Bacon.

Marzano, R. J. (2000). *Transforming classroom grading.* Alexandria, VA: Association for Supervision and Curriculum Development.

Marzano, R. J., Pickering, D., & McTighe, J. (1993). *Assess student outcomes: Performance assessment using dimensions of learning model.* Alexandria, VA: Association for Supervision and Curriculum Development.

Marzano, R. J., Pickering, D., & Pollock, J. E. (2001). *Classroom instruction that works: Research-based strategies for increasing student achievement.* Alexandria, VA: Association for Supervision and Curriculum Development.

McIntyre, C.V. (1992). *Writing effective news releases...: How to get free publicity for yourself, your business, or your organization.* Colorado Springs, CO: Piccadilly Books.

McMillian, J. H. (2001). *Classroom assessment: Principles and practice for effective instruction* (2nd ed.). Needham Heights, MA: Allyn & Bacon.

McMillian, J. H. (2001). *Essential assessment concepts for teachers and administrators.* In Guskey, T.R. & Marzano, R.J. (Series Eds.). Experts in Assessment. Thousand Oaks, CA: Corwin Press, Inc.

McREL. (1995-2002). *Classroom assessment, grading, and record keeping.* Aurora, CO: Author.

McTighe, J., & Ferrara, S. (1998). *Assessing learning in the classroom.* Washington, DC: National Education Association.

Merrow, J. (2001). *"Good enough" schools are not good enough.* Lanham, MD: Scarecrow Press.

Microsoft. (2003). Available: http://www.microsoft.com.

National Staff Development Council. (2002, October). Scientifically-based research as defined by NCLB. *Results.* Oxford, OH: Author.

Northwest Evaluation Association (NWEA). (2002). Available: http://www.nwea.org.

O'Connor, K. (1999). *The mindful school: How to grade for learning.* Arlington Heights, IL: Skylight Professional Development.

Oshry, B. (2000). *Leading systems: Lessons from the power lab.* San Francisco, CA: Berrett-Koehler Publishers.

Oosterhof, A. (1999). *Developing and using classroom assessments* (2nd ed.). Upper Saddle River, NJ: Prentice Hall, Inc.

Parsons, B. A. (2002). *Evaluative Inquiry: Using evaluation to promote student success.* Thousand Oaks, CA: Corwin Press, Inc.

Patten, M. L. (1997). *Understanding research methods: An overview of the essentials.* Los Angeles, CA: Pyrczak Publishing.

Payne, R. K., & Magee, D. S. (1999). *Meeting standards and raising test scores when you don't have much time or money.* Highlands, TX: RFT Publishing Company.

Perone, V. (Ed.). (1991). *Expanding student assessment.* Alexandria, VA: Association for Supervision and Curriculum Development.

Peterson, K. D. (1999). *Shaping school culture: The heart of leadership.* San Francisco, CA: Jossey-Bass Publishers.

Peterson, R. A. (2000). *Constructing effective questionnaires.* Thousand Oaks, CA: Sage Publications, Inc..

Popham, W. J. (1999). *Classroom assessment: What teachers need to know* (2nd ed.). Needham Heights, MA: Allyn & Bacon.

Popham, W. J. (2001). Standardized achievement tests: Misnamed and misleading. *Education Week, 21*(3), 46.

Preuss, P. G. (2003). *School leader's guide to root cause analysis: Using data to dissolve problems.* Larchmont, NY: Eye on Education, Inc.

Quellmalz, E., & Burry, J. (1983). Analytic scales for assessing students' expository and narrative writing skills. (CSE Technical Report No. 5). Los Angeles, CA: University of California, Center for Research on Evaluation, Standards and Student Testing (CRESST).

Rauhauser, B., & McLennan, A. (1995). *America's schools: Making them work.* Chapel Hill, NC: New View.

Rauhauser, B., & McLennan, A. (1994). *America's schools: Meeting the challenge through effective schools research and total quality management.* Lewisville, TX: School Improvement Specialists.

Rauhauser, B., & McLennan, A. (1995). *Research design: Qualitative, quantitative, and mixed methods approaches.* Thousand Oaks, CA: SAGE publications.

Rogers, S., & Graham, S. (2000). *The high performance toolbox: Succeeding with performance tasks, projects, and assessments* (3rd ed.). Evergreen, CO: Peak Learning Systems.

Sanders, J. R. (2000). *Evaluating school programs: An educator's guide.* Thousand Oaks, CA: Corwin Press, Inc.

Schafer, W. D., & Lissitz, R. W. (1987). Measurement training for school personnel: Recommendations and reality. *Journal of Teacher Education, 38*(3), 57-63.

Schmoker, M. (2001). *The results fieldbook: Practical strategies from dramatically improved schools.* Alexandria, VA: Association for Supervision and Curriculum Development.

Senge, P., Cambron-McCabe, N. H., Lucas, T., Smith, B., Dutton, J., & Kleiner, A. (2000). *Schools that learn: A fifth discipline fieldbook for educators, parents, and everyone who cares about education.* New York, NY: Doubleday Dell Publishing Group, Inc.

Senge, P., Kleiner, A., Roberts, C., Ross, R. B., & Smith, B. (2000). *The fifth discipline fieldbook: Strategies and tools for building a learning organization.* New York, NY: Doubleday Dell Publishing Group, Inc.

Shepard, L. A. (2000). *The role of classroom assessment in teaching and learning.* (CSE Technical Report No. 517). Los Angeles, CA: University of California, Center for Research on Evaluation, Standards and Student Testing (CRESST).

Smith, J. K., Smith, L. F., & DeLisi, R. (2001). *Natural classroom assessment: Designing seamless instruction & assessment.* In Guskey, T.R. & Marzano, R.J. (Series Eds.). Experts in Assessment. Thousand Oaks, CA: Corwin Press, Inc.

Solomon, P. (2002). *The assessment bridge: Positive ways to link tests to learning, standards, and curriculum improvement.* Thousand Oaks, CA: Corwin Press, Inc.

Statistica. (2003). Available: http://www.statsoft.com.

Stiggins, R. J. (2000). *Student-Involved classroom assessment* (3rd ed.). Englewood Cliffs, NJ: Prentice Hall.

Stiggins, R. J. (1999). Assessment, student confidence, and school success. *Phi Delta Kappan,* November, 191-198.

Stigler, J. W., & Hiebert, J. (1999). *The teaching gap: Best ideas from the world's teachers for improving education in the classroom.* New York, NY: The Free Press.

Strong, R. W., Silver, H. F., & Perini. M. J. (2001). *Teaching what matters most: Standards and strategies for raising student achievement.* Alexandria, VA: Association for Supervision and Curriculum Development.

TetraData. (2002). Available: http://www.Tetradata.com.

Trice, A. D. (2000). *A handbook of classroom assessment.* Needham Heights, MA: Allyn & Bacon.

Tufte, E. R. (2001). *The visual display of quantitative information.* (2nd ed.). Cheshire, CT: Graphics Press.

Tufte, E. R. (1997). *Visual explanations: Images and quantities, evidence and narrative.* Cheshire, CT: Graphics Press.

Tufte, E. R. (1990). *Envisioning information.* Cheshire, CT: Graphics Press.

U. S. Department of Education. *No child left behind.* Available: http://www.ed.gov.

Visual Mining, Inc. (2003). Available: http://www.visualmining.com.

Wahlstrom, D. (1999). *Using data to improve student achievement: A handbook for collecting, analyzing, and using data.* Virginia Beach, VA: Successline Publications.

Whitaker, T., Whitaker, B., & Lumpa, D. (2000). *Motivating and inspiring teachers: The educational leader's guide for building staff morale.* Larchmont, NY: Eye on Education.

Wiggins, G. (1998). *Educative assessment: Designing assessments to inform and improve student performance.* San Francisco, CA: Jossey-Bass, Inc.

Wiggins, G., & McTighe, J. (1998). *Understanding by design.* Alexandria, VA: Association for Supervision and Curriculum Development.

Wilson, L. W. (2002). *Better instruction through assessment: What your students are trying to tell you.* Larchmont, NY: Eye on Education, Inc.

Wittrock, M. C., & Baker, E. L. (Eds.). (1991). *Testing and cognition.* Englewood Cliffs, NJ: Prentice Hall.

Wormeli, R. (2003). *Day one & beyond: Practical matters for new middle-level teachers.* Portland, ME: Stenhouse Publishers.

Worthen, B. R., White, K. R., Fan, X., & Sudweeks, R. R. (1999). *Measurement and assessment in the schools* (2nd ed.). Needham Heights, MA: Allyn & Bacon.

Yero, J. L. (2002). *Teaching in mind: How teacher thinking shapes education.* Hamilton, MT: MindFlight Publishing.

Yin, R. K. (2003). *Case study research: Design and methods.* (3rd ed.). Thousand Oaks, CA: Sage Publications, Inc.

Zemelman, S., Daniels, H., & Hyde, A. (1998). *Best practice: New standards for teaching and learning in America's schools* (2nd ed.). Portsmouth, NH: Heinemann.

INDEX